The Life of the Author: Nathaniel Hawthorne

THE LIFE OF THE AUTHOR

This new series aims to transform literary biography from its status as a resource for facts and details to that of a dynamic, innovative aspect of teaching, criticism, and research. Outside universities lives of writers are by far the most popular genre of books about literature, but within them they are neglected as a focus for interpretation and as frameworks for advanced research. *The Life of the Author* will reverse this imbalance by exploring new questions on how and why our conception of the author frames our evaluation and understanding of their work.

New books in this series

The Life of the Author: Nathaniel Hawthorne
The Life of the Author: John Milton
The Life of the Author: Maya Angelou
The Life of the Author: Shakespeare

The Life of the Author

Nathaniel Hawthorne

Dale Salwak

Series editor
Richard Bradford

WILEY Blackwell

Registered Offices
John Wiley & Sons, Inc., 111 River Street, Hoboken, NJ 07030, USA
John Wiley & Sons Ltd, The Atrium, Southern Gate, Chichester, West Sussex, PO19 8SQ, UK

Editorial Office
The Atrium, Southern Gate, Chichester, West Sussex, PO19 8SQ, UK

For details of our global editorial offices, customer services, and more information about Wiley products visit us at www.wiley.com.

Wiley also publishes its books in a variety of electronic formats and by print-on-demand. Some content that appears in standard print versions of this book may not be available in other formats.

Library of Congress Cataloging-in-Publication Data applied for
ISBN Paperback 9781119771814

Cover Design: Wiley
Cover Image: Portrait of Nathaniel Hawthorne (1840) by Charles Osgood, photographic reproduction, Wikimedia Commons, public domain

Set in 9.5/12.5 STIX Two Text by Straive, Pondicherry, India
Printed and bound by CPI Group (UK) Ltd, Croydon, CR0 4YY

C114196_041022

To the Memory of my Parents

Stanley F. Salwak
1920–2005
Frances H. Salwak
1922–2021
remembered with gratitude and love.

Contents

Acknowledgments

Many of the ideas in this book were nourished over a lifetime in conversations with my remarkable parents, to whom this book is dedicated, and with my brother, Glenn, who shared our first life-changing visit to Salem and the House of the Seven Gables when we were only youngsters; and there isn't a page here that hasn't benefited from the fine ear and keen mind of my mother, who regrettably passed away before I had completed the final draft.

I owe a special debt to Valerie Meyers, whose superb editorial skills have made this a better book; to Jason Kline and my colleague Rudy Saldaña for their careful work with the manuscript in its early stages; to my colleagues Dr. David Overly and the late Eun Kang for their moral support during my research; to Samuel Smith for his unfailing words of encouragement during our many late-night telephone calls; to Jeffrey Meyers for his valued feedback during the book proposal stage; to John E. McLaughlin, William H. Pritchard, and a third (anonymous) reader, who took time from their own work to give this effort of mine their detailed attention; and to my wife, Patti, for her steadfast encouragement during my five-year journey from inception to completion of this book.

My gratitude extends to the selection committee, Board of Trustees, Dr. Gina Hogan, former Dean of Language Arts and Library, and Dr. Geraldine Perri, former President/Superintendent of Citrus College, for granting me a sabbatical leave in the fall of 2021 that freed me from my teaching duties to complete the final draft.

This project would not have been conceivable, however, without the brilliance of the many scholars, editors, and enthusiasts who have, for more than 150 years, illuminated Nathaniel Hawthorne's work and life, not to mention the dedicated historians who have paid scrupulous attention to his canonical status in nineteenth-century American literature. Listed among my references are many of the publications from which I have benefited including, above all, The Ohio State University Center's *Centenary Edition of the Works of Nathaniel Hawthorne* – a major achievement of contemporary scholarship whose 23 volumes will continue to sustain future generations of Hawthorneans. Unless otherwise stated, all references to Hawthorne's work are taken from this edition.

It is also a pleasure to acknowledge the following research institutions that have preserved unpublished materials connected to the story of the Hawthorne family: Henry E. Huntington Library, San Marino, California; Bancroft Library, University of California at Berkeley; Department of Special Collections, Stanford University Libraries, Stanford, California; Massachusetts Historical Society, Boston; Department of Rare Books and Manuscripts, Boston Public Library; George J. Mitchell Department of Special Collections and Archives, Bowdoin College Library, Bowdoin College, Brunswick, Maine; Amherst College and Special Collections, Amherst, Massachusetts; Concord Free Public Library, Concord, Massachusetts; Houghton Library, Harvard University, Cambridge, Massachusetts; Hawthorne-Manning Collection, Phillips Library (formerly Essex Institute), Peabody Essex Museum, Salem, Massachusetts; Henry W. and Albert Berg Collection, New York Public Library; Pierpont Morgan Library, Rogers Collection, New York Historical Society; Alderman Library, University of Virginia, Charlottesville; Library of Congress, Washington, DC; Beinecke Rare Book and Manuscript Library, Yale University; and Archivi Musei Capitolini, Rome.

Lastly, I am greatly obliged to Wiley-Blackwell, Publishers, for commissioning me to write this book. From the beginning, the care and enthusiasm of Managing Editor Liz Wingett and Commissioning Editor Nicole Allen, along with the guidance of series editor, Richard D. Bradford, have been an indispensable part of the process of getting this book into shape. I also cannot say enough for the many thousands of students that I have been privileged to work with since 1973, when I began my academic career.

List of Illustrations

Introduction

Given the astonishing volume and variety of publications on Nathaniel Hawthorne, which have been appearing since his death in 1864, someone coming across the title of my study might ask, "Why another?" It's a fair question and easy to answer: we need a new biographical approach to Hawthorne.

It's been said that we write the books we want to read. Indeed, this is one such book: free from what Henry James (1934) referred to as the "shackles of theory" (383), aimed at the general reader with little knowledge of Hawthorne. It is written from my personal perspective, from my own experience – just as I teach his life and work.

My portrait of the author is intended to ignite greater interest in his writings and his psyche. By drawing on my own 45 years of studying and teaching the literature written by and about him, visiting the places where he lived and worked, and reading what he read, I want to bring new readers close to the private man. By exploring the circumstances that led him to become a writer, I hope to enable others to gain insights into his innermost thoughts and ideas. Most crucially, I want to convince my audience that Hawthorne still matters.

For almost a century and a half, ingenious scholars have labored to decipher the truth behind the man and his work, which explains why we have so many theories about his life and art. Ruminating on his first and only visit with the author in 1860, William Dean Howells (1968 [1900]) wrote: "[W]e are always finding new Hawthornes" (52). Close one eye, and he is a Puritan, a Romantic, a Transcendentalist, a socially-conscious humanitarian, an aristocrat, a realist. Close the other eye, and he is a rebel against Puritanism, an anti-Romantic, a critic of Transcendentalism, an introverted aesthete, a democrat, an idealist (Abel 1963: 189). What readers make of Hawthorne depends on their contemporary viewpoint.

There is something eerie, almost magical, about a famous writer who wrote so much and yet gives so little away about himself. "Hawthorne withdraws from the

The Life of the Author: Nathaniel Hawthorne, First Edition. Dale Salwak.
© 2023 John Wiley & Sons Ltd. Published 2023 by John Wiley & Sons Ltd.

biographer," wrote Brooke Allen (2003), "as successfully as he did from his family and friends." "I love Hawthorne, I admire him; but I do not know him," remarked Jonathan Cilley, his college classmate. "He lives in a mysterious world of thought and imagination which he never permits me to enter" (Cleaveland and Packard 1882: 303). Henry James (1984 [1879]) alluded to the elusive character that reveals itself in all of his writings: "He was silent, diffident, more inclined to hesitate – to watch, and wait, and meditate – than to produce himself, and fonder, on almost any occasion, of being absent than of being present" (21). Even his wife, Sophia, wrote: "To the last, he was in a measure to me a divine mystery" (Hawthorne 1884: II, 352–353). Hawthorne increased this mystique by burning much of his correspondence (while entreating his family members and friends to do the same) and all early drafts of his prose.

Nevertheless, I welcome the challenge. If every word written by authors divulges some new facets of themselves, we can find the elusive Hawthorne not only in the testimonies from his ever-watchful family members and friends but also through the veil of his own words, both published and unpublished. These writings encompass five novels (or "romances" to use his term); 100 tales and sketches from newspapers, magazines, and gift books (published anonymously until 1836); his American notebooks (spanning the years 1835–1853); three journals comprising his impressions during extended trips to England (1853–1857), France and Italy (1858–1859); a campaign biography of Franklin Pierce; a memoir of his time spent in England; six children's books; and hundreds of letters that somehow survived the flames.

Despite all that has and continues to be written about Hawthorne, he is the best guide to his own life and work. For this reason, I take seriously what *Newsday* editor, Alan Hathaway, advised Robert Caro (2019) as he was about to embark on the writing of a biography of Lyndon Baines Johnson: "Just remember. Turn every page. Never assume anything" (11). I needed to explore everywhere and everything before I could ascertain what to use and what to discard.

It is not well known that Hawthorne had a penchant for exploring uncomfortable, even contentious issues. He confronted in himself with the deepest secrets of the human heart, including the most fundamental themes of good and evil, body and soul, and expressed those secrets in his work. "That blue-eyed darling Nathaniel knew disagreeable things in his inner soul," wrote D.H. Lawrence (1977 [1923]). "He was careful to send them out in disguise" (89). "[D]eep as Dante," Herman Melville would say of "Young Goodman Brown" in its penetration into the mystery of evil (Crowley 1970: 123). In 1883, when Julian Hawthorne visited Melville with a view to seeking credible information for his father's biography, the latter remarked (as Julian remembered) that he was convinced Hawthorne had all his life "concealed some great secret, which would, were it known, explain all the mysteries of his career" (Parker 2002: 855–856).

In this regard, "negative capability," the phrase coined by John Keats (2002 [1877]) in a letter to his brothers George and Tom, is particularly useful. Keats distinguished writers like Shakespeare, who exemplified this quality, from others, such as Samuel Taylor Coleridge, who did not: "[A]t once it struck me, what quality went to form a Man of Achievement especially in Literature," he wrote. "I mean *Negative Capability*, that is when a man is capable of being in uncertainties, Mysteries, doubts, without any irritable reaching after fact & reason" (60). Keats takes Shakespeare as the great example of a poet who, inspired by the external world, was receptive to the contradictions of experience and gave free rein to his imagination.

This was true for Hawthorne, also. He didn't set out to change the world, to make a point, or even to send a message, yet his stories transcend mere imitations of life. Like Emily Dickinson, who greatly admired him, in a letter to his publisher William D. Ticknor (dated 19 January 1955), he spurned the overly topical or commercial, sneered at what he called the "d–d mob of scribbling women'" – the soon-to-be-forgotten middlebrow authors of his time who, with the exception of Fanny Fern, whose work he admired, commented on social issues, not timeless truths of the human heart (*Works* XVII, 304).

Hawthorne was content to remain in a state of ambivalence as he explored "an enduring sense of mystery and chaos just beneath the surface of everyday life, of the burden of the past borne by the present, of the persistence of evil whether the world believes in original sin or not" (Cryer 2004). He did not feel obligated to illuminate his mysteries. Instead, he was secure enough to allow his readers to form their own judgments about him and his characters.

Few writers have represented and encapsulated the ambiguities of moral choice so fully. Did Young Goodman Brown really meet the Devil? Did Arthur Dimmesdale in *The Scarlet Letter* really have a fiery scar on his breast? What finally became of Miriam and her lover in *The Marble Faun*? To his credit, Hawthorne does not give us clear answers. As readers, we are asked to do what great literature has always required: question everything. As with every art form where ambiguity is a dominant feature, it is perhaps more useful to investigate *how* this condition is achieved and what it means rather than attempting to resolve it.

Each tale or novel becomes, therefore, a kind of mirror or Rorschach test in which we get to see not only our physical reflection, but our innermost being, even our soul, but only if we dare to look. Hawthorne's fiction demands that we examine ourselves incisively and determine what we intend to do with this self-knowledge. It is for us (as it was for Hawthorne) a means of unleashing the imagination, to reach the deepest recesses of our hearts that are otherwise locked away from us. We get out of his work the more we put into it. "The sources of the truest truths," said Saul Bellow, "are inevitably profoundly personal" (Bloom 1987: 12).

I approach this project as if I were preparing a seminar for a new generation of intelligent college students disillusioned by perfunctory scholarship and unfriendly theories (though I hope specialists may profit in passing here and there). At one time, we could reasonably expect them to demonstrate some understanding of Hawthorne's writings and their vital role in America's literary history. Today this is not the case. For most students, exposure is limited to a forced (and superficial) reading of *The Scarlet Letter* and a handful of tales, unlike my postwar generation, which began to read him during high school before continuing through our college and graduate years. It is disheartening to find so many students since the mid-1980s indifferent to this great writer.

The reasons for this decline in interest are apparent. There is a prevailing attitude among many teachers that Hawthorne's relevance to our times is steadily dwindling. They contend that we cannot be bothered with unraveling the "impenetrable" mysteries of a nineteenth-century writer, a dead white Western male at that, who has historically "proven" to be inaccurate, insufficiently philosophical, sexist, misogynistic, racist, insular, and elitist. I heard one prominent scholar complain at a conference, "Well, we historians don't take Hawthorne seriously." When I questioned the rationale behind her inference, she said, "Students can't relate to him and his invented facts" – the basis of all fiction. When students (and their teachers) proclaim that they cannot relate to Hawthorne, they do so because they cannot relate to the way he has been taught to them. They are also essentially conceding that they are misreading or unwilling to put in the work his writings demand from them. For reasons I shall explore in greater detail, Hawthorne does matter today – perhaps even more so now than he did to his nineteenth-century readers.

Hawthorne was one of the most acute observers of Puritan life in colonial New England. His understanding of Calvinism, with its emphasis upon predestination and a wrathful, judgmental God, was profound, although he didn't accept most of its doctrines. Without his insights, no modern reader can claim to understand the texture of early American history, with its myriad distortions and delusions, its incendiary, judgmental and unforgiving impulse.

If there's harm associated with Hawthorne, or any of the classics for that matter, it comes from *not* teaching him. Not teaching Hawthorne undervalues the power of his art and undermines the ability of our students to appreciate and be deepened by it. Students suffer poverty of language and cultural references and, worse, they don't even know it.

We can also look at Hawthorne as a guiding force as we think through our contemporary dilemmas; what mattered to him is not devoid of consequences for us as well. The timeless concerns of the effects of sin (both secret and disclosed), guilt and penitence, religious hypocrisy, sexuality, history and national identity, art and the imagination are always encrypted in his works of fiction – hidden, yet visible if we know how to look – as they are, somewhere, in our thoughts. The truths he conveys hit close to home with the reader. "Make no mistake," said Robert Frost, an admirer of Hawthorne's: "A true piece of writing is a dangerous thing. It can change your life" (Wolff 2003: 47).

I always knew that I'd write this book. My interest in Hawthorne goes back to 1957 when, as a youngster, I made my first journey with my family from Amherst (where I was raised) to Salem, Massachusetts. I picked up a small blue copy of *The House of the Seven Gables* in a bookshop, opened to chapter one, and read in a state of exaltation the first mesmerizing sentence: "Half-way down a by-street of one of our New England towns, stands a rusty wooden house, with seven acutely peaked gables facing towards various points of the compass, and a huge, clustered chimney in the midst" (*Works* II, 5). This passage struck a deep chord within me, possibly because I had just returned from that memorable visit, and when I went back to Salem four years later, I realized that Hawthorne had accurately described the dark ancestral house. After many decades, the novel continues to resonate in my memories of musty smells and haunting sounds and sights.

I kept a worn copy of that volume, published by Classic Books, with my penciled annotations in the margins and endpapers. Since then, I have been perpetually curious about this enigmatic, shy, consummate artist whose life of solitude, mystery, and later marriage to Sophia Peabody never ceases to intrigue and attract visitors to his homes in Salem and Concord.

Such is the personal attachment we tend to develop for the authors and works we admire. The sheer joy of reading Hawthorne and now writing about him has impelled me to ponder deeply as to why I have been drawn to him since childhood and why I still am, albeit in different ways and from a different perspective – as shall be revealed in the chapters to follow.

1

Under the Spell of Hawthorne

Hawthorne's birthplace, 27 Union Street, Salem. Source: Library of Congress.

> *A man of a deep and noble nature has seized me in this*
> *seclusion. His wild, witch-voice rings through me; . . .*
> —Herman Melville (Crowley 1970: 111)

When those of us with an unbounded love for literature begin reading, we enter the psyche of another and allow our own world to be subsumed in the world created by the author. In so doing, there are times when we are touched within by some sort of awe, even euphoria. We feel edified. We feel transformed. We feel more fully and pleasurably alive.

We call such flashes of intense insight "aha" moments – as in *now I see, now I know, now I understand*. Christianity refers to them as "epiphanies" – from the Greek *epiphaneia*, meaning "a manifestation" (Petridou 2016: 6). Virginia Woolf

The Life of the Author: Nathaniel Hawthorne, First Edition. Dale Salwak.
© 2023 John Wiley & Sons Ltd. Published 2023 by John Wiley & Sons Ltd.

(1976) called them "moments of being" (70), and William Wordsworth (2012 [1805]) referred to them as "spots of time" in *The Prelude* (XI, line 257).

Whatever we call them, once these eureka moments occur and we have considered them afterward in calm reflection, we find ourselves in sync with the rhythm of life in a fresh way: the world is put into clearer perspective; we begin to move in a direction that is different from anything we'd ever imagined, a direction that we know is *just right* for us. This describes fairly accurately how many of us respond (as did Herman Melville) to the life and work of Nathaniel Hawthorne. But why? What is it about this particular author's temperament and artistry that casts such a powerful (almost hypnotic) spell, one that draws us in so quickly and holds us so tenaciously? Why is it that the novels and tales give so many of his devoted readers such a personal experience? Why does Brenda Wineapple's (2003) assessment – "Once read, his stories never vanish" – ring so very true? (381)

Certainly, his appeal to the reading public lies partly in his fulfillment of what Vladimir Nabokov (1980) identified as the fundamental requirements of any great writer: he is a storyteller, a teacher, but above all, an astute enchanter (5). He points us in the direction of a new discovery, a new conquest, a great new adventure. He often catches us unaware, transporting us to a world we are fascinated by but never knew existed. He speaks to anyone at any age and in any state of mind who is willing to press the pause button and listen. As he specifies in his preface to *The House of the Seven Gables*, Hawthorne strives both to present "the truth of the human heart" – his great subject – and to connect "a by-gone time with the very Present that is flitting away from us" (*Works* X, 1, 2).

"[E]very man and woman contains the truth of every man and woman who has ever lived," wrote Robertson Davies (1997), "and that truth is cloaked in the muddy vesture of everyday life" (137). The context may be different from our own, and on the surface, the characters may be quite unlike us, but what remains constant is the human heart. What separates one generation from another is superficial. We share with Hawthorne's characters identical needs, desires, fears, and potential for good or, alas, evil. C.S. Lewis (1961 [1942]) refers to this as the doctrine of "The Unchanging Human Heart," and my belief in it underscores what I say both in the classroom and in this book (62). Quite remarkably, Hawthorne meets us at our point of need.

The seductive appeal of his works, including those that were aimed at children, lies in their invitation to each of us to read as if we, and not solely the characters therein, were its true subject. We find ourselves unraveling a mystery that we've always known but didn't know we knew. Hawthorne very often creates a story with a setting and characters so enchanting and so seemingly real that we end up disregarding the fact that it is fiction.

The Russian poet Kornei Chukovsky (1971) showed the vital importance of enchantment to the growth of the intellect. He described a policy instituted by the

Soviet government in the 1920s that banned all fantasy from the education of children in favor of simple, realistic, factual stories. One of the educators, curious about the effects of this ruling, began to keep a diary of her own child's development. She found that her son began to make up his own fantasies as if to compensate for what he was being denied. He had never heard a fairy tale, never read a ghost story, but talking tigers, birds, and bugs, as well as beautiful maidens, castles, and underground cities, soon consumed his imaginative world. Chukovsky concluded: "Fantasy is the most valuable attribute of the human mind and it should be diligently nurtured from earliest childhood, as one nurtures musical sensitivity and not crushed" (116–117).

Hawthorne never outgrew his need for creative play, and neither do we; many mature and rational adults enjoy imaginative tales, ghost stories, and science fiction. In his writings, events and situations oftentimes occur beyond the realm of the ordinary. He associated the paranormal and the ghostly with the genre of romance in which the purely imaginary could co-exist alongside the mundane. It is "a neutral territory," he wrote in "The Custom-House," "somewhere between the real world and fairy-land, where the Actual and the Imaginary may meet, and each imbue itself with the nature of the other. Ghosts might enter here, without affrighting us" (*Works* I, 36). The eerie atmosphere in *The House of the Seven Gables* raises the question, "What does it mean to be haunted by the past?" We are drawn into the tale by its realistic elements, then surprised by weird and abnormal details that convince us that the supernatural affects everyday life. He uses the classic techniques of the ghost story for serious, moral purposes.

Hawthorne's tales also offer perhaps the most eloquent instances of the gratifying triumph over fear – what H.P. Lovecraft (1994 [1927]) called "the oldest and strongest emotion" of humankind (1). Horror stories and tales of the supernatural are a means by which both children and adults can bravely confront frightening adversaries, such as death, ghosts, and the unknown, by reading about them in a safe, even light-hearted context. Hawthorne's characters and settings and mysterious plots express a variety of ideas about the relationship of the individual to the culture. Some reveal human fragility; some satirize and therefore deflate certain stereotypes about death; others make compelling statements about our own worst nightmares. Any horror loses at least some of its magnitude once we have looked squarely upon it. "When we become the dark," said American novelist P. D. Cacek, "the shadows seem less frightening" (Bannatyne 2011: 42).

One of my colleagues makes Hawthorne a centerpiece of the semester as his students examine the dark side of the literary imagination. Mary Shelley's gothic novel *Frankenstein* (1823), Robert Louis Stevenson's *The Strange Case of Dr. Jekyll and Mr. Hyde* (1886), and Bram Stoker's *Dracula* (1897), or the hauntings of Henry James's *Turn of the Screw* (1898) are just a handful of obvious examples his students explore to accompany Hawthorne. It's a short leap from discussions about horror to the witches in Shakespeare's *Macbeth* (1606) or the ghost in *Hamlet* (1599/1601) – both of which Hawthorne had read as a child. The course also places the works of Edgar Allan Poe, an enthusiastic promoter of Hawthorne, within a literary tradition of supernatural tales that goes beyond entertaining to deeper emotional and moral concerns. As Hawthorne did early on, the students are encouraged to keep a fear journal – in which they write down their nightmares and discover how wicked other people are or could be.

So, what did Hawthorne discover? "There is evil in every human heart," he wrote in an early journal entry (dated 25 October 1836), "which may remain latent, perhaps, through the whole of life; but circumstances may rouse it to activity. To imagine such circumstances. A woman, tempted to be false to her husband, apparently through mere whim, – or a young man to feel an instinctive thirst for blood, and to commit murder" (*Works* VIII, 29–30). Hawthorne's early notebooks are replete with "morbid anatom[ies]" of the human heart (McFarland 2004: 22). Ghosts appear with a purpose – to warn, to encourage, to punish, or to provide an alter ego.

In their power and subtlety, these stories create a gripping, tension-laden atmosphere. For some spirits, like myself, curling up in the safety of our beds with a terrifying book will do the trick: as the wind blows and a barren branch taps at the window, we can experience once again, without warning, and as if from a reservoir not of years but of centuries, the haunting memories of childhood fears that Hawthorne brings to life so vividly. This brings me to another reason we fall under Hawthorne's spell: A sense of place is at the heart of everything he wrote. He rendered physical settings with such dreamlike clarity that we never doubt their actual existence. We never want to. We enter them as if they are our own.

When I announced in one of my literature classes that I needed to return to Salem, Concord, and Boston to complete a chapter for a book I was writing, one student remarked, "Why bother? That's why we have the Internet. You can do your research that way and save yourself a lot of time and money." Although expressed completely without guile or malice, that student's seemingly tacit acceptance of the computer over "see-touch-feel" strangely disquieted me. My response, acerbic as it may have sounded, was as follows: "I'm going there because life is not found on the bloodless Internet. Life is found in real places."

For decades, acting on this belief has deepened my insights into the reading and study of authors whose works become better illuminated by experiencing firsthand the physical spaces they knew and drew from. I cannot claim for others, but that has certainly been my experience with Hawthorne. I wanted to see the fully textured physical and psychic landscape – its warp and woof – where some of my favorite stories, novels, and essays were conceived and written. I went to see the beds on which Hawthorne slept, the tables where he ate, the desks where he wrote, the halls he paced, and the windows he must have stared through when the right words did not come.

In fact, I did much of my early thinking about this book while on the grounds of his Concord homes, The Old Manse and The Wayside, or late at night at the Hawthorne Inn (now permanently closed) across the road from Bronson Alcott's Orchard House, while sipping from a glass of wine, a favorite beverage of Hawthorne's, and almost sensing as if he were there with me, guiding every word.

Hawthorne could never have written *The Scarlet Letter* or *The House of the Seven Gables* under the glare of bright sunshine. Autumn and winter months were the optimal times for his writing – as they are for me. He had to write in the shimmer of candlelight or by the glow of a coal-fire, haunted and inspired by the deep shadows of antiquity. Darkness is primal; it soothes, invites, and relaxes. Voices lower. Thoughts emerge with greater care, ease, and openness. "[B]road daylight dispels shadow just as wakefulness dispels dream; a world of fact crowds out fiction" (Martin 1983: 31).

We might understand what the scenes in a novel or tale say and portend, but we need to transcend the verbal surface of what we read. Perhaps only standing where the author had stood can we do justice to and bring home to our imagination the physical realities of his life and times. Perhaps even more importantly, it is only then that we are able to connect our own reality with the one he strove to create in his work. Every journey outward is a journey inward. I needed to be there, not only in Salem, Concord, and Boston but also in Brunswick, Maine, the Berkshires, Lennox, West Newton, West Roxbury, Liverpool, London, Paris, Florence, and Rome. All these places were important to Hawthorne's development and, as a consequence, to my understanding of him.

I often tell my students of my unabashedly romantic pilgrimages to other sites as well: Ralph Waldo Emerson's two-story clapboard mansion where, with the curator's permission, I touched the bed on which the sage of Concord had drawn his last breath; or upstairs at Orchard House where I lingered at the semicircular fold-down shelf-desk upon which Louisa May Alcott had composed *Little Women* (1868/1869) in just 10 weeks; or the Church of the First Parish from which I walked to Author's Ridge atop Sleepy Hollow Cemetery while envisioning the funeral and Hawthorne's procession. Standing at his gravesite, it dawned upon me that this would be the closest I'd ever get to shaking his hand.

Memory and imagination – tools all writers share – are sheltered inside the walls of homes, said Gaston Bachelard (1964) in *The Poetics of Space* (3). I find it fascinating that we're never quite sure as to what hints, pointers, suggestions, or promises we will discover about our readings, thoughts, and dreams, when we examine the environs where some of the most brilliant minds in history produced their creative gems. Surrounded by their space, we may catch a glimpse, as the authors once did, of humanity in its depths. "Behind every door," wrote Anna Quindlen (2004), "there are stories, behind every one ghosts. The greatest writers in the history of the written word have given them substance, given them life" (160).

And so, I describe for my students the powerful resonance I felt within the clapboard walls of The Old Manse. Here, from the flurry of family life, Hawthorne collected impressions he later used to develop the interior scenes for some of his memorable tales. Running her hand over Hawthorne's desk and wiping off the dust, one colleague naively sighed, "Oh, that some of his genius might rub off on me!" How many of us have done and said something similar about the authors we care for?

My travels have given me interesting ways to engage my students with Hawthorne. I visited Rome and Florence, where he spent a little more than a year, and I learned that he did most of his preparatory thinking there for his final completed and published romance, *The Marble Faun*. I relate how, upon entering his third-floor study at The Wayside in Concord, I sensed the pain, the isolation, and the frustration as he tried unsuccessfully to compose a new novel after his return from Europe while his family, directly beneath, tended to daily domestic affairs.

I reveal how I have stood at noon at the approximate spot where, on 9 July 1845, the day of the Hawthorne's third wedding anniversary, 19-year-old Martha Hunt, the superintendent of a district school, had left her bonnet and shoes neatly arranged on the shore, and, after hours of pacing the banks, had walked to her death in the Concord River. Later that evening, Hawthorne set out in his boat with Ellery Channing and two other men. As they paddled and dragged the river, they recovered the girl's body. (Several years later, one of her sisters also committed suicide in the river and another died by accidental drowning.)

I explained to the students how standing there connected me emotionally to Zenobia's suicide by drowning in *The Blithedale Romance*, particularly the lines: "Of all modes of death, methinks it is the ugliest. Her wet garments swathed limbs of terrible inflexibility. She was the marble image of a death-agony. Her arms had grown rigid in the act of struggling, and were bent before her, with clenched hands; her knees, too, were bent, and – thank God for it! – in the attitude of prayer. Ah, that rigidity! It is impossible to bear the terror of it" (*Works* III, 235). Until he had written about this mortifying, heart-wrenching scene, Hawthorne could not make peace with the Hunt tragedy. This is one of the many instances in his life where Hawthorne's refusal to let go of a painful episode had positive results in his work.

Discussions that follow elicit useful questions as we speculate about the various ways in which geography informed Hawthorne's works. Every place is inexorably linked to an open-ended question. What does it mean, for example, to say that he will forever be connected with Salem or Concord? What was transpiring in Hawthorne's mind as he walked at dusk, lost in nostalgic contemplation in the green seclusion of the outskirts of Salem? Or while alone in the darkest regions of Liverpool and London? Or within the cathedrals and museums of Rome? His novels and tales indeed capture the spirit of the locale, but in order to appreciate how he uses a particular place, it can help to visit it, as I have done, and experience there the fairy-tale mystery that intrigued Hawthorne himself.

No website or video can capture this magic: the shaded, plain wooden bench perched on a path above the garden behind his house, The Wayside; the buzz of bees feasting on nearby apple and wild rose; the warm breeze wafting gently from the valley spread out below, bearing with it the cleansing scent of fresh-cut grass of which he wrote in his American journal.

I hope that such discussions not only engage my students but, ultimately, inspire them to set out with high expectations on their respective journeys to make a connection with writers such as Hawthorne. Seeing the sparse tower room upstairs at his Concord home, The Wayside, where he wrote late in life, or the lake, near to the Hawthorne's home, where Sophia slipped and miscarried her child, might kindle or renew an interest in his books.

To some of my colleagues, all this is but a fool's errand, a snooping obsession that borders on the ridiculous – literary idolatry of sorts. "What if the information about the places isn't accurate?" someone said. "What if the guides aren't telling the truth?" My answer is that the tourist information really doesn't matter; I go for the atmosphere of the places. After visiting them, I am moved beyond words to turn to the books and tales again, and my reading is infused with a new, more pungent essence derived from visiting these homes and villages. Regardless of the extent to which they have changed over time, the places Hawthorne captured and drew from continue to live in his work. "Our emotions are somehow stirred," wrote Cicero, "in those places in which the feet of those whom we love and admire have trodden" (Hendrix 2009: 14).

More than his enchanting storytelling or unforgettable characters, his use of ambiguity and impeccable irony, his taste for the supernatural, and his sense of place, Hawthorne's most memorable gift was his voice – a narrative voice that speaks to each one of us in a uniquely enthralling manner.

Unsentimental and wise, the voice behind his characters beguiles us, humors us, and refuses to let go. There is truth in every line he wrote, almost as if he were incapable of uttering a falsehood. This is the voice of reason, of moderation, of intellectual honesty, and prudence. In the preface to *The Ambassadors*, Henry James (1934) refers to this narrative voice as the reader's friend or confidante (*ficelle*) because it invites us to suspend our disbelief and enter into a world that is different from our own (322).

Suspension of disbelief, a notion introduced into English literature by Coleridge, is central to our pleasure in reading Hawthorne. When we temporarily suspend disbelief, we enjoy the work on its own terms, allowing ourselves to think of the characters as real. We play along in this enchanted world and rarely doubt whose voice we are hearing. Hawthorne's narrator wins and retains our trust.

Although no amount of academic study will ever explain why we prefer one writer's voice over another's, what we do know, as noted by John Le Carré (2005), is that "partly it has to do with trust, partly with good or bad manners of the narrator, partly with his authority or lack of it. And a little also with beauty, though not as much as we might like to think" (xiii). For these reasons and many more, Hawthorne's writings have the iron of permanence. Once under his spell, we never escape.

Bowdoin College, 1823, oil by John G. Brown (Bowdoin College Museum of Art). Source: Artokoloro/Alamy Images.

2

The Formative Years (1804–1825)

In early adolescence we're primed for
life-altering experiences . . .

—Joyce Carol Oates (2005: 364)

On a return trip to Salem, Massachusetts, after a ten-year absence, I stood in front of the house where Nathaniel Hawthorne had been raised, and thought: What if, as an adult, he had been unable to remember where he was born or where he had lived as a child? What if he had forgotten his father's name, his mother's, his sisters', or his grandparents', aunts', uncles', and cousins' names? Would he have been the same person? The answer must surely be no because he wouldn't have had a story to tell. For a story is nothing less than an integral part of the soul, and he would have lost part of his soul.

"Most of us know the parents or grandparents we come from," said V.S. Naipaul (1995) in *A Way in the World*. "But we go back and back, forever; we go back all of us to the very beginning; in our blood and bone and brain we carry the memories of thousands of beings" (11). Similarly, the sixteenth century Michel de Montaigne (whose essays Hawthorne counted among his favorites) wrote, "What a wonderful thing it is that that drop of seed from which we are produced bears in itself the impressions, not only of the bodily shape, but of the thoughts and inclinations of our fathers!" (Jacob 1993: 20).

Hawthorne was destined to be a writer and driven to understand a past that sat heavily on his mind and spirit. To better appreciate the effect of his family history, we should look at his childhood and youth. As is true of so many authors, he felt the need to write early on.

Born on 4 July 1804 in the upstairs bedroom at 27 Union Street in Puritan-haunted Salem, he was the second of three children of the seagoing Nathaniel (1775–1808) and the raven-haired beauty, Elizabeth Clarke Manning Hathorne (1780–1849), as the name was then spelled. Notably, he belonged to one of Salem's

The Life of the Author: Nathaniel Hawthorne, First Edition. Dale Salwak.
© 2023 John Wiley & Sons Ltd. Published 2023 by John Wiley & Sons Ltd.

first families, but they had witnessed a gradual decline in both fortune and social importance.

Many years later, Hawthorne added a *w* to his last name in order to distance himself from the stain of his forefathers' conduct: his paternal great-grandfather, John Hathorne (1641–1717), who sat in judgment on and then sentenced to death hundreds of the accused during the hysteria of Salem's witch trials of 1692 (an event Hawthorne poignantly used in *The House of the Seven Gables*); and his paternal great-great grandfather, the magistrate William Hathorne (c. 1606/1607–1681), a brutal prosecutor of the nonconforming Quakers, who went on to become the Speaker of the House of Delegates in Massachusetts.

We do not know for sure if Nathaniel believed his family had been cursed. What we do know is that as an adult, he was troubled by a fiendish problem: there were times when he felt haunted and desperately unhappy. He also thought that at least two events in his life suggested there were supernatural causes for his misery. Were the deaths at sea of both his father and his sister, Louisa, he wondered, the result of a family curse? (Hartley 1967: 57) In this regard, his testimony in "The Custom-House" introductory essay to *The Scarlet Letter* is revealing:

> I know not whether these ancestors of mine bethought themselves to repent, and ask pardon of Heaven for their cruelties; or whether they are now groaning under the heavy consequences of them, in another state of being. At all events, I, the present writer, as their representative, hereby take shame upon myself for their sakes, and pray that any curse incurred by them – as I have heard, and as the dreary and unprosperous condition of the race, for many a long year back, would argue to exist – may be now and henceforth removed. (*Works* I, 9–10)

He clearly believed his family's bad luck arose from these "cruelties," and that he bore a great burden of guilt for his ancestors' crimes. He intended his work to be a way of expiation.

We also know that Puritan parochialism, intolerance, and harshness horrified him. In *The Scarlet Letter*, Hester Prynne is victimized by "the whole dismal severity of the Puritanic code of law" (*Works* I, 52). At the conclusion of the introduction, he wrote: "Henceforth, [Salem and its Puritan legacy] ceases to be a reality of my life. I am a citizen of somewhere else" (*Works* I, 44). The world has changed since the Colonial era, but we still hear about or even witness cruel punishments inflicted on women by a community full of religious hubris and convinced of its own moral rectitude. Sometimes, as Hawthorne knew all too well and as he would demonstrate through his fiction, people use their beliefs as an excuse for satisfying their own evil passions (Russell 1946).

"There is always one moment in childhood," wrote Graham Greene (1954), "when the door opens and lets the future in" (7). For Nathaniel, it occurred in early 1808, after the birth of his younger sister. His father, a sea captain, died of yellow fever at the age of 32 in Dutch Guiana (now Suriname), leaving his four-year-old son, the only male heir on both sides of the family, abandoned and fearful for his family's safety. This cataclysmic loss was understandably the lightning bolt in young Nathaniel's emotional life, the catalyst for the beginning of a lifelong yearning for the absent father. Such longing he never revealed to anyone, "at least not directly, only behind veils" (Miller 1991: 25, 36).

The captain's impoverished wife, left with an estate of only $427.02 (of which she spent nearly $200 on funeral expenses), moved her family to the home of her parents at 12 (now 10 1/2) Herbert Street, directly behind the house where Nathaniel was born and close to the wharves. There (except for occasional visits to family members and three years spent in Raymond, Maine) she slipped into seclusion, dressed always in black, and mourned for the rest of her life. Hawthorne's young life was blighted by his mother's grief. In his unfinished, posthumously published novel, *The Dolliver Romance* (1876), he describes such a woman as follows: "a forlorn widow, whose grief outlasted even its vitality, and grew to be merely a torpid habit, and was saddest then" (*Works* XIII, 457). In "The Wives of the Dead" (1831), a character's husband is reported drowned at sea. She falls asleep with a look upon her face "as if her heart, like a deep lake, had grown calm because its dead had sunk down so far within" (*Works* XI, 196). It's no surprise that death at sea became a recurring image in his work. As early as 16, he published the following in his own family newspaper, *The Spectator*: "The billowy Ocean rolls its wave, / Above the shipwreck'd Sailor's Grave, / Around him ever roars the Deep, / And lulls his wearied form to sleep, / Low in the deep Sea's darkest dell, / He hears no more the tempest swell" (Chandler and Hawthorne 1931: 324).

Through her letters, Hawthorne's mother seemed to express affection and kindness to her son and showed a keen interest in his welfare. According to Mark Van Doren (1949), she was "an excellent cook, an attentive mother, and an interesting talker about things past and present" (9). However, a perceptible reserve between mother and son soon developed. "I love my mother," Hawthorne recorded in his journal on 29 July 1849, shortly before she died, "but there has been, ever since my boyhood, a sort of coldness of intercourse between us, such as is apt to come between persons of strong feelings, if they are not managed rightly" (*Works* VIII, 429).

"Absorb these details," I say to my students, "and you'll begin to understand the man behind the work." At the heart of all his compositions are the father he barely knew and the mother he yearned to draw close to. It is almost as if his artistic proclivity was born out of the need to express loss and its concomitant feelings: nostalgia, loneliness, despair, and the desire for reconciliation. This early sadness helps to explain why he would be so ambitious, so driven; and why so much of what he would do in his life would be to make his absent parents proud.

For the next ten years, young Nathaniel and his sisters – Elizabeth "Ebe" Manning (1802–1883) and Maria Louisa (1808–1852) – lived in the company of the Manning grandparents, four maternal aunts and four maternal uncles (all unwed), a great-aunt, occasional servants, as well as two cats – whose names, Apollyon and Beelzebub, came from one of his favorite books, John Bunyan's *Pilgrim's Progress* (1678).

Nathaniel occupied the third story of the house which he loved, as Jorge Luis Borges (1968) wrote, "with the sad love inspired by persons who do not love us, or by failures, illness, and manias" (48). In a letter to his wife Sophia dated 10 November 1845, he wryly referred to the cheerless place as "Castle Dismal" (*Works* XVI, 129). At the age of 16, he threatened (but didn't act upon it) to go away to sea and never return. All his fiction is preoccupied with isolation and loneliness, with the predicament of someone who has parted company with his fellows and suffers from a protractedly tormented conscience (Hartley 1967: 62).

But he consoled himself by attending concerts and the theater and read constantly. Throughout his life, he read and reread Sir Walter Scott, his boyhood favorite among novelists, whose influence we will see in his work, beginning with *Fanshawe*. "[A] hearty devourer of books," his future publisher James T. Fields (1872) called him, "and in certain moods of mind it made very little difference what the volume before him happened to be" (62). Austin Warren (1935) wrote: "Never a collector of books, never a professional critic, possessed of no desire to judge the work of others or even to articulate his impressions except by the way in brief, he was, however, always a bookman, eager and catholic" (497). According to his sister Elizabeth, in later years after his return home from college, "He read a great many novels; he made an artistic study of them" (Hawthorne 1884: I, 125).

I encourage my students to let themselves be drawn into Nathaniel's world, as if they were literally born to it. "Rid yourselves," I say, "of the notion that you are studying someone far removed from you by time, place, or culture." His world was different from our own, but it was replete with people very much like us and with problems and challenges very much like our own.

"Picture yourselves sprawled out on the floor with him," I add, "while reading the books that Elizabeth had acquired for him from the local library." Dante, Shakespeare, Milton, Pope, James Thomson's *The Castle of Indolence* (1748), Bunyan's *Pilgrim's Progress* (1678), Byron, Samuel Johnson, Rousseau's *Confessions* (1782) and *La Nouvelle Héloïse* (1761), the sermons of Laurence Sterne, and the novels of G.P.R. James and Anthony Trollope were among his favorites. Let us imagine Nathaniel identifying with the melancholic protagonists peopling their works – so closely did they parallel at times the author-to-be.

Many of his stories originated in the idea of someone, usually a man, unwilling or unable to identify himself with what Rousseau referred to as the General Will, the idea that society collectively aims for the common good, and the individual's interests should be subordinate to it. Hawthorne termed this unwillingness, or inability, the sin of pride. His judgment precipitated agony-ridden guilt and frustration. The worst thing one could do, he thought, is to lose "his hold of the magnetic chain of humanity" (*Works* XI, 99). But he also had a Calvinist Protestant side to him – he believed in the innate wickedness of the heart of man.

Nathaniel was also an attentive reader of Renaissance allegorical poetry, particularly Edmund Spenser's *The Faerie Queene* (1590/1596 – the first book he purchased with his own money) and Sir Philip Sydney's *Arcadia* (1593). "It is of the very nature of thought and language," wrote C. S. Lewis (1958), "to represent what is immaterial in picturable terms. What is deemed good or happy has always been considered high like the heavens and bright like the sun. Evil and misery were deep and dark from the first" (44). Hawthorne would often use allegory in his work. In his satirical "The Celestial Rail-road" (1843), for example, constructed on the model of *Pilgrim's Progress*, he uses conventional devices of allegory, such as symbolic names (Gathergold, Dryasdust, Mr. Smooth-it-away), stereotypes (the Cynic, the Seeker), and gives personification of abstract values, such as Purity or Honesty. In some stories, a central symbol dominates – for instance, a veil, the maypole, a birthmark, and the scarlet letter – and creates meaning and coherence.

When he turned 14, Nathaniel was sent to boarding school in Stroudwater, near Portland, Maine. Given his love for books, it seems odd to find his reluctance to attend classes, as shown in his letter to Richard Henry Stoddard in 1852. "One of the peculiarities of my boyhood," he wrote, "was a grievous disinclination to go to school, and (Providence favoring me in this natural repugnance) I never did go half as much as other boys, partly owing to delicate health (which I made the most of for the purpose), and partly because, much of the time, there were no schools within reach" (Hawthorne 1884: I, 95). But then we learn why he felt this way: It was not the studies that he found unwelcome, but the accompanying pressures to converse and socialize. Consequently, some acquaintances called him secretive, although that was definitely not the case. He was shy and watchfully self-aware of the words that he spoke while communicating with others, and when and how, because he didn't want to offend. He wanted to learn by observing others. He absorbed everything.

To Nathaniel's relief, a foot injury suffered in the fall of 1813 while playing ball at school, and the subsequent lameness, prevented him from attending classes for the next 14 months and confined him to crutches for another three years. (Later, he would use this experience to write of a lame six-year-old child, a Quaker boy named Ibrahim, in the story, "The Gentle Boy.") Biographers are of the view that the protracted result of his injury was psychosomatic. Perhaps some underlying psychological weakness caused him to imagine that he'd suffered greater harm and disability than was really the case, or perhaps he perceived that his persistent lameness might gain sympathy and increase attention from his immediate circle. "In either case, this injury served Nathaniel's preference to evade the unpleasant rigors of schooling, to satisfy his appetite for voluminous reading, and to cultivate the attention of his mother, his sisters, and a series of physicians" (Valenti 2004: 15). Or was it, along with his father's death, further evidence of the family curse with which Nathaniel was obsessed?

As a result, he was homeschooled in the evenings by Dr. Joseph Emerson Worcester, the future lexicographer, whose dictionary was intended to "preserve the richness and succulence" of English (Cantwell 1948: 36). Given Hawthorne's love of language, it is pertinent to note that the young Nathaniel studied under a man "to whom English words were like precious heirlooms of inestimable value, each to be polished and weighed, treasured as long as it had meaning" (Cantwell 1948: 36). By October 1815, his condition had improved considerably, and for physical therapy he was allowed to attend the dance studios of William Turner and John M. Boisseaux and subsequently return to school.

In the summer of 1816, the 12-year-old Nathaniel experienced some relief from Salem's pressures when along with his two sisters he went to live with their mother along with Aunt Mary and Grandmother Manning in Raymond, Maine, a remote wilderness village near Lake Sebago, where Elizabeth owned property. For the next three years he "ran quite wild" – walking (one of his favorite pastimes) along the shore, swimming, fishing salmon trout, tracking bears in the snow, and hunting hen-hawks and partridges in the woods (Woodberry 1902: 10). This memory of exploring the countryside is something that he cherished as the brightest part of his boyhood. As he matured, he grew ever closer to the natural world and it became, as it had for Wordsworth and the Romantic poets, his teacher, guide, and source of support. Wordsworth's thoughts from "Lines Composed a Few Miles above Tintern Abbey" (1798) became Nathaniel's as well: "Therefore am I still / A lover of the meadows and the woods / And mountains; and of all that we behold / From this green earth" (lines 102–106).

"Ah," he exclaimed years later, "how well I recall the summer days when, with my gun, I roamed at will the woods of Maine. I lived like a bird of the air, so perfect was the freedom I enjoyed" (Fields 1872: 20). His feelings for nature were never tepid.

But even during this otherwise blissful period, he purportedly acquired his "cursed habits of solitude" which turned near-obsessive in later years and figured prominently in his fiction (Fields 1872: 113). In a society much like our own in which many people have lost possession of what Emily Dickinson called "[t]he appetite for silence" (1873), his characters feel a tug-of-war between the solitude they need for contemplation and the social interaction they seek for inspiration. In "On Solitude" (1820), written when he was 16, we can better gauge this conflict:

> Man is naturally a sociable being; not formed for himself alone, but destined to bear a part in the grand scheme of nature. All his pleasures are heightened, and all his griefs are lessened, by participation. It is only in Society that the full energy of his mind is aroused, and all its powers drawn forth.
>
> Apart from the World, there are no incitements to the pursuit of excellence; there are no rivals to contend with; and therefore there is no improvement. Perhaps life may pass more tranquilly, estranged from the pursuits and the vexations of the multitude, but all the hurry and whirl of passion is preferable to the cold calmness of indifference.
>
> The heart may be more pure and uncorrupted in Solitude, than when exposed to the influence of the depravity of the world; but the benefit of virtuous examples is equal to the detriment of vicious ones, & both are equally lost. (Chandler and Hawthorne 1931: 293)

He traced his tendency to solitude to his father – a silent, stern man. "Granite," he noted, "was my legacy" (Hawthorne 1884: I, 96).

Many biographers have been unfair to this aspect of Hawthorne's character as if his appetite for privacy should be considered a secret vice. I've never quite understood this approach. Solitude is the most fundamental of disciplines in any creative person's life and pursuits. Every story or novel we read, every song we hear, and every painting we enjoy is the result of many hours spent by the artist in quiet – and alone.

"If you want to live creatively," I tell my students, "you had better like being alone." As Hawthorne discovered, there is no other way. He became a solitary man who preferred to be in the company of his books, his writing, and his imagination. He made friends, but on his own terms. Even when married, he lived according to Emerson's principle in "Society and Solitude" (1870): "people are to be taken in very small doses" (*Complete Works* VII, 8). Like Emerson, he could be quite ruthless about protecting his privacy.

From 1818 to 1820, while living with Manning relatives and under the guardianship of his Uncle Robert (whose credo was practicality and hard work), he attended Samuel Archer's school in Salem. He then went on to prepare for college under the tutelage of the deeply learned scientist and inventor of telescopes and lenses, the 60-year-old Dr. Benjamin Lynde Oliver, Jr. Nathaniel quickly gained proficiency in Latin and Greek, thus exemplifying his latent abilities. He also worked in his Uncle William Manning's stagecoach office and as a beekeeper, for which he was paid one dollar a week.

As a diversion from his studies, he founded in June 1820 (continuing until August 1821) the Pin Society made up of two members, himself (as secretary) and Louisa. They met weekly and formulated elaborate rules of procedure kept in a little blue-covered manuscript book. Between 21 August and 25 September of 1821, he also produced and circulated among his immediate family six issues of a hand-printed weekly newspaper, *The Spectator*, an imitation of two of his favorite authors, Joseph Addison (1672–1719) and Richard Steele (1672–1729). The newspaper contained Maria Louisa's poetry and Nathaniel's wry, satirical essays, short poems, news items drawn from both Salem and Raymond, as well as editorials on themes such as death, sorrow, passage of time, ambition, nature, and God, that foreshadow his subsequent work (Woodson 1986: 1–2).

In 1821, he passed the entrance examination and, with the financial support and encouragement of his uncle, entered Bowdoin College in Brunswick, Maine, becoming the first member of his family to pursue a higher education. This was an ideal site because it was inexpensive and a mere 30 miles from his mother and sisters, who had been living in Raymond since 1818.

Founded in 1794, the state's oldest college, Bowdoin began instruction in 1802 with a class comprising eight students. It was named after James Bowdoin (1726–1790), a statesman and first president of the American Academy of Arts and Sciences, and much of its initial endowment came from his son. Women were not admitted until 1971. Following Harvard's model, the curriculum focused on the classics and on religion, which is not surprising, given that the majority of American colleges were originally created to educate ministers.

Situated on a sandy plain near the falls of the Androscoggin River, Bowdoin stands against a background forest of deep-needled pine and oak groves where wild pigeons feed. In Nathaniel's time the college had three buildings, 38 students, and five faculty members. Two four-story, red-brick Georgian-style structures (Maine and Massachusetts Halls) served as recitation halls and dormitories. An unpainted and unheated two-story wooden chapel also functioned as a library with 4000 books.

I have walked the length and breadth of the campus, have sat where he sat, and have attempted to visualize the young student: "a slender lad, having a massive head, with dark, brilliant, and most expressive eyes, heavy eyebrows, and a profusion of dark hair" (Bridge 1893: 4). Ellery Channing added: "Tall, compacted figure, / ably strung, / To urge the Indian chase, or point the way" (Higginson 1879: 3). In his preface to *The Snow Image* Hawthorne described "gathering blue-berries, in study-hours, under those tall academic pines; or watching the great logs, as they tumbled along the current of the Androscoggin; or shooting pigeons and gray squirrels in the woods" (*Works* XI, 4).

Contrary to popular notions of Hawthorne, he made friends quickly in his class. "I am very well contented with my situation," he wrote to his mother on 17 October.

"I have a very good Chum, and find College a much pleasanter place than I had expected" (*Works* XV, 157). His classmates included Henry Wadsworth Longfellow, Horatio Bridge (who encouraged him to write), Alfred Mason, Jonathan Cilley (who was later elected to Congress and died in a political duel with William J. Graves), and, a year ahead, Franklin Pierce – the future representative to the New Hampshire House of Representatives and US congressman, Brigadier General in the Mexican War, and, later, the fourteenth president of the United States. Along with Bridge, he remained Hawthorne's confidant for the rest of his life.

With his newfound friends, all destined for distinction in their chosen fields, Nathaniel played cards, drank champagne at Ward's Tavern (which still stands), smoked cigars, and violated other college rules, sometimes getting caught and fined 50 cents. He also joined a literary society and, together with five colleagues, formed a secret group which they named "The Pot-8-O Club," dedicated to weekly poetry readings, eating, and drink (its name a reference to the abundance of potatoes grown in Maine) at Ward's Tavern (Tapley 1931: 225–233). All this seems to suggest that as a young man, Hawthorne was not the morbid, dangerously introspective recluse as portrayed by some of his early biographers. Indeed, he found enjoyable the student activities and congenial company.

Hawthorne took the same set of required courses everyone else did. It would be fascinating to know more about the lessons he must have received in Greek, Latin, mathematics, the physical sciences, and philosophy. Never shy about his likes and dislikes, of these years he said he loved to read but resisted formal instruction, neglected recitations (calling for students to recite verbatim poems or essays in front of class), and skipped public worship. "I was an idle student, negligent of college rules and the Procrustean details of academic life," he wrote to his friend Richard Stoddard in 1853, "rather choosing to nurse my own fancies than to dig into Greek roots and be numbered among the learned Thebans" (*Works* XVI, 523; Hawthorne 1884: I, 96; Stoddard 1853: 18).

While at college, he felt pressured to choose a particular profession. Like most of us, Hawthorne lived in a world preoccupied with early achievement, as if that were the best indicator of being successful in later life. But this idea is both untrue and discouraging. To his credit, Hawthorne bristled against the pressure. He was, to use a modern expression, a late bloomer. In an irreverent but prescient letter to his mother dated 13 March 1821, he dismissed any suggestion of becoming a minister, lawyer, or physician (the predictable male professions at the time), and pointed out: "What do you think of my becoming an Author, and relying for support upon my pen. Indeed I think the illegibility of my handwriting is very author-like. How proud you would feel to see my works praised by the reviewers, as equal to the proudest productions of the scribbling sons of John Bull" (*Works* XV, 139).

Neither she nor her son could have predicted that he would eventually become one of America's great novelists, or that for a time, he would support himself and his family by working at the Custom Houses in Salem and Boston, or that he would serve as Consul to Liverpool under President Franklin Pierce. But he was ambitious, hungry for fame, and sought freedom from monetary concerns. A spark from within pushed him to explore the less-traveled path.

This was a courageous (some said foolhardy) declaration to be sure, for then the self-sustaining American writer was rare. Except in very few cases, authors were paid little, rarely on time. In "The Custom-House," he imagined his Puritan ancestors mocking his chosen profession:

> "What is he?" murmurs one gray shadow of my forefathers to the other. "A writer of story-books! What kind of a business in life, – what mode of glorifying God, or being serviceable to mankind in his day and generation, – may that be? Why, the degenerate fellow might as well have been a fiddler!" Such are the compliments bandied between my great-grandsires and myself, across the gulf of time! And yet, let them scorn me as they will, strong traits of their nature have intertwined themselves with mine. (*Works* I, 10)

Most writers back then, just like their modern counterparts, had lingering self-doubt, not only about their talent but especially about their ability to make a living. Until his breakthrough with *The Scarlet Letter* in 1850, this describes Hawthorne. He soon began to write fiction, albeit with little success, working on *Fanshawe: A Tale*, whose setting is reminiscent of Bowdoin College, along with a series of stories entitled *Seven Tales of My Native Land* (both of which he later burned).

He graduated on 7 September 1825, 18th in his class of 37. Gorham Deane, the second scholar of the class, had died of overwork and disregard for his health (the diagnosis was tuberculosis) on 11 August. This tragic event moved Hawthorne profoundly, and he would base his central character in *Fanshawe* on Deane. He realized the irony of someone spending so much time and energy acquiring the knowledge that he would never live to apply. "[W]here was the happiness of superior knowledge?" the narrator asks (*Works* III, 350). Fanshawe was a type that always fascinated Hawthorne – excessively studious, brilliant, but suffering the consequences of poor health and a sedentary lifestyle. Another classmate, Zenas Caldwell, also died unexpectedly at about the same time.

At graduation exercises, Hawthorne's ears must have perked up when he heard the president of the college, the Reverend William Allen, deliver the following words on the topic of "Humility":

> To all who are engaged in literary pursuits, and especially to them whose course of study in this Seminary is now finished, it may be said: – It is the order of providence, that you should be distinguished above many others; – it cannot be necessary that you should shrink from that sphere, in which

> God has placed you, but it should be your most anxious care that in that sphere you may carry with you a deep sense of your unworthiness and guilt . . .. (Hawthorne 1940: 278)

Always "a diligent reader of the Bible" (Fields 1872: 94), with deep faith and moral sense, he must have heard in Allen's words a confirmation of his own piety and humility in the face of the inscrutable ways of God. Guard against falling into pride, Allen warns, as you commit to a higher calling. This was a theme that Hawthorne would turn to repeatedly in the writings to come.

Fifty years later, Longfellow recalled nostalgically their college days in his poem titled *Morituri Salutamus* (1876): "The love of learning, the sequestered nooks, / And all the sweet serenity of books; . . . / Something remains for us to do or dare" (lines 88, 90). We find a similar ambition in an autobiographical passage from *Fanshawe*:

> He called up in review the years, that, even at his early age, he had spent in solitary study – in conversation with the dead – while he had scorned to mingle with the living world, or to be actuated by any of its motives . . . Fanshawe had hitherto deemed himself unconnected with the world, unconcerned in its feelings, and uninfluenced by it in any of his pursuits. In this respect he probably deceived himself. If his inmost heart could have been laid open, there would have been discovered that dream of undying fame, which, dream as it is, is more powerful than a thousand realities. (*Works* III, 350)

Unlike Fanshawe, however, who dies at age 20, Hawthorne would live to just shy of 60 and realize his dream of fame. His own books went on to pay him handsomely, though profits from *The Scarlet Letter* and *The House of the Seven Gables* were still 20 years off.

The motivation for making art is the prompting of not just *love* – but also *longing*. The first rule is that creation is *always* the successful resolution of internal conflict or anxiety – the artist's, to begin with, and then perhaps of those who appreciate what they have created. Ironically, some writers are at their best in public when they are at their saddest or most conflicted in private. Disconcerting and sadistic as it may sound, the reader's pleasure is derived from the artist's pain.

My students are unsurprised, therefore, to discover that some of the traumas Hawthorne experienced at an early age – including his father's death, the pain of separation, the weight of his Puritan past, his mother's remoteness, his poverty, the sudden passing of a fellow student, and his manifold insecurities – played out in the adult's work. Like his characters, he could not escape the trappings of the past. A seemingly living force in his psyche continued to influence his thoughts, feelings, and behavior. No comforting amnesia of childhood here.

3

Fanshawe: A Tale (1828)

> *He left a world for which he was unfit; and we trust, that,*
> *among the innumerable stars of heaven, there is one where he*
> *has found happiness.*
>
> —*Fanshawe: A Tale* (*Works* III, 113)

"Why *Fanshawe*? Am I missing something?"

These were the words of a colleague after I mentioned adding Hawthorne's first published novel to my students' reading list.

"It would be a mistake not to consider it," I said. "My students find it to be a very easy novel to enjoy, and so do I. It reminds me of some of what I learned about myself during my own time in college."

Had the opportunity presented itself, I would have added that it's the first novel of academic life in American literature and a remarkably mature achievement for a 24-year-old author. In it, we come across themes that eventually go on to gain prominence in his later fiction. These include the role and nature of the artist, the burden of guilt, disguised identities, the undying dream of fame, a romantic fascination with death, and the redemptive/transformative power of love. Clearly, there's something here for everyone.

Although, like my colleague, many of Hawthorne's later critics have never quite known what to make of it, for the most part, *Fanshawe* has had its defenders. On 6 November 1828, for example, John Neal in the *Yankee and Boston Literary Gazette*, acknowledging the book's "considerable merit," its "powerful and pathetic" parts, and its "excellent descriptive penciling," portended "a fair prospect of future success" for the author. The unsigned reviewer for the *Boston Weekly Messenger* said on 13 November: "To the elegance of language which frequently occurs in this volume, we are pleased to bear testimony. There are some beauties of more than an ordinary kind, and they give promise of better things hereafter." Meanwhile, Sarah Josepha Hale, editor of the *Ladies' Magazine*, urged in the

The Life of the Author: Nathaniel Hawthorne, First Edition. Dale Salwak.
© 2023 John Wiley & Sons Ltd. Published 2023 by John Wiley & Sons Ltd.

November issue: "Purchase it, reader. There is but one volume, and trust me that is worth placing in your library" (Crowley 1970: 42, 43, 44). Much later, the novelist Robert Cantwell (1948), noting its "formal excellence" and its "engaging and easy" humor, summed up its appeal as follows: "under the smooth surface of the story the power of genius shows like the muscles of a rare horse held in check" (121, 123).

Part of the novel's charm lies in its clever plot and deftly crafted character motivation. The setting is the secluded Harley College (not unlike Bowdoin) in the year 1745. Fanshawe, a dedicated student who has forsaken the commercial life for books and his "dream of undying fame" (*Works* III, 350), falls in love with the beautiful and sweet Ellen (whose mother and aunt have passed away). The 18-year-old daughter of an affluent merchant, Michael Langton, who has been living in England for many years for business purposes, she is under the care of the affectionate head of the college, Dr. Melmoth, and his wife, who have no children of their own.

Over time, Fanshawe's alter ego, Edward Wolcott, begins to compete for Ellen's affection. He, too, is a respected scholar and class poet, but the similarities end there. Unlike Fanshawe, he is a man of the world – tall and good-looking, polite, groomed by family and money. But Wolcott is not impervious to human frailties; for instance, he drinks too much, has a propensity for picking fights, and is both headstrong and reckless. Thus, we have what it takes to constitute a classic love triangle: the introvert versus the extrovert, both attracted to the same woman.

Further complications develop when we meet Hugh Crombie, the proprietor of the Hand and Bottle tavern close to the college. A reformed pirate who has fled inland to escape hanging, he has married Sarah Hutchins, the tavern keeper's widow. Just before Ellen's father returns from England, Butler, "a lawless and guilty man" (*Works* III, 436) and an old shipmate of Crombie's from the *Black Andrew* (who had been in Langton's employment before he turned to crime), enters the fray. Hoping to secure her fortune, he blackmails Crombie into facilitating the kidnapping of Ellen at midnight on the pretext of taking her to her father, who, he lies, is ruined in business and needs her at once. He also deceives Melmoth with a false story planted in the newspaper reporting Langdon's death in a shipwreck. Butler then takes her to a mysterious cave and threatens to rape her.

Just in time, Fanshawe rescues Ellen and witnesses the villain's accidental fatal fall from a high rocky ledge – a version of a plot device that Hawthorne would use again in *The Marble Faun*. Fanshawe is finally able to save the life of a noble and modest woman, and he returns her to the arms of her recently arrived father. But when in sympathy for Fanshawe, she offers herself in marriage as a reward, he refuses because he does not see normal married life as compatible with the scholarly life. He is fully cognizant of the ramifications of such a choice. They "must part now and forever," he proclaims. Immediately, Fanshawe resumes his studies,

Faust-like, with "the same absorbing ardor," cut off from humankind (*Works* III, 459). Almost inexorably, he passes away, frustrated and despairing, before turning 20.

Four years later, Walcott puts aside his own scholarly ambitions and marries Ellen, whose "gentle, almost imperceptible, but powerful influence, drew her husband away from the passions and pursuits that would have interfered with domestic felicity; and he never regretted the worldly distinction of which she thus deprived him." The narrator goes on to add: "Theirs was a long life of calm and quiet bliss; – and what matters it, that, except in these pages, they have left no name behind them?" (*Works* III, 460).

We do not know as to when exactly Hawthorne wrote this novel, although the general consensus is that he began working at it while in college and finished it upon his return to Salem. But completing the novel was one thing; successfully getting it into the hands of a publisher was quite another. There was no way for a fledgling writer to be conversant with the rituals and personalities through which literary business was conducted at that time.

After several firms had rejected the manuscript, Hawthorne had to pay at least $100 (perhaps as much as $270) to the Boston firm of Marsh and Capen in order to publish it anonymously. It came out in late October 1828 in an edition of 1000 copies. Although it was actively promoted by numerous New England booksellers and in general reviewed favorably, Hawthorne had a change of heart soon after its release. In a fury, he burned his own copy (just as he had obliterated drafts of his early fiction and correspondence) and as many others as he could find, never informing his wife of its existence and refusing to discuss the book in the years to come.

"We were enjoined," said Elizabeth in a letter to his son Julian after her brother's death, "to keep the authorship a profound secret, and of course we did, with one or two exceptions; for we were in those days almost absolutely obedient to him" (Hawthorne 1884: I, 124). His future publisher James T. Fields (1872), reported that in 1851, Hawthorne referred to *Fanshawe* "with great disgust" (48) and informed him that it would be in their "mutual interest to conceal" it and "other follies of my nonage" (*Works* XVI, 383). The "utterly disheartened" Hawthorne also shared his dismay with his friend, Horatio Bridge (1893): "I'm a doomed man" (68). At the author's request, Bridge burned his own copy and never spoke of the work again. Three years later, a warehouse fire destroyed the many copies that had gone unsold.

Hawthorne nearly succeeded in sinking the book in oblivion. Fortunately for his readers and the literary world at large, the family discovered a surviving copy 12 years after his passing. James R. Osgood, who had released George Parsons Lathrop's *A Study of Hawthorne* two years earlier, republished the novel in 1876 as *Fanshawe and Other Pieces* – four years after Sophia's death while living abroad. (To her dying day, she had innocently denied her husband's authorship.)

For the most part, reviews of the re-issue were favorable. Bayard Taylor, writing in the 7 July 1876 issue of the *New York Daily Tribune*, typified the reactions when he wrote: "[it] is a work which derives the interest wholly from its author's later masterpieces. It has the slightest possible plot, the characters are imperfectly presented, the descriptions are commonplace to the verge of triteness yet one who reads the story carefully will easily detect the weak and timid presence of all Hawthorne's peculiar powers" (Idol and Jones 1994: 383). Ever since, it has attained cult status and never fallen out of print.

I have yet to read or hear a satisfactory explanation for Hawthorne's profound dissatisfaction with the novel. Given that he had to pay to publish it, and it made therefore little or no impression on the popular audience (which he ostensibly had in mind when writing it), the lack of response, along with a couple of negative reviews (despite its generally cordial reception), may have stung him. On 31 October 1828, Joseph T. Buckingham, editor of the *New England Galaxy,* called the book "A love story" which has, "like ten thousand others, a mystery, an elopement; a villain, a father, a tavern, almost a duel, a horrible death, and – heaven save the mark! . . . an end." In the 22 November 1828 issue of *The Critic: A Weekly Review of Literature, Fine Arts, and the Drama*, William Leggett declared that "The mind that produced this little, interesting volume, is capable of making great and rich additions to our native literature," but conceded that "the book has faults," including an improbable plot, stilted sentences, and wooden characters (Crowley 1970: 41, 45–46). Like all artists, Hawthorne was sensitive to criticism. It left him feeling beleaguered. Ironically, his publisher, Samuel Goodrich, once told him that it would have been a success had its printer had any way of selling the copies. "The bane of your life," Bridge (1893) would tell him on 25 December 1836, "has been self-distrust" (73).

Furthermore, low sales may have convinced Hawthorne that, from a marketing perspective, his timing was off. Possibly, this campus story was ahead of its era. The novel-reading public was skeptical of higher education and its pursuit of reason, of contemplation – the very subjects the novel explores. The public did not relish the life of the cerebrally inclined, drawing an equivalence between Fanshawe's need for academic solitude and laziness, inactivity, and non-productiveness. Study without action was worse than action without study. This attitude is not unexpected when we consider the fact that America began as a rural nation. Most people lived on farms or in small towns and villages. Most authors at the time were not university-educated. "Meek young men grew up in libraries," Emerson would lament in "The American Scholar" (1903–1904 [1837]). "Books [with specific reference to the Bible] are for the scholar's idle times. When he can read God directly, the hour is too precious to be wasted in other men's transcripts of their readings" (*Complete Works* I, 91). More than a generation would pass before the college novel took hold in America, starting with the publication of Thomas Hughes's *Tom Brown at Oxford* in 1861.

Still, others have suggested that Hawthorne rejected the book because some of its characters, along with the setting itself, bore a strong resemblance to reality, and he feared a backlash as a result. Ellen Langton, for example, may have been inspired by Jane Appleton, a member of a prominent Federalist family who married Franklin Pierce. In Walcott, there were echoes of Pierce or Bridge, whereas Dr. Melmoth's character may have been derived from the college's president William Allen and his predecessor, Jesse Appleton. Hawthorne might have concluded that in creating Fanshawe, he would perhaps be accused of exploiting the tragic life of one of his classmates, Gorham Deane, the brilliant but sickly young man who had died of tuberculosis a few weeks before Commencement. Jane Appleton's cousin Alfred Mason, who was also Hawthorne's old roommate, died in New York of yellow fever. This connection, too, may have caused Hawthorne to become disillusioned with his story. Robert Cantwell (1948) also made a strong case that the unflattering description of Harley College was modeled in part after Dartmouth, given its rural remoteness, its setting in 1745 (long before the founding of Bowdoin), and the references to a number of Indian students. This is significant because Dartmouth was originally an Indian school (119–120).

Given the book's confessional nature, however, it seems plausible that the author's primary reason for rejecting it was not just that it fell short of his high standards, but that he believed he had revealed much more of his private self through his protagonist than he intended. That would explain its anonymous publication. "Writers are generally fated to commit the truest parts of themselves to the page," said Maria Bustillos (2013), "whether they choose to own their work in public or not. That is the ultimate vulnerability, and it is inescapable." Charlotte Brontë (1816–1855), when asked why she concealed her own identity, asked a counter-question, "What author would be without the advantage of being able to walk invisible?" (Brontë 2000: 141). I can imagine Hawthorne thinking along similar lines.

This novel, like all of his work, also has autobiographical origins. L.P. Hartley (1967), who was influenced by Hawthorne, spotted this immediately upon reading *Fanshawe*. According to him, the novelist's world "must, in some degree, be an extension of his own life; its fundamental problems must be his problems, its preoccupations his preoccupations – or something allied to them" (2). While it is "unsafe to assume that a novelist's work is autobiographical in any direct sense," it is nonetheless "plausible to assume that his work is a transcription, an anagram of his own experience, reflecting its shape and tone and tempo, and its main preoccupations" (62).

Throughout his life, Hawthorne was concerned about the possibility of revealing too much of what he called the "inmost Me" (*Works* I, 4). In a letter written after her husband's death, Sophia spoke of a veil her husband had drawn around himself – a recurring theme in many of his tales, notably "The Minister's Black Veil" (1836). Thus, his portrayal of Fanshawe as a gifted, pensive, solitary young man, apprehensive about his lack of progress as a writer, who dies young without any successful display of his genius, may have been too close to the grain. It is also notable that in appearance (darkly dressed, Byronically handsome), temperament (melancholy, preoccupied by death and immortality), and ambition (intensely hungry for fame combined with a fear of failure), he reminds us of the author. Fanshawe confined himself "sedulously to his chamber, except for one hour – the sunset hour – of every day. At that period, unless prevented by the inclemency of the weather, he was accustomed to tread a path that wound along the banks of the stream" (*Works* III, 352). All these traits were strongly associated with the author himself. In that case, is the name "Fanshawe" a variant of "fantasy of Hawthorne"?

Both also felt deeply a sense of the impermanence of this world and a longing for the next. Subconsciously, did Hawthorne himself explore the thoughts of an early death, perhaps by his own hand? (He once said that he expected to die before 25.) After all, the demise of his father at such a young age had, in a mysterious sense, granted his son the "permission" to die young, too, if he so chose – much in the way that an alcoholic or divorced parent unwittingly grants the child permission to drink too much or turn too readily to divorce. At the time, the parallels drawn between the author and the character must have been cathartic. I tell my students, "Don't think yourself odd if, after finishing the book, you spend hours if not days in a reverie of alienation. Hawthorne has made profound art out of estrangement and loneliness."

Other than the inevitable interest in early work by a famous writer, what else recommends the book to my students? I place *Fanshawe* within the genre of popular gothic-horror fiction and romances – with their Victorian ideals of secrecy and restraint along with elements of terror, mystery, the supernatural, and extremes of good and evil. A closer look reveals clear connections with gothic authors such as Sir Walter Scott, William Godwin, and especially Charles Robert Maturin, whose *Melmoth the Wanderer* (1824) suggests a strong resonance with Hawthorne's book in terms of major plot elements and character portraits (Goldstein 1945: 2). The presence of pirates and runaways, escapes, and coincidences suggests the influence of Robert Louis Stevenson. All this indicates that at the time, Hawthorne prioritized entertaining the reader over anything else. "The storyteller's intention," said Paul Theroux (2011), "is always to hold the listener with a glittering eye and riveting tale" (viii). Indeed, Hawthorne keeps his readers enraptured even to this day.

He achieves this not only with an entertaining, mysterious plot and well-motivated characterization but also through the intervention of an omniscient narrator who comes across as intelligent, considerate, articulate, and unassuming.

The following humorous asides between Melmoth and his wife, sprinkled sporadically at just the right moment, poignantly exemplify the role he plays:

> Doctor Melmoth, at the time when he is to be introduced to the reader, had borne the matrimonial yoke (and in his case, it was no light burthen) nearly twenty years. (336)

> [His study] was the only portion of the house, to which, since one firmly repelled invasion, Mrs. Melmoth's omnipotence did not extend. (337)

> But, by long disuse, she had lost the power of consenting graciously to any wish of her husband's. (339)

> "I think I may be trusted, Doctor Melmouth," replied the lady, who had a high opinion of her own abilities as a comforter, and was not averse to exercise them. (403)

> "Well, I thank Heaven for his safety," said Mrs. Melmoth; "but truly, the poor gentleman could not have chosen a better time to be drowned, nor a worse one to come to life, than this." (404)

> You must not spare for trouble – no, nor for danger – now, oh! if I were a man – (405)

> Mrs. Melmoth was appeased by the submission with which the Doctor asked her counsel; though, if the truth must be told, she heartily despised him for needing it. (406)

The above laugh-out-loud lines are conveyed by a friendly, well-meaning, tactful narrator whose gentle irony infuses life into each entertaining scene. He quickly establishes a confidential relation with the reader, whom he *addresses* as "the reader." Hawthorne's naive observer allows characters such as Mrs. Melmoth to reveal themselves more effectively than an intrusive narrator could. The imagination that would create *The Scarlet Letter* and *The House of the Seven Gables* was anchored in a unifying concept of reader engagement. With Hawthorne, we never feel that he is being dogmatic, narrow-minded, and doctrinaire.

Closer to my students' experience, too, is a medical theory running through the novel, suggesting that one could die from an overdose of studying. Edwin Haviland Miller (1991) discovered that in 1828, Hawthorne borrowed Chandler Robbins' *Remarks on the Disorders of Literary Men* (1825) from the Salem library. The book discusses the case of a Boston man who died in 1820 "by too great love of learning" (80) – a prominent theme in Hawthorne's later work ("Ethan Brand," for example) known as the "Unpardonable Sin."

More specifically, Hawthorne believed that people with over-developed intellects sacrifice their emotional life. This often leads to "the violation of the individual soul or the probable exposure of certain secret places in the human heart and consciousness, which might otherwise remain unrevealed" (Coale 2001: 72). To allow one's heart to become "withered," "contracted," and "hardened," he wrote in "Ethan Brand," is the most damaging approach to life someone can adopt (*Works* XI, 99). That is the takeaway of *Fanshawe*, whose central character, we are told, is "unconnected with the world, unconcerned in its feelings, and uninfluenced by it in any of his pursuits" (*Works* III, 350). Friedrich Nietzsche (1844–1900) called such a scholar "a cold demon of knowledge" (2019 [1874]: vi).

On our first encounter with the protagonist, it becomes apparent that he is reading himself to death. Melmoth has sent him to wander among the woods so that he can recover his sanity and health. The narrator calls him a victim of "a blight, of which his thin, pale cheek and the brightness of his eye were alike proofs" (*Works* III, 346). His solitary studies are "destructive labor," a "conversation with the dead" (*Works* III, 350). After Fanshawe's demise, his epitaph features words borrowed from Nathaniel Mather's (the brother of Cotton Mather) grave, which Hawthorne passed by often as a boy and whom he may also have had in mind while creating Fanshawe. "[I]n his almost insane eagerness for knowledge and in his early death," the narrator tells us, "Fanshawe resembled. THE ASHES OF A HARD STUDENT AND A GOOD SCHOLAR" (*Works* III, 460).

Hawthorne knew from his own life that the outcome of an over-developed intellect that causes or paves the way to the neglect of emotions is never pleasant. If he were here today, I can imagine him saying to my ambitious students, "Write all the books you care to write, read all that you want to read, give of yourself to every creative compulsion, but try not to let your busy professional life irreparably skew your sense of proportion and balance." Granted, there is a lot to lose if we fail to fulfill our professional aspirations, but even more to lose, as is evident with Fanshawe, if in pursuing those dreams, we end up neglecting what should be our deepest concern: our innermost self.

The literary world is replete with examples of those like Fanshawe, but the one that comes immediately to mind is Goethe's *Doctor Faust* (1790/1806), with which Hawthorne was well acquainted. He would later adapt the story in "Young Goodman Brown" (1835), "The Birth-mark" (1843), "Rappaccini's Daughter" (1844), and "Ethan Brand" (1850). Unlike the doctor, Fanshawe doesn't enter into a pact with the Devil, but Hawthorne creatively draws upon the Faustian myth, using words that echo the author's concerns about himself:

> The books were around him, which had hitherto been to him like those fabled volumes of Magic, from which the reader could not turn away his

eye, till death were the consequence of his studies . . . He called up in review the years, that, even at his early age, he had spent in solitary study – in conversation with the dead – while he had scorned to mingle with the living world, or to be actuated by any of its motives. He asked himself, to what purpose was all this destructive labor, and where was the happiness of superior knowledge. He had climbed but a few steps of a ladder that reached to infinity – he had thrown away his life in discovering, that, after a thousand such lives, he should still know comparatively nothing. He even looked forward with dread – though once the thought had been dear to him – to the eternity of improvement that lay before him. (*Works* III, 350)

Fanshawe, therefore, becomes a cautionary tale for its readers. What overwhelms the protagonist could entrap any of us if we turn a blind eye to the needs of our inner self. Intellectual and spiritual torpor (a favorite word of Hawthorne's), indifference, and lethargy take root; sensibilities wither; and relationships with people become stunted.

Like Fanshawe, we can also become emotionally disconnected, which manifests in our inability to draw sustenance from the life we have chosen to live. A chronic lack of enthusiasm, a refusal to take risks, a lost capacity to feel – are all symptoms of a greater malaise. Unless we are careful, we can easily succumb to a life that is fixated on and dictated only by our studies.

Ironically, Fanshawe rejects the one opportunity that might have helped him to attain some degree of balance in his life – Ellen – whose love temporarily regenerates him. For a brief time, he is not entirely hopeless or utterly lost. In her presence, "he felt the first thrilling of one of the many ties, that, so long as we breathe the common air (and who shall say how much longer?) unite us to our kind. The sound of a soft, sweet voice – the glance of a gentle eye – had wrought a change upon him . . . The recollection of his ruined health – of his habits, so much at variance with those of the world – all the difficulties that reason suggested – were inadequate to check the exulting tide of hope and joy" (*Works* III, 350–351). Yet Fanshawe also acknowledges the intrinsic hopelessness of his love for Ellen. Hawthorne dramatizes his inner struggle in this conversation. Ellen appeals to his noble spirit:

> "Yours is a heart, full of strength and nobleness; and if it have a weakness –"
> "You know well that it has, Ellen, – one that has swallowed up all its strength," said Fanshawe. "Was it wise, then, to tempt it thus – when, if it yield, the result must be your own misery?" (*Works* III, 458)

Even the *idea* of marriage to Ellen causes Fanshawe to experience inner anguish, anticipating Parson Hooper ("The Minister's Black Veil," 1835), Wakefield

("Wakefield," 1835), Richard Digby ("The Man of Adamant," 1836), Arthur Dimmesdale (*The Scarlet Letter*, 1850), and Miles Coverdale (*The Blithedale Romance*, 1852) – all of whom isolate themselves, often questioning or abandoning the prospect of married love.

When Ellen extends her hand to Fanshawe, we are told, "to refuse it was like turning from an angel, who would have guided him to heaven. But, had he been capable of making the woman he loved a sacrifice to her own generosity, that act would have rendered him unworthy of her" (*Works* III, 458). Hawthorne knew this of himself. It would be years before he would meet and accept the extended hand of *his* "Ellen" (which in Hebrew means "my God is abundance") – in the person of Sophia Peabody.

Fanshawe is admittedly an apprentice work from which Hawthorne would learn valuable lessons as an author. Novels oftentimes come from what we are unknowingly worrying about, from what Martin Amis (2020) referred to as "long-marinated and unregarded anxiety, from silent anxiety" (19). They are the *donnée* or gift from the subconscious. Something is consuming the author from within, but it's subliminal. He gets a glimpse of this world, experiences a "shiver" or a "throb" and thinks, "Here is something I can write a novel about," and he does, because he must (Amis 2014: 422; Riviere 1998: 9).

To write *Fanshawe*, Hawthorne looked into a mirror – not just any mirror, but a magical mirror that every aspiring writer, if fortunate, discovers. The genesis of this idea goes back to an ancient story. "Once upon a time there was a king, and the king commissioned his favourite wizard to create a magic mirror. This mirror didn't show you your reflection – it showed you who you really were. The wizard couldn't look at it without turning away. The king couldn't look at it. The courtiers couldn't look at it. A chestful of treasure was offered to any citizen in this peaceful land who could look at it for 60 seconds without turning away. And no one could" (Amis 2014: 34). No one can look at the mirror, because they cannot bear to see what lies beneath the surface of the 5% that is visible to them, much like the tip of an iceberg. Inexorably, the remaining 95% remains hidden.

In writing a novel, however, the author searches for that which is hidden. The experience is a staggering surprise – for himself, of course, but also for the reader. This is precisely what Shakespeare had in mind when he emboldened Hamlet to lecture the actors. The moral purpose of theater, he says, is to hold "the mirror up to nature" (III.ii.22) so that the performance reveals virtues and vices reflected back to us in their true shape. Shakespeare's art, at least as Hamlet understands it, entails mirroring reality, in representing "nature," the world, as it viscerally is. This is what we call *mimesis*, or imitation of life, and it held true for Hawthorne as well. He presented his characters as if established in a theater, "a little removed from the highway of ordinary travel, where the creatures of his brain may play their phantasmagorical antics" (*Works* III, 1). *Fanshawe* needed to be written before its author could move on, with growing confidence, in his journey toward self-discovery. He would continue to find a haven in his imagination.

4

The Dark Years (1825–1837)

I have made a captive of myself and put me into a dungeon;
and now I cannot find the key to let myself out – and if
the door were open, I should be almost afraid to come out.
—Hawthorne to Longfellow, 4 June 1837 (*Works* XV, 251)

From graduation in 1825 until the publication of *Twice-Told Tales* in 1837 and marriage to Sophia Peabody in 1838, Hawthorne (as he now spelled his name) lived a reclusive life, shielding himself from scrutiny in a drab attic room on the third floor of the Manning house at 12 Herbert Street in Salem, the quaint home of his childhood. He lived with his mother (who had since returned from Raymond), adoring spinster sisters Elizabeth and Louisa, and a number of cats. In this "dismal chamber," with a modest inheritance that allowed him to defer employment, his imagination ripened and "FAME was won" (*Works* VIII, 20). Hawthorne remembered these years as a time of darkness and isolation.

We think of isolation as negative, even a punishment, and value the company of others. But to Hawthorne, these ostensibly obscure and lonely years were not all gloomy. True, his struggles predisposed him to sporadic bouts of melancholy, but that is not necessarily tantamount to being sad or depressed – which he was not. "Dark" to Hawthorne meant delving deeper into unexplored facets of his life and psyche, and embracing the melancholy that inevitably accompanied his ineffable journey. Hawthorne preferred being alone. There were times when he would just stare out the window, daydreaming or brooding. Equally, he relished the process of researching. During these years, he read over seven hundred nonfiction books that Elizabeth borrowed for him from the Salem Athenaeum. He developed a fascination for early New England history which would go on to influence much of his work. This is where he felt most at home. He was always listening, learning, and writing.

The Life of the Author: Nathaniel Hawthorne, First Edition. Dale Salwak.
© 2023 John Wiley & Sons Ltd. Published 2023 by John Wiley & Sons Ltd.

He wrote every morning, interrupted his work to have lunch, and then worked some more through the afternoon, saving the evening hours after tea for a solitary walk. He often enjoyed wandering by the seashore or in the forest, when no one could observe him, or hiding in the woods rather than face a passer-by. Sometimes, a village bonfire or public event drew him out to lurk at the edges of the crowd (Fields 1872: 66). In a letter to Sophia (dated 4 October 1840), he conceded:

> [I]f I had sooner made my escape into the world, I should have grown hard and rough, and been covered with earthly dust, and my heart would have become callous by rude encounters with the multitude . . . But living in solitude till the fullness of time was come, I still kept the dew of my youth and the freshness of my heart . . . I used to think that I could imagine all passions, all feelings, all states of the heart and mind; but how little did I know. . . Indeed, we are but shadows – we are not endowed with real life, and all that seems most real about us is but the thinnest substance of a dream – till the heart is touched. (*Works* XV, 495)

He had a lot to explore. Given the death of his father, the shame associated with his family's Puritan Past, the absence of any literary encouragement from most of his Manning relatives (who, with the exception of the always loyal Elizabeth, preferred the security of the business world), the intensifying neuroticism of his ineffectual mother, his pressing financial constraints, and the challenges in finding publishers and readers for his early work, it is not difficult to understand why, like Hilda in *The Marble Faun*, "the riddle of the Soul's growth, taking its first impulse amid remorse and pain," preoccupied him and deepened with time (*Works* IV, 381). It is no wonder that writing brought on occasional bouts of sadness and bitterness over the fleeting nature of all that is beautiful. Like Joyce Carol Oates (2003), who has written glowingly of his journals, he had to concede, "the more we are hurt, the more we seek solace in the imagination" (140).

For him, writing became effortlessly cathartic. Each day, as he entered the sanctuary of his upper room and closed the door, he would try to leave behind the din of daily life. He allowed tranquility to settle upon him and embraced the pleasure of composition – "an enjoyment," he wrote, "not at all amiss in its way" (*Works* IX, 3). To borrow a phrase from Emerson's essay "Nature" (1836), he wanted to "unlock" his thoughts and become "acquainted" with himself (*Complete Works* I, 21). "I sat down by the wayside of life, like a man under an enchantment," Hawthorne reflected in 1851, "and a shrubbery sprung up around me, and the bushes grew to be saplings, and the saplings became trees, until no exit appeared possible, through the entangling depths of my obscurity" (*Works* XI, 5). By his own admission, his early writings were "the memorials of very tranquil and not unhappy years" (*Works* IX, 6).

The idea of a room as a sanctuary is fundamental to understanding Hawthorne as a writer. Without such a refuge, distractions threatened to intrude upon his thoughts and impede his progress. When his door closed, it served to draw him in and keep him focused on the work at hand. Unfettered from others and free to observe and investigate his primal thoughts and feelings, he progressed toward an ever-deepening familiarity with himself and his art.

All of us, but especially my students, need opportunities for productive withdrawal. On our campus, there sits an easy-to-miss, gray-stone chapel that provides a small place for prayer and meditation. One has to stoop like a child to enter a room just large enough to accommodate five or six people. Everything about its interior – the wooden beams that rib the ceiling, the dark green carpeting, the gingerbread-colored pew benches – is suffused with an atmosphere of tranquil happiness. During their undergraduate years, some of them go there during the week, sometimes alone, sometimes with two or three members of their weekly study group. They go with their needs – they talk, they pray, they listen. Some read or work on assignments. After an hour or so, they feel refreshed and strengthened, as if they have just returned from a mountain retreat.

And so, my students understand when I say that I feel at ease sitting alone in Hawthorne's third-floor room, as I have done on several occasions. True, the window of his room was "miserably small," and the interior conjured memories of "the most unprepossessing of attic rooms," but this only enhanced the effect Hawthorne desired (Clarke 1913: 69). Everything about the interior was designed to promote a relaxed, fully focused atmosphere. He kept distractions at a minimum. There was no glittering decoration. The walls, covered with homely old paper, lacked even a nail to hang a picture or photograph. A brownish carpet covered the floor. Dimmed lighting helped to create restful shadows to stimulate self-reflection, vulnerability, and openness. There were no intrusions: just himself, a mahogany desk, books and periodicals and papers and pens and bottles of black ink. Reason and imagination could have free play in this treasured room-of-his-own. Characters sprouted, plots evolved, and imaginative distances bridged.

For the form of his early work, he chose the tale. Its great strength, wrote Poe (1950 [1846]) in "The Philosophy of Composition," is that it may be read at a single sitting and creates a unified impression (421). Henry James (1907) argued in the preface to *The Turn of the Screw* that singleness of effect is essential to the genre – a detached incident, "short and sharp and single, changed more or less with the compactness of anecdote" (xvi). More subjective than dramatic, it is often a mere sketch or "a personal essay with a backbone of narrative" (Abel 1963: 190). Within his "disciplined isolation" (to borrow from Ernest Hemingway [Meyers 1985: 137]), new ideas gravitated to him. At the onset, he perceived what seemed to be a fleeting thought, but he knew he had to grasp that wisp of an idea and work on it slowly and deliberately, cultivate and nurture it. Often, he would devote all morning to write a single perfect paragraph but then would be inundated by a deluge of new ideas for possible future use – as his journal entries from the time reveal. "It needs long thought with me," he told Pierce on 9 June 1852, "in order to produce anything good" (*Works* XVI, 545).

Notwithstanding this admirable energy and dedication, however, publishers' reception of his first collection, *Seven Tales of My Native Land*, was poor, and so, "without mercy or remorse" or subsequent regret, he burned up the manuscript – all "dull stuff," he wrote, which yet "possessed inflammability enough to set the chimney on fire!" (*Works* IX, 4). Only his tale of witchcraft and inherited guilt, "Alice Doane's Appeal," survived to be revised and published in 1835 in the *Token and Atlantic Souvenir*, before being reprinted in the posthumous collection, *Sketches and Studies*, published by Houghton Mifflin in 1883. Around 1829, he planned another collection, *Provincial Tales*, and in 1834 a third, *The Story Teller*, both of which were rejected, much to his chagrin. As it turned out, publishers were uninterested in collections of short stories written by an obscure young writer.

But encouraging signs began to emerge as well. In a conscious effort to find his audience, at a decisive stage in his writing career, Hawthorne began to issue anonymously and piecemeal more than 40 works under a variety of signatures (including Ashley, A. Royce, the Rev. A.A. Royce, Oberon), or a tag ("by the author of . . .") when referring to a previously published story. In 1830, for example, he published "The Hollow of the Three Hills" and "An Old Woman's Tale," besides three biographical sketches from New England history in the *Salem Gazette*. Those led to more opportunities. From 1830 to 1833, Samuel H. Goodrich published others, including "Sights from a Steeple" in his annual gift book, *The Token and Atlantic Souvenir*. In 1832, Hawthorne published in *The Token* "The Wives of the Dead," "My Kinsman, Major Molineux," "Roger Malvin's Burial," and "The Gentle Boy." In 1833, more sketches and stories would appear in *The Token*. These tales, he later noted, "opened the way to most agreeable associations, and to the formation of imperishable friendships" (*Works* IX, 7).

Taken as a group, these early pieces evoke an atmosphere of "beauty, melancholy, mystery, or terror" – traits that would eventually become Hawthorne's signature (Baym 1976: 31). Each tale explores one or more universal themes that he would return to throughout his career. His mastery of New England Colonial and pre-Colonial history, as well as the moral and political ramifications of Puritanism, are ubiquitous. Although the language belongs to the nineteenth-century era, each tale takes us to places we didn't know existed yet somehow feel familiar. They could have happened yesterday.

The terrible burden of remembered guilt and shame, for example, pervades his first published tale, "The Hollow of the Three Hills," a brief dreamscape influenced by the gothic, shaped by the Faustian myth, and aptly reminiscent of a fairytale with its opening words, "In those strange old times" (*Works* IX, 199).

At sunset, a beautiful but troubled young woman, "smitten with an untimely blight in what should have been the fullest bloom of her years," meets with "an ancient and meanly dressed" old crone (suggestive of Satanic darkness) who has outlived any ordinary human life (*Works* IX, 199).

The young woman kneels at the crone's feet in a subversive act of genuflection, offering her life in exchange for knowledge of the fate of her loved ones that the title's three lonely hills represent: her aged parents (whom she had deserted), her husband (whom she had betrayed), and her child (whom she had left to die). As a result of these grotesque betrayals, her heart has become hollow, like the basin. The conjurer summons such forceful fragmentary visions of the consequences of her sin that they render their listener lifeless: "when the old woman stirred the kneeling lady, she lifted not her head." Says the withered crone, chuckling to herself, "Here has been a sweet hour's sport" (*Works* IX, 204).

Life's vicissitudes are unpredictable. Not for the last time, Hawthorne suggests that the past may cast an eerie light on the present. History haunts us. We are left quivering and unsure of what its effects have in store for us. Distant, intangible, unreliable, lost, our histories are, at best, half-remembered and, at worst, actively misrepresented. Hawthorne's characters are driven by a combination of knowing and not-knowing. "The past is a foreign country," wrote Hartley in *The Go-Between* (1953); "they do things differently there" (17). Hawthorne would agree.

Events also linger like dreams in the surreal "An Old Woman's Tale." It is framed by an ostensibly autobiographical sketch wherein the author recalls paying rapt attention as a child to the tale narrated by an elderly servant. We meet a penniless young couple, David and Esther, cuddling in the moonlight, unable to marry because they cannot afford the fee. The two happen to live in a town where the residents periodically succumb to a magical one-hour's "simultaneous slumber" (*Works* XI, 241). On one such moonlit evening, the sleeping couple seems to be overtaken by a strange dream of long-deceased villagers, a parade of ghostly characters "like a group of shadows flickering in the moonshine" (*Works* XI, 246). It's almost as if they have come in the fashions of yesteryear to inspect the current state of the town.

One of them, an old woman wearing "spangled shoes and gold-clocked stockings" (*Works* XI, 248), attempts to dig in the ground with an iron shovel. Three times she tries to turn, albeit unsuccessfully, the "stubborn turf" (*Works* XI, 249). Then, just as suddenly, the couple awaken, discover the shovel, and seek the actual site where the dream-woman was digging. Seizing it, the young man plunges it into the earth. "Oho! – What have we here?" he cries as he scoops away the soil, evidently unearthing the old woman's long-hidden treasure from the past, just as Hawthorne himself sought to do through his fiction (*Works* XI, 250).

With its troubling portrait of the isolate (or artist), the pressing need to pry into others' lives is at the heart of the sketch, "Sights from a Steeple." One summer afternoon from high atop an urban church, the unnamed first-person narrator watches keenly the scenes unfolding before him: the countryside, the endless sea, the stately mansions, the busy wharf, a solitary young man, two pretty young girls and their father, a prosperous merchant, soldiers, schoolboys, and a funeral procession. "The full of hope, the happy, the miserable, and the desperate," the narrator says, "dwell together within the circle of my glance" (*Works* IX, 196). He yearns to uncover the latent secrets of their hearts, but knowing it is impossible, can only guess.

The narrator is a mute spectator, just as we are as readers, and brazenly feeds his innate human urge to observe. Are we, too, gazing merely to stay connected? Or are we gazing, like the narrator, out of a bit more than just curiosity? The sun-filled clouds, with which his explication commences, are soon followed by darker cousins, a thunderstorm and, eventually, a rainbow. Looking in, which reading offers, becomes for us, too, a source of vicarious pleasure.

Death and loss permeate "The Wives of the Dead," a story whose title crystallizes Hawthorne's intent as clearly as any we can find. Two young wives, the lively and irritable Margaret and the timid Mary, learn that their respective husbands, a landsman, and a sailor, have just died. They seek to comfort each other before drifting into a troubled sleep in a house they occupy together. Each is awakened separately at different hours of the night and given the joyful news (in one case by Goodman Parker, a fatherly innkeeper; and by Stephen, a former suitor, in the other) of her husband's safe return.

Each believes the opposite to be a widow and leaves her alone, not telling her the good news out of respect for her grief. Each is sleeping restlessly; each is awakened by someone outside; each hears that her husband is alive; and each stops herself from waking the other. The final ambiguous sentence comes across as particularly striking: "But her hand trembled against Margaret's neck, a tear also fell upon her cheek, and she suddenly awoke" (*Works* XI, 199). Who is "she"? If it is Mary, then they both have been dreaming. Did they share a dream of their husbands' survival? Did the messengers actually come, or were they just figures in a night's dream? Hawthorne leaves it to the reader to decide.

"My Kinsman, Major Molineux" is an initiation story that charts a *naif*'s journey to maturity. Eighteen-year-old Robin Molineux, the son of a rural clergyman, travels with an eager eye from the country all the way to Boston in search of his famous and wealthy kinsman, the Major, hoping that he will help him to get established and prosperous in life. During his search, Robin encounters a cross-section of the community: an elderly man, an innkeeper, a pretty young woman, a watchman, a prostitute, desperadoes, rebels, prostitutes, and friends wearing disguises. He stops a passer-by to ask his way to the Major's house, only to discover that one side of his face is painted red and the other black, symbolic of two devils coalesced into one entity, "a fiend of fire and a fiend of darkness" (*Works* XI, 220). Everyone he encounters either ignores his request for information or reacts with anger or impatience. Tired, beleaguered, and almost out of money, Robin waits on the church steps together with a gentleman who begins to feel sorry for him.

Suddenly on this moonlit evening, from around the corner marches the "counterfeited pomp," "senseless uproar" and "frenzied merriment" of a mob, "trampling all on an old man's heart," likened to "fiends that throng in mockery round some dead potentate, mighty no more" (*Works* XI, 230). At the center of the crowd is the Major, tarred and feathered, having been driven out of the colonies as a despised representative of royal authority (we are never told why). "His face was pale as death, and far more ghastly; the broad forehead was contracted in his agony, so that his eyebrows formed one grizzled line; his eyes were red and wild, and the foam hung white upon his quivering lip. His whole frame was agitated by a quick, and continual tremor, which his pride strove to quell, even in those circumstances of overwhelming humiliation" (*Works* XI, 228–229). When Robin sees all the people in the crowd whom he's asked for directions, he joins in the shouts and jeers. He realizes that he has no hope of advancement from his disgraced kinsman and decides to go home.

Robin then reflects on his own residence and sees his father "holding the Scriptures in the golden light that shone from the western clouds." There would have been a thanksgiving for "daily mercies" and "supplications for their continuance." There was a time when Robin would have listened to these words wearily; now, amidst all that is false or artificial, they are among his "dear remembrances" (*Works* XI, 223). Unsettling and humor-laden in equal measure, the plot draws its energy from Robin's overbearing desire to leave his family and make his mark in a larger world that is fraught (just as America must separate itself from England). He sets out in search of fame and fortune, only to realize that his true self is to be found at home with his father.

Hawthorne undertakes a deeper exploration of guilt in "Roger Marvin's Burial." The story is set in the context of the 1725 battle at Lovewell Pond. Captain John Lovewell, along with 46 men, massacred ten Pequawket sleeping warriors to avenge the death of his family (and to collect scalps). Thereafter, they were ambushed by a large group of Indians, who left three of their wounded for dead. These men survived and told their stories of abandonment.

In Hawthorne's tale, Reuben Bourne, returning with Roger Malvin from the ambush (which Hawthorne calls Lovell's fight, not Lovewell's), is compelled to leave the badly wounded older man behind. If Reuben remains, both are certain to perish. "For me there is no hope; and I will await death here," Malvin says. "I have loved you like a father, Reuben, and, at a time like this, I should have something of a father's authority. I charge you to be gone, that I may die in peace" (*Works* X, 339). Reuben promises to return, to send a party to rescue or, which seems more likely, to bury him.

But Reuben is prevented from keeping his promise because he collapses due to exhaustion and his own wounds. After being nursed to health by Malvin's daughter Dorcas, and marrying her, a kind of moral cowardice composed of pride (from fear of losing his wife's affection) and dread (of universal scorn) prevents him from admitting that he had not stayed with Malvin until the end. He is haunted by guilt, by "the miserable and humiliating torture of unmerited praise," and by "a haunting and torturing fancy, that his father-in-law was yet sitting at the foot of the rock, on the withered forest-leaves, alive, and awaiting his pledged assistance" (*Works* X, 348, 349). His strength dissipates; he becomes a sad, downcast, and irritable man and also loses the farm he had inherited from Malvin.

Eighteen years later, a voice seemingly commands him to go forth and redeem his vow. Together with his wife and their 15-year-old son, Cyrus (Persian for "one who bestows care"), in whom he sees what he himself had been in happier days, Reuben sets out for the wilderness to clear land for another farm. Ironically, he stops at the exact spot where his companion had passed away 18 years earlier.

In search of food, he fires at a movement in the bushes and kills Cyrus. Why does he do it? Insanity? Unintentional sin? Filial disobedience? Irrational guilt? Unconscious compulsion? An array of possibilities exist, but the one that resonates the most with my students is suggested by the final line of the story: "His sin was expiated, the curse was gone from him; and, in the hour, when he had shed blood dearer to him than his own, a prayer, the first for years, went up to Heaven from the lips of Reuben Bourne" (*Works* X, 360). That is, he absolves himself from the guilt of abandoning his father-in-law by killing his own son (Newman 1979: 281, 282).

Puritan persecution of the early Quakers, who began to appear in New England in 1656, is dramatized in "The Gentle Boy" – Hawthorne's "quintessential child-scape, composed of his memories of loneliness, feelings of rejection and loss, and . . . 'moments of deep depression'" (Miller 1991: 37–38). On the deepest level, "The Gentle Boy" engages many of my students who, like Hawthorne, yearn for a father or mother, a home, caressing hands, and genuinely caring peers. In January 1839, Sophia made a drawing of the central character, Ilbrahim, for a separate edition published later that year. It became Hawthorne's most popular tale for its celebration of a mother's love. Writing for the April 1842 issue of the *North American Review*, Longfellow said it was "on the whole, the finest thing he ever wrote" (Crowley 1970: 82).

Six-year-old Ilbrahim is the Quaker child of a martyred father and a banished mother. Tobias Pearson, a large-hearted Puritan, finds the boy weeping bitterly on his father's grave and takes him home to his wife, Dorothy. He explains to her that Christian men had left him out to die, and "his heart had prompted him, like the speaking of an inward voice," to take the boy home (*Works* IX, 75). However, their action only alienates the community's iron-hearted Puritans. They hiss and hoot and begin to persecute the Pearsons as backsliders.

One Sabbath day, they take him to public worship at the meetinghouse. Catherine, the boy's rebellious Quaker mother who, after her husband's execution, had been banished into the wilderness to perish, suddenly stands up and denounces everyone present, including the governor: "Woe to them that slay! Woe to them that shed the blood of the saints! Woe to them that have slain the husband, and cast forth the child . . . and have saved the mother alive, in the cruelty of their tender mercies! . . . Lift your voices, chosen ones, cry aloud, and call down a woe and a judgment with me!" (*Works* IX, 82).

When she sees Ilbrahim and realizes he is her son, alive, she embraces him and concedes her failure as a mother. Ilbrahim wants to go with her, but Dorothy takes the boy's hand. "The two females, as they held each a hand of Ibrahim, formed a practical allegory; it was rational piety [Dorothy] and unbridled fanaticism [Catharine], contending for the empire of a young heart" (*Works* IX, 85). Then Catherine hears a voice emanating from within that instructs her to "[b]reak the bonds of natural affection" and abandon her child (*Works* IX, 87). She leaves Ilbrahim, entrusting him to the Pearsons, and then continues to preach the Quaker faith.

Despite slipping into a deep depression and while continuing to be the object of ridicule and scorn in the community, the boy becomes "more childlike" under the Pearsons's care, and his "airy gaiety" is "like a domesticated sunbeam" (*Works* IX, 88, 89). One day the Pearsons take in a Puritan child two years older, who had been injured in a fall from a tree near their home. Ilbrahim grows close to the boy as if to compare his own fate with that of the sufferer and entertains him as he convalesces.

Later, Ilbrahim encounters him among a group of other Puritan boys. Upon seeing Ibrahim, they turn into "baby-fiends" and pelt him with stones, exhibiting "an instinct for destruction, far more loathsome than the blood-thirstiness of manhood" (*Works* IX, 92). The invalid offers his hand, but then the "foul-hearted little villain" lifts his crutch and strikes Ilbrahim on the mouth. Ilbrahim, a sensitive boy, suffers not merely bodily injuries, but his spirit is aggrieved beyond measure. A few neighbors intervene and return him to Pearsons's home (*Works* IX, 92, 93).

Years pass and Catharine returns on a stormy night. Covered with snow, the cold-hearted mother finally brings good tidings: King Charles II has sent letters to stop any further executions. Upon finding her son to be ill, however, she blames the Pearsons for his condition and demands custody. But alas, it is too late by now. The child dies in her arms, but not before saying, "Mourn not, dearest mother. I am happy now" (*Works* IX, 104). She runs off again in fear of persecution, only to return again in order to settle down. It is as if when Ibrahim's spirit "came down from heaven to teach his parent a true religion, her fierce and vindictive nature was softened by the same griefs which had once irritated it" (*Works* IX, 104). She is pitied by those who used to persecute her and is eventually buried beside the gentle boy.

Memorable as these tales are, with their haunting, alarming visions, yet it was only Bridge along with a few New England friends and fellow writers, who knew the identity of the author. In *The New-England Magazine* (dated October 1835) and *The Token* (1936), Park Benjamin referred to him as "the most pleasing writer of fanciful prose, except [Washington] Irving, in the country" (Crowley 1970: 48). To Bridge, they were "as good, if not better, than anything else I get" (*Works* IX, 490). But few reviews appeared until they were freshly gathered for the public in *Twice-told Tales* (1837, 1842), causing Hawthorne to refer to their "kindly, but calm, and very limited reception" (*Works* IX, 4). For a variety of reasons, they did not capture the attention of readers, most of whom were weary working souls who craved diversion, rather than challenging, discomfiting tales.

With renewed confidence and vigor, however, he continued writing, and in 1835 we first see the reclusive Hawthorne getting into print under his own name at last. He published four of his most enduring tales – "The Minister's Black Veil: A Parable," followed by "The Wedding Knell" and "The May-Pole of Merry Mount" in *The Token* and "Young Goodman Brown" in *The New-England Magazine* in 1836.

"The Minister's Black Veil" is a crowning achievement about secret sin set during the Great Awakening, the revival of fervent Christian belief among the Colonists in the mid-seventeenth century. One Sunday morning, the young Parson arrives at the meeting house with his face wrapped in a black crape veil which he refuses to lift or explain. At first, his ghostlike appearance frightens and confuses his congregation. Only his wife, Elizabeth, dares ask him to remove it, but Hooper points out that the veil is "a type and a symbol," a sign of mourning, and he is "bound to wear it ever, both in light and darkness, in solitude and before the gaze of multitudes" (*Works* IX, 46). When he refuses to lift the veil and look at her, she says goodbye, leaving Hooper lonely and frightened, isolated from humanity. Yet the veil has the strange effect of making his sermons and his spiritual leadership, in general, more powerful. When he dies, still veiled and isolated, while being nursed by the calm and affectionate Elizabeth, who has since returned, his dying words take us to the heart of Hawthorne: "I look around me, and, lo! on every visage a Black Veil!" (*Works* IX, 52).

The tale suggests that on some level, all of us are like Hooper. To avoid exposing our true selves, we hide behind a socially-acceptable mask. We are afraid of being seen for who we truly are. Thus, the story is a parable (hence the sub-title) about the common practice of hiding behind appearances rather than facing the truth of ourselves. Even social and religious institutions can mask (or reveal) their true nature. Those who reveal their true selves can alarm themselves and others. Parson Hooper's fear of his own sinful nature is so great that he does not dare show his face.

Lost youth and the vanity of life is the focus in "The Wedding Knell" set in New York. Mr. Ellenwood is 65 and, not unlike Fanshawe, has led "an aimless and abortive life" as a bachelor and scholar (*Works* IX, 28). He is about to marry Mrs. Dabney, a wealthy but childless widow who has been married twice before. During the ceremony, just as she reaches the altar, the church bell peals a deep funereal knell, seeming "to fill the church with a visible gloom, dimming and obscuring the bright pageant, till it shone forth again as from a mist" (*Works* IX, 31). Apprehensive, the widow admits that she expects her first two husbands as groomsmen to accompany her bridegroom into the church.

A dark procession makes its way up the aisle consisting of her former friends, now old and withered. The bridegroom enters in his burial garment. He invites his bride to marry him and then accompany him to their coffins: "other husbands have enjoyed your youth, your beauty, your warmth of heart, and all that could be termed your life," he complains. "What is there for me but your decay and death?" Upon realizing that her life is gone, "in vanity and emptiness," she implores him to marry her for eternity. At the end of the ceremony, the organ's "peal of solemn triumph" drowns the wedding-knell. The two immortal souls are finally united. "The young have less charity for aged follies," writes Hawthorne, "than the old for those of youth" (*Works* IX, 32, 35, 36).

"The May-Pole of Merry Mount" (1836) is set in 1630 at the time of the first English colonies of the New World. It depicts an incident in the feud between the Plymouth Puritans at Salem under Governor Endicott and a pre-Puritan, rival settlement called Merry Mount that was founded by Thomas Morton. These two settlements signify different stances toward the world. "Jollity and gloom were contending for an empire" (*Works* IX, 54).

At the beginning of the tale, the people of Merry Mount are celebrating the spring by dancing around their maypole. Their party is to culminate in the marriage of Edith and Edgar. In the middle section, Hawthorne offers a fuller description of the origins of Merry Mount's hedonistic philosophy and the dour features of Puritanism. The Merry Mount people pursue happiness to the extreme (their presiding god is Comus, the child of Dionysus and deity of revels and bawdy mirth), but it is a false joy, manufactured mirth and delight camouflaging an underlying deeper, almost prescient despair. The Puritans, aspiring to reach purity and holiness in all affairs of daily life, see the revelers as spirits of the devil, as pagans defiling the land that should be removed.

Who shall reign in New England? By the end of the third part, we know the answer as the narrator describes a Puritan raid upon Merry Mount. The zealot Endicott and his followers chop down the maypole, the emblem of bliss, and erect a whipping post. The votaries are whipped and placed in stocks. The high priest is arrested. The dancing bear is killed. As for the newlywed couple, Endicott, a man of iron, is softened by their mutual support, affection, and willingness to die for the other. He dresses them in more modest clothing, cuts the youth's hair to resemble the shape of a pumpkin (often linked with rebirth and fertility), and includes them into the Puritan community, thinking that he will make a good worker and warrior and that she will make a nurturing mother. The severest Puritan salvages gather up the roses and place them over the heads of the newly-weds. Merry Mount is not sustainable. Puritanism will not die. Then as now, we are surrounded by Endicotts – sanctimonious purifiers and pleasure-haters.

This brings us to the measure of Hawthorne's genius, found in his unsurpassed masterpiece, another story of initiation, "Young Goodman Brown." I first read this fine tale in high school and have been haunted by its images ever since. To introduce it, I tell my students of an experience I had in the autumn of 1969, after my arrival from Indiana to begin my PhD program at the University of Southern California.

On Friday evenings, I usually took time off from my studies to drive to Hollywood, sometimes with a friend, sometimes alone, to visit the local book-shops, sightsee, and have dinner. One evening, as I left the restaurant, I noticed an open door across the street, next to a magician's supply store. Since childhood, an open door has been an invitation to me. So, after crossing the street, I entered and began to climb the dimly lit stairs. Despite feeling a growing discomfort, I was too curious to go back.

Upon reaching the top stair, to my right, through another open door, I could hear chanting. I peeked inside and saw a roomful of people, all dressed in black, sitting with their eyes focused on a man who was speaking from the front of the room. Suddenly, someone the size of a football linesman blocked my path and said, "What do you want?"

> I answered with something profound, such as, "Oh, nothing."
> And then, he spoke the most important words I would hear
> that evening: "Well, you don't belong here. Get out."
> I should have quietly left, but my curiosity got the better of me,
> and so, I asked, "What's going on here?"
> "We worship the Satan," he said, without irony. "Get out."

Anybody watching as I walked away would have noticed that my pace quick-ened with each step. Even though I tried to convince myself it hadn't happened, the nagging, persistent, and unavoidable memory of it has never really left me.

A chill of fear, of dread, overpowered me at that moment. Suddenly, I had an intimation of something I wasn't familiar with, an awareness I have carried with me from that moment on. I felt as if a suffocating woolen blanket had enveloped me. Milton's timeless words from *Paradise Lost* (1667/1674) came to mind: "dark-ness visible" (I, line 62). In that instant, I understood the absence of good, an awareness that Hawthorne evokes powerfully in "Young Goodman Brown." The mood and words of the tale ring true as having been written by someone who had himself been in close proximity to the heart of darkness. Herman Melville shared that insight and thus was able to proclaim, with "Young Goodman Brown" in mind, Hawthorne's "great power of blackness" (Crowley 1970: 116).

Like many of Hawthorne's tales, this one follows a reversal on the classic structure of the hero's journey as identified by Joseph Campbell in *The Hero with a Thousand Faces* (1949) – wherein the hero leaves the known world, enters the unknown, confronts and surmounts adversities, gains something of value, and returns home. Young Goodman Brown leaves the village of Salem at dusk, saying goodbye to his wife of three months, Faith, with pink ribbons in her cap, and enters the darkening forest. After having crossed the threshold of the home, he moves into what Campbell referred to as a "dream landscape of curiously fluid, ambiguous forms" where he faces a succession of trials (81).

There, by appointment, he meets a stranger, soon identified as the devil (a departure from the protective figure who usually appears in the classic hero's story), who tries to persuade him to attend a meeting of devil-worshippers. He says that Brown's father and grandfather have often done so and that the leaders of the Puritan community are generally in attendance. Brown refuses, but his faith is shaken when he sees, or thinks he sees, his catechism teacher, Goody Cloyse, on the path ahead and learns that she, too, is on her way to the meeting. Yet he refuses to continue the journey. His faith is further shaken when he hears and sees, or thinks he does, the minister and Deacon Gookin riding through the forest toward the same destination. His resolve is shattered when a heavy cloud passes over, and he hears the voices of people he knows in Salem, including that of his wife, and sees her pink ribbon fluttering down.

"My Faith is gone!" he shrieks while running like a madman through the forest until reaching the fire-lit clearing where the witch meeting is being held (*Works* X, 83). At the end of the clearing is a rock used as an altar or pulpit, "surrounded by four blazing pines, their tops aflame, their stems untouched, like candles at an evening meeting. The mass of foliage, that had overgrown the summit of the rock, was all on fire" (*Works* X, 84). Brown is taken aback to see that the congregation includes many presumably virtuous people, as well as "men of dissolute lives and women of spotted fame," and he finds it "strange to see, that the good shrank not from the wicked, nor were the sinners abashed by the saints" (*Works* X, 85). He feels a "loatheful brotherhood" between himself and the others "by the sympathy of all that was wicked in his heart" (*Works* X, 86).

Brown and Faith are led to the altar where the devil, in the guise of a Puritan minister, proposes to divulge the surreptitious deeds of their neighbors: "'how hoary-bearded elders of the church have whispered wanton words to the young maids of their households; how many a woman, eager for widow's weeds, has given her husband a drink at bed-time, and let him sleep his last sleep in her bosom; how beardless youths have made haste to inherit their fathers' wealth; and how fair damsels . . . have dug little graves in the garden, and bidden me, the sole guest, to an infant's funeral'" (*Works* X, 87).

As the congregation welcomes the "converts" to the communion of evil, the setting becomes even more ominous: "A basin was hollowed, naturally, in the rock. Did it contain water, reddened by the lurid light? or was it blood? or, perchance, a liquid flame? Herein did the Shape of Evil dip his hand, and prepare to lay the mark of baptism upon their foreheads, that they might be partakers of the mystery of sin, more conscious of the secret guilt of others, both in deed and thought, than they could now be of their own" (*Works* X, 88).

All this becomes way too overwhelming for Brown. He rejects evil and commands Faith to "Look up to Heaven, and resist the Wicked One!" (*Works* X, 88). Instantly, the scene disappears, and Brown finds himself "amid calm night and solitude," while the foliage that had been blazing with fire now sprinkles him "with the coldest dew" (*Works* X, 88). After awakening and noticing that the strange things have departed, he returns home.

When he looks again in daylight at his Salem neighbors, Brown can't stop thinking about how they seemed to behave the night before. He now sees the world through changed eyes. It is as if the veil has been lifted, enabling him to explore the depths of their hearts. Are they what they seem to be (venerable, tender, loving)? Or had he indeed beheld them in the forest? Brown's journey has shattered his trust in mankind and bedevils him for the rest of his life. His identity and even his consciousness have been fractured by disillusionment. He shrinks away from the minister, wonders what god Deacon Gookin is praying to, snatches a child away from Goody Cloyse, and passes his wife in the street without any explanation. Through the remainder of his long life, Goodman Brown is "A stern, a sad, a darkly meditative, a distrustful, if not a desperate man," and when he dies, "they carved no hopeful verse upon his tombstone; for his dying hour was gloom" (*Works* X, 89, 90).

As we reflect on Hawthorne's years of obscurity and some of his dark, brooding tales written and published up through 1837, we must avoid falling into the trap of concluding that he was a recluse, morbidly inner-directed, or distant, as suggested by some of the early critical consensus. The testimony of his correspondence from this period suggests the opposite – that he was capable of warmth, enthusiasm, and especially humor with his friends and family. In the words of his daughter, Una, her father was "capable of being the gayest person I ever saw. He was like a boy. Never was such a playmate as he in all the world" (Auster 2003: xxxii).

One set of American journal entries, written while the Hawthornes lived in Lenox, Massachusetts, covers the period from 28 July to 16 August 1851. Later published separately as *Twenty Days with Julian & Little Bunny By Papa* (2003), these pages tell us more about a warmhearted, affectionate father who delighted in writing of some of his experiences at home and alone with his five-year-old son, Julian, as his wife, Sophia and daughter Una, visited with her parents in West Newton.

In his private travel journals, too, we discover snippets of an adventurous Hawthorne as he uses the concept of travel as a metaphor for living a life. From June to September 1832, Hawthorne took a solo extended trip into New Hampshire and Vermont and conceived of an itinerant narrator whose experiences would serve as the frame for "The Story Teller," later published in various magazines, 1834–1837. This quasi-autobiographical tale marked a turning point in his work, as he moved away from the study of history to an exploration of the present, and away from the gothic, historical romances to more realistic sketches of contemporary life. Other trips – to New Haven, New Hampshire (1828) and a Shaker village at Canterbury (1831), Maine with Horatio Bridge (1837), Western Massachusetts (1838), and The Isle of Shoals (1852) – continued to stimulate his imagination and spawned later work.

"The wish to travel seems to me characteristically human," wrote Paul Theroux (2011): "the desire to move, to satisfy your curiosity or ease your fears, to change the circumstances of your life, to be a stranger, to make a friend, to experience an exotic landscape, to risk the unknown, to bear witness to the consequences, tragic or comic, of people possessed by the narcissism of minor differences" (vii). Hawthorne would agree. The "importance of elsewhere," as Philip Larkin put it in a poem by that title (1945), is true for Hawthorne's characters. Why should it be any less true for the author himself, who traveled throughout his life? This included his final journey in 1864 with his friend, Franklin Pierce, at the end of which he would die in his sleep.

His energetic spirit reached out to other projects as well. From March to August 1836, Hawthorne edited (with the help of Elizabeth) and wrote for Goodrich's the *American Magazine of Useful and Entertaining Knowledge* (his first regular employment, promising $500 for four months' work). He shifted to Boston in order to assume his duties, but the magazine went bankrupt in the month of June. Along with Elizabeth, he went on to compile and publish the two-volume *Peter Parley's Universal History, on the Basis of Geography* in 1836.

All this being said, it cannot be denied that Hawthorne had a melancholic streak, to which I alluded at the beginning of this chapter. But this tendency is not attributable to general realities or events in his life. It visited him uninvited and inevitable, like a mist, a vapor, a fog, while he wrestled with his work. "[I]t was the melancholy of a mind conscious of power, but as yet doubtful whether that power could be so used or adjusted as to leave its mark upon mankind" (Hawthorne 1884: I, 126). Implied here is a degree of ambiguity that any creative endeavor thrives on – captured poignantly by John Keats (1991 [1819]) in the last stanza of his "Ode on Melancholy":

> She dwells with Beauty – Beauty that must die;
> And Joy, whose hand is ever at his lips

Bidding adieu; and aching Pleasure nigh,
Turning to poison while the bee-mouth sips:
Ay, in the very temple of delight
Veil'd Melancholy has her sovran shrine,
Though seen of none save him whose strenuous tongue
Can burst Joy's grape against his palate fine;
His soul shall taste the sadness of her might,
And be among her cloudy trophies hung. (21–30)

Like the poet, Hawthorne learned to embrace melancholy by actively acknowledging its presence, knowing that it is a fundamental part of beauty, joy, and pleasure. We value some of the finest examples of perfect beauty – a blooming morning rose, a rainbow – because we know their existence is fleeting. That's why beauty contains and even intensifies melancholy. This, in turn, makes anything good in a life replete with sadness even before it is over. The best response to this inescapable reality is simply to embrace it. Hawthorne understood, heart-deep, that melancholy is a profound, often necessary part of life.

He will break free from his self-imposed dungeon like a butterfly from a cocoon. Positive reviews, especially from his friend Longfellow, the wisdom and love and beauty of Sophia Peabody, whom he will marry, as well as a renewed spirit of confidence in himself and his work, will become the keys to his release. But for now, he must continue to develop his voice and find his audience.

5

A Voice Refined (1837–1842)

Above all ideal personalities with which the poet must learn
to identify himself, there is one supremely real which is the most imperative of all;
namely, that of his reader.

—Dante Gabriel Rossetti (1887: 489)

When we truly read a book, we enter into a state of trust and intimacy with its writer; we hear a human voice in the words. To Saul Bellow (1994), "It seems to issue from the bosom, from a place beneath the breastbone. It is more musical than verbal, and it is the characteristic signature of a person, of a soul" (xii). These words might well apply to Hawthorne himself, whose narrative voice is exclusively his own. Consider, for example, the iridescent opening to "The White Old Maid" (1835):

> The moonbeams came through two deep and narrow windows, and showed a spacious chamber, richly furnished in an antique fashion. From one lattice, the shadow of the diamond panes was thrown upon the floor; the ghostly light, through the other, slept upon a bed, falling between the heavy silken curtains, and illuminating the face of a young man. But, how quietly the slumberer lay! how pale his features! and how like a shroud the sheet was wound about his frame! Yes; it was a corpse, in its burial-clothes. (*Works* IX, 370)

The quiet ease, the haunting quality, the fluidity of language imbued with darkness, the mysterious textures: we have come to associate all these soul-stirring attributes with Hawthorne's tales. This is the type of beauty we feel upon hearing a melody sung by a beautiful voice that seems to *live the song*. It lingers in the sensitive reader's mind, said Walter Pater of drama, as a sort of ballad, "an

The Life of the Author: Nathaniel Hawthorne, First Edition. Dale Salwak.
© 2023 John Wiley & Sons Ltd. Published 2023 by John Wiley & Sons Ltd.

intangible residuum of pleasure; a cadence, a quality of voice that is exclusively the writer's own, individual, unique" (Winters 1993: 54).

As our intimacy grows with a writer, so does our awareness of that familiar voice. "Give me ten unsigned passages from ten, nineteenth century American writers, one of them Hawthorne," I say to my students, "and I will distinguish his passage from the others." Why? Because I have been reading his tales for so long that I know his narrative voice. In the same way, if ten women were to call me one evening and say, "I am your mother," I would instantly be able to identify *her* voice from the others.

By way of illustration, I tell my students of how, as a youngster of ten or eleven, I loved to explore the woodland behind my home in Amherst, Massachusetts, for an hour or so before suppertime. Prior to setting out on my journey, I never forgot to turn on the lamp in my bedroom upstairs. As long as I could see the light, I knew I could find my way back. One day, I ended up in an unfamiliar area, farther than I had wandered before. Suddenly, the forest appeared ominously dark and convulsive with shadows. The air was thickly oppressive. Worse still, I couldn't see my bedroom light. No matter how I turned, I lost track of my way, as if I were trapped in some dark corridor that endlessly twists and turns and doubles back on itself. My heart was pounding.

During previous journeys, I had always been disappointed to hear my mother's voice calling for me because that signaled the time to stop what I was doing and return home. But now, I yearned for that dear sound. Upon hearing my name, faint but audible, I recognized the voice and ran in its direction. Before long, I saw the familiar sights that had never seemed more precious: the chimney, the tiled slope of the roof, the main body of my brown-shingle house with its green shutters and, finally, a bright light shining from the second-floor window. Within minutes, and with an enormous sense of gratitude, I had found my way home.

Since childhood, my mother's reassuring voice has remained an undeniable presence within me. The same can be said of Hawthorne. This inimitable voice takes us into his confidence and involves us in a paradoxical world where the fate of his heroes seems inexplicable. According to Kristin Brady (1985), it is a haunting voice too, which "gathers his materials, all of them potentially unreliable but also richly mysterious, and then engages in a sort of conversation with the reader, offering him choices, enlisting his impressions and opinions" (35).

As we have seen, Hawthorne found his distinctive voice early in his career. Once he did, the writing flowed. We heard it, for example, in *Fanshawe: A Tale* as the narrator insightfully and often ironically reveals how several characters think in relation to the affairs of the protagonist. We heard it in "The Minister's Black Veil" as the narrator relates the story of the young minister who wears a black veil, "a type and a symbol" of the "hoarded iniquity of deed or thought" which everyone carries in the heart (*Works* IX, 40, 46). Here the narrator tells the tale as if he were a member of the congregation, observing the events without passing judgment. His voice is cold, objective, yet sympathetic to the confused townspeople and the minister's wife. This objective tone makes the minister's pain sharper and his end more tragic. We also heard it in "The May-Pole of Merry Mount" in which the inquiring and observing narrator describes the contrast between jollity and Puritan gloom, between a carefree lifestyle bordering on juvenility and the adult responsibilities of maturity.

Now we hear it, cumulatively and powerfully, in a collection of eighteen pieces entitled *Twice-Told Tales* published by Goodrich in 1837. Its title is a self-deprecating allusion to the Dauphin's lines in Shakespeare's *King John* (1623): "Life is as tedious as a twice-told tale / Vexing the dull ear of a drowsy man . . ." (III. iv. 108–109). The collection, with Hawthorne's name finally appearing on the title page, was secretly subsidized by his Bowdoin classmate, Horatio Bridge (and reissued in expanded editions of 39 tales in 1842 and 1851), thereby giving the author hope and the coveted opportunity "to open an intercourse with the world" (*Works* IX, 6). Ideas that had teased his mind for years – mortality, guilt, the germ of evil inhabiting every human heart, and the risk of losing life-giving sympathy with humanity (the Unpardonable Sin) – predominate. After years of struggling for recognition, for the freedom to write as he wished, he no longer felt impelled to sprinkle his tales anonymously in an assortment of journals and magazines. Without a doubt, 1837–1842 were his breakthrough years when he published stories with an identifiable voice.

With each of his characters, Hawthorne enters into morally agnostic intercourse with another mind, another heart, another soul, another voice of a human being who is not himself but comprises parts of himself. Whether this happens, for example, to be a man ("Wakefield," 1835) or a woman ("Lady Eleanore's Mantle," 1838), the old ("The White Old Maid," 1835) or the young ("The Ambitious Guest," 1841), in every story the author makes an imaginative leap.

We begin with "Wakefield," a haunting tale that warns against the horror of isolating oneself from humanity. Kafka-like in its bizarreness, it compels us to address our own unacknowledged desires and latent fears of being rendered powerless to understand or control what is happening. Set in London, the story introduces an apparently ordinary man named Wakefield who, one October evening, leaves his wife of 10 years on a perverse whim. Although he tells her he is embarking on a business trip, in reality, he moves into a flat one street away from their residence.

Disguised in a red wig and old clothes, he takes refuge both literally and figuratively. He does not return home, but watches her in secret, until the 10th year of his absence, when he comes face-to-face with her in a crowded street. However, she does not recognize him. He has become a "meager" man with "small and lustreless" eyes; she is now a "portly female" with a prayer book in one hand and "the placid mien of settled widowhood" on her face (*Works* IX, 137). Wakefield rushes back to his flat, wonders if he has gone mad, and continues to live the life of a hermit, having given up "his place and privileges with living men, without being admitted among the dead" (*Works* IX, 138).

Another 10 years pass, and again on a whim, chilled and wet, he returns home one rainy night. In contrast to his cheerless, lonely life, he sees the "good fire to warm him, and his own wife [who] will run to fetch the gray coat and small-clothes" for him (*Works* IX, 139). As he crosses the threshold, the narrator draws a moral lesson: "Amid the seeming confusion of our mysterious world, individuals are so nicely adjusted to a system, and systems to one another, and to a whole, that, by stepping aside for a moment, a man exposes himself to a fearful risk of losing his place forever. Like Wakefield, he may become, as it were, the Outcast of the Universe" (*Works* IX, 140). Hawthorne stops here and leaves us to imagine their reunion.

We are sure of what happens next, but we are not sure why. Who among us hasn't had the impulse to escape from their life for a moment and vanish into thin air? Many have surely fantasized about walking away from someone they care for, only to spy without detection upon the one they have abandoned. For reasons, they can't explain, "Wakefield" gives my students nightmares and haunts their days as well. "One of my jobs as professor," I say, "is to challenge you with ideas that will keep you up at night, thinking and re-thinking." With "Wakefield," Hawthorne has certainly accomplished that for me. Its first-person omniscient voice describes mysterious events as they unfold, often giving opinions about how the characters feel or think while simultaneously speaking to the reader. Sometimes he directly addresses Wakefield.

The narrator in "Lady Eleanore's Mantle," a moral tale that warns of the consequences of hubris, uses the traditional diction and style of a fairy tale. Lady Eleanore Rochcliffe, "a young lady of rank and fortune," comes to Boston from London in order to live in the Province House under the care of her guardian, Governor Shute (*Works* IX, 273). She is envied for her beauty, accentuated by her lovely embroidered but sinister mantle, rumored to possess "magical properties of adornment" (*Works* IX, 274). Upon her arrival in the colony, as the bell of the Old South Church begins to toll for a funeral, an unfortunate and portentous sign, she brazenly disdains those she perceives as her inferiors.

To celebrate her arrival, Governor Shute hosts a ball and invites everyone of importance within the colony. She gives the cold shoulder to most of the guests, including a young man named Jervase, who has been maddened by his love for her ever since their first meeting in London. He offers her a goblet of wine, then urges her to cast off her mantle; she curtly refuses both requests. She deludes herself into believing that she has control over her fate, even to the point of ignoring the idea of death. A short time later, the tragic smallpox plague of 1721 hits the city. The rich and poor, the snobbish and compassionate alike, are felled by the disease. Lady Eleanore herself is stricken and languishes from a disfiguring disease that may have been spread by her cursed mantle.

One day, Jervase insists on entering Lady Eleanore's chamber. He finds her hidden behind the curtains of her canopied bed, complaining of thirst. Struggling to conceal her face, she says, "the curse of Heaven" has struck her because she "would not call man [her] brother, nor woman sister" (*Works* IX, 287). By her own admission, she has wrapped herself in "PRIDE as in a MANTLE, and scorned the sympathies of nature." She goes on to add, "and therefore has nature made this wretched body the medium of a dreadful sympathy" (*Works* IX, 287). The embittered Jervase snatches the mantle from her. That night, bearing the red flag of pestilence, he leads a torchlight procession with her effigy, enveloped in her mantle, which the crowd burns in front of the Province-House. The pestilence abates, but a "legend" persists that a mysterious, ghost-like presence still haunts a certain chamber of the dwelling.

Few nineteenth-century writers have written more unblinkingly about old age and mortality than Hawthorne. We recall "The Wedding Knell," "The Hollow of the Three Hills," and "The Minister's Black Veil." It is easy for anyone to ignore the reality of death from the safe distance of a passive observer. Until death greets us personally, none of us can claim to truly know it. When we are at our most vulnerable, then and only then do our lives change powerfully. As a keen observer of mortality, Hawthorne understood this very well.

Undoubtedly mindful of his own father's passing, Hawthorne was deeply moved by the death of his college friend, Jonathan Cilley, by then a member of Congress. On the morning of 24 February 1838, he was killed in a duel with William J. Graves, a Whig congressman, over a political dispute, leaving behind his wife and six children. In a memorial issue for the *Democratic Review*, Hawthorne (3 September 1838) commended Cilley's moral rectitude and political success while condemning those who had wrongfully silenced him: "Alas, that, over the grave of a dear friend, my sorrow for the bereavement must be mingled with another grief – that he threw away such a life in so miserable a cause!" (75).

As in "Lady Eleanore's Mantle," in his next nightmarish tale, "The White Old Maid," Hawthorne's narrator tells a story of guilt and enchantment, though its plot is more mysterious and ambiguous. In a noble mansion, we are introduced to two beautiful women, one haughty and stately but unnamed, the other, Edith, gentle and fragile. Both are tearfully hovering over the body of a young man for whom they had been rivals. The proud one has apparently committed a transgression of sorts, perhaps the murder of her lover who lies before her, although it is never divulged. The proud one laments, "Thou hadst him living! The dead is mine!" She asks, "Wilt thou betray me?" Edith replies: "Till the dead bid me speak, I will be silent . . . Leave us alone together! Go, and live many years, and then return and tell me of thy life. He, too, will be here! Then, if thou tellest of sufferings more than death, we will both forgive thee." When the proud woman asks for a token, the other answers, "This lock of hair," as she lifts "one of the dark, clustering curls that lay heavily on the dead man's brow" (*Works* IX, 371).

The two agree to meet in the same place "far, far in time to come," and separate (*Works* IX, 371). Edith becomes the "Old Maid in the Winding-Sheet," spending her entire life dressed in white, attending every funeral, a familiar figure in the town.

Years later, a coach arrives, bringing a mysterious widow to the old mansion, now empty and derelict. An aged clergyman and his attendant ascend the steps and arrive before a closed oak door on their left and an open door on their right. The clergyman points to the left and recalls, a whole lifetime earlier, sitting within the chamber where the dead man had lain. Throwing it open, he discovers, to his horror, the corpse of the stately widow, in her hand a lock of hair, once sable but now covered with greenish mold, on her knees before the corpse of the Old Maid in the Winding-Sheet. He exclaims, "Both dead! . . . Then who shall divulge the secret? Methinks it glimmers to-and-fro in my mind, like the light and shadow across the Old Maid's face. And now, 'tis gone!" (*Works* IX, 382).

Now we come to a tale concerning the futility of human ambition that originated in an actual event. On 28 August 1826, a landslide in the White Mountains of New Hampshire caused the death of the Samuel Willey family. They left their home, which they thought would be in the path of the slide, and ran to a shelter for safety, only to perish there. A flurry of articles, poems, songs, and artwork was produced to interpret the ironic tragedy, made even more ironic because the family had escaped a landslide earlier that month by running to the shelter. In 1832 Hawthorne visited the site of the tragedy and, by 1835, had published a short story chronicling the family's tryst with death. He added to the story by inventing a visitor, a young educated man with high hopes for his future.

In "The Ambitious Guest," a contented family resides in the Notch of the White Hills of New Hampshire, where they are often startled by the ominous sound of stones tumbling down from the mountain. Sometimes, travelers stop at their tavern home for a night's food and lodging and meet with the generous family. One evening, a melancholic young man appears and made welcome. Following dinner, he talks about his desire not to be buried and forgotten after his death. "I cannot die till I have achieved my destiny," he says. "Then, let Death come! I shall have built my monument!" (*Works* IX, 328).

As the talk turns to future hopes, death, and even funerals, a sense of unease grips the family. The daughter tries to steer the conversation away from this dark topic and says that "[i]t is better to sit here, by this fire . . . and be comfortable and contented" (*Works* IX, 328). The grandmother says that she has already assembled her burial clothes, but asks that they hold up a mirror when she is in her coffin, so that she can see that everything is perfectly arranged. The father speaks about his dreams of a house at the base of the mountain, a good farm, and a "slate gravestone . . . with just my name and age, and a verse of a hymn, and something to let people know, that I lived an honest man and died a Christian." The stranger affirms, "it is in our nature to desire a monument, be it slate, or marble, or a pillar of granite, or a glorious memory in the universal heart of man" (*Works* IX, 329).

Suddenly, they hear the sounds of sliding stones and the entire family rush out to their emergency retreat, prepared when an earlier landslide had threatened them. But this time, the avalanche makes an unpredictable turn. The cottage survives, but the family perishes. Their bodies are never discovered. A mound of snow is their only marker.

Not long ago when I learned about the actual event this tale was based on and visited the site, I couldn't help but think about the tragedy of the landslide and the series of well-intentioned but erroneous decisions that led to everyone's death. The story serves as a stark reminder of how vulnerable we human beings are – perhaps most of all when we overestimate our own capacity to direct our fate. Hawthorne portrays Nature as not only powerful but also indifferent. He wonders if all our ambitions, humble or exalted, are essentially meaningless.

Twice-told Tales turned out to be a critical success. Longfellow, to whom Hawthorne had sent a copy, praised it as a "sweet, sweet book" in an unsigned notice in the July 1837 issue of the *North American Review*. These tales and sketches, he wrote, "have been gathered fresh from the secret places of a peaceful and powerful heart . . . The book, though in prose, is written nevertheless by a poet. He looks upon all things in the spirit of love and with lively sympathies"; . . . It comes from the hand of a man of genius, "a friendly man" with a pleasant philosophy and quiet humor who feels "a universal sympathy with Nature, both in the material world and the soul of man, . . . [one who] has wisely chosen his themes among the traditions of New England" and whose style is "as clear as running water." Everything [*sic*] about it has the freshness of morning and of May." This work was also hailed by none other than Poe himself: "Mr. Hawthorne's distinctive trait is invention, creation, imagination, originality – a trait which, in the literature of fiction, is positively worth all the rest . . . Mr. Hawthorne is original at *all* points" (Crowley 1970: 56, 58, 91).

Despite his artistic successes, Hawthorne's fiction had made him little money up to now. In 1838, therefore, he became an active contributor to the *United States Magazine and Democratic Review* (publishing twenty-four tales and sketches over the next seven years at $5 per page) edited by his friend, John Louis O'Sullivan. Then in January 1839, through friends in the Democratic Party, Elizabeth Peabody (older sister of his future wife, Sophia), along with noted historian George Bancroft, Collector of the Port, secured his appointment as Weigher and Gauger of salt and coal in the Boston Custom House at an annual salary of $1500 (a poor substitution for the position he had actually sought as historian to an expedition to the Antarctic under Commodore Wilkes). Reference to his piece on Cilley had been included in Hawthorne's appointment letter and helped secure this assignment, but he did not find this position gave him enough time to write. In a letter to Sophia dated 15 March 1840, he called it "a very grievous thraldom" (*Works* XV, 422). But he remained there until early the next year because he needed the income. Then in 1841 he invested $1000 in the Rev. George Riley's utopian community of Brook Farm, where he lived while hoping to prepare a place for his future wife, only to leave toward the end of the year for reasons I will make clear in Chapter 11.

It is worthwhile pausing briefly to consider another source of income: his work written over a period of almost two decades for an established juvenile market. In 1838, conversations between Hawthorne (as proposed contributor) and Longfellow (as proposed editor) resulted in the idea of collaborating on a book of fairy tales to be called *The Boys' Wonder-Horn* – named after the famous collection of German folksongs, *Des Knabens Wunderhorn* (1805–1808), by Ludwig Achim von Arnim and Clemens Brentano. In a letter dated 21 March 1838, Hawthorne wrote, "Possibly we may make a great hit, and entirely revolutionize the whole system of juvenile literature . . . [we] will twine for ourselves a wreath of tender shoots and dewy buds" and, perhaps, make some money (*Works* XV, 266–267). Although this project did not come to fruition, Hawthorne's interest in the field continued to engage him, as it had ever since the early 1930s.

Along with publishing shorter pieces – including "The Gentle Boy" (in *The Token*, 1832), "Little Annie's Ramble" (*Youth's Keepsake*, 1834/1835), "Little Daffydowndilly" (*Boys' and Girls' Magazine*, 1843), "A Good Man's Miracle" (*The Child's Friend*, 1844), and "The Snow Image: A Childish Miracle" (*The Memorial*, 1851) – he had served as a ghostwriter for a book in Samuel Griswold Goodrich's educational Peter Parley series, the two-volume *Peter Parley's Universal History on the Basis of Geography, for the Use of Families* (1836). Additionally, he worked as an editor for Goodrich's *American Magazine of Useful and Entertaining Knowledge* from January through June 1836, editing the March through August issues of that year (Laffrado 2010: 28).

Looking ahead, in 1851, he published *Grandfather's Chair*, a child's history of New England during colonial and revolutionary times (we shall return to this in Chapter 10), *Famous Old People,* and *Liberty Tree*. As he continued to master the art of writing for juveniles, he published in 1852 *A Wonder-Book for Boys and Girls* (a retelling of six classical myths), *Tanglewood Tales, For Girls and Boys: Being A Second Wonder-Book*, and *Biographical Stories for Children* in which a father conveys to his son (whose eyes remain bandaged because of a disease) the stories of famous people including Queen Christina, Benjamin Franklin, Oliver Cromwell,

Samuel Johnson, Sir Isaac Newton, and Benjamin West. In a prefatory note, he wrote with an unabashedly loving, domestic tone:

> This small volume, and others of a similar character, from the same hand, have not been composed without a deep sense of responsibility. The author regards children as sacred, and would not, for the world, cast anything into the fountain of a young heart, that might embitter and pollute its waters. And, even in point of the reputation to be aimed art, juvenile literature is as well worth cultivating as any other. The writer, if he succeed in pleasing his little readers, may hope to be remembered by them till their own old age – a far longer period of literary existence than is generally attained, by those who seek immortality from the judgments of full grown men. (*Works* VI, 214)

Hawthorne's ideal images of children are drawn from observing (and keeping a journal about) his own offspring and, indubitably, from the happiest phases of his own childhood. In promoting the spiritual and intellectual growth of children into adults, he was doing all he could to resist acquiescing to the moments of despair and bitterness from his past.

Critics agreed. "The spirit of the book," wrote the anonymous reviewer (probably Edwin Percy Whipple) in the January 1852 issue of *Graham's Magazine*, "is so essentially sunny and happy, that it creates a jubilee in the brain as we read" (Crowley 1970: 233). Another critic (probably Evert A. Duyckinck) made the following observation for the 29 November 1851 issue of *Literary World*: "Natural, because he is sincere, his stories for children are at once entertained by the youthful mind – a home where all crude thoughts, half conceptions, bungling style, and made up stuff, knock in vain for admittance . . . Life, from whatever view he paints it, always comes forth an harmonious picture from Hawthorne's pen" (Idol and Jones 1994: 181).

Underlying this sunny theme is Hawthorne's firm belief, which makes its presence felt through most of his juvenile writing, that a child's mind should be preserved as a wellspring of hope, joy, curiosity, exuberance, magic, faith, and unfettered potential. On this subject, Plato (375 BC), whose *Republic* Hawthorne was fascinated by and learned from, had much to say in this dialogue from Book II:

> You know that the beginning of everything we undertake is the most important, especially in any young, tender creature? Then is when it is most malleable and when whatever character you desire to be stamped on the individual is fixed . . . Are we going to allow our children to hear any old stories so easily created by any passerby, and to let into their souls opinions which are for the most part the opposite of those which we think they ought to have when they're grown up? (2013: 193, 195)

Hawthorne would surely agree that our children need to be allowed to live out their childhood – untainted and unblemished from adult influences. We would not inject them with some substance that might render their senses numb to the tart crispness of a freshly picked apple, the cool relief of a clear lake's waters on a hot August day, or the nurturing, protective comfort of a parent's arm. Similarly, the last thing we should be doing is to deaden their imaginations or anesthetize their capacity for wonder.

Having lost his own direct connection with innocence at such an early age, Hawthorne appreciated and relished it that much more. His sunny outlook in these works reveals an undercurrent of utopianism – as if stocking up on optimism during childhood prepared him for the myriad challenges he would face in adulthood. He was more than familiar with the world of children. His relationship with his own, moreover, was built on love, mutual give and take, and gentle authority – in stark contrast to the stern, dictatorial method of raising children in Colonial New England when, as he writes in *The Scarlet Letter*, "[t]he frown, the harsh rebuke, the frequent application of the rod, enjoined by Scriptural authority" were used not only for punishment, "but as a wholesome regimen for the growth and promotion of all childish virtues" (*Works* I, 91).

An entire course could (and should) be taught on this aspect of his career. Indeed, when students do express such an interest, I encourage them to begin with Laura Laffrado's "Hawthorne's Literature for Children" in the Spring 2010 issue of the *Nathaniel Hawthorne Review,* along with Calvin Earl Schorer's groundbreaking unpublished dissertation, *The Juvenile Literature of Nathaniel Hawthorne* (University of Chicago, 1948), and Hugo McPherson's *Hawthorne as Myth-Maker* (University of Toronto, 1969). For a historical introduction, a reliable source would be the appendix to the Ohio University's Centenary edition of the writings, Volume VI, *True Stories from History and Biography*.

Scenes of "a grown man entering the public sphere hand in hand with a young child" are depicted throughout Hawthorne's fiction, including *The Scarlet Letter* and "The Artist of the Beautiful," as if Hawthorne wanted to publicly express his connection with childhood (Sanchez-Eppler 2004: 143). Further evidence of his sensitivity and sensibility is found in "Little Annie's Ramble," for example, published in *Youth's Keepsake*, 1835. This story evokes strong responses and provocative questions among my students as the first-person narrator journeys into the realm of strangeness.

The story opens with the town crier ringing his bell and loudly announcing the arrival of the circus. Little Annie, standing on her father's doorstep, feels an "impulse to go strolling away – that longing after the mystery of the great world – which many children feel" (*Works* IX, 121). The narrator, with whom she is acquainted, impulsively invites her to accompany him. Despite traversing a throng of people and a "tumult" of horses and trucks and carts, Annie "passes on with fearless confidence." Her eyes "brighten with pleasure" at the sight of an organ grinder, playing on the street, "the silks of sunny hue" glowing in shop windows, the pies and cakes at the confectioner's, and the doll at the toy shop (*Works* IX, 122, 123).

They then enter the circus. Annie begins looking with great interest at the exotic circus animals, such as the elephant and tiger. Meanwhile, the narrator imagines the animals' thoughts. The polar bear, for instance, is "absorbed in contemplation" and misses his iceberg and cubs. On the other hand, the monkeys are "unsentimental" and "ill-natured." Annie does not love them, for their "ugliness shocks her pure, instinctive delicacy of taste" and "bears a wild and dark resemblance to humanity" (*Works* IX, 127).

As they move through the boisterous crowd, the town crier rings his bell again, this time screaming that a little girl of five is missing, "in a blue frock and white pantalettes, with brown curling hair and hazel eyes" (*Works* IX, 128). The narrator realizes he had forgotten to tell her mother that he was taking her along on a ramble. As they hurry home, he is struck by the revelation that the "charm of childhood" has revived his spirits. He commends the "free and simple thoughts" and "native feeling" of children. In fact, he expresses the desire to become a child again. Since that is impossible, it has been "good to steal away from the society of bearded men, and even of gentler woman, and spend an hour or two with children" (*Works* IX, 129).

Here a parallel can be drawn with the experience of Wordsworth, a lifelong influence. In the winter of 1799, Coleridge convinced Wordsworth and his sister, Dorothy, to accompany him on a trip to Germany. Unlike his friend, Coleridge spoke German. Depressed and isolated, Wordsworth suddenly found himself writing poems about his childhood. Incidents from his boyhood flooded back to him, crowding out crabbed, inhibited false starts. What triggered his sudden burst of creativity was a memory of when, at the age of four, he was bathing in the River Derwent in the Lake District, an image resembling the narrator's vision of children in "Little Annie's Ramble": Their "fountains of still fresh existence is a tonic for aged men . . . All this by thy sweet magic, dear little Annie!" (*Works* IX, 129). What unites the vision of Wordsworth and that of Hawthorne is a sense of being at home in the world, untrammeled, under the influence of remembered childhood.

From experiences involving his own children, too, Hawthorne would learn that the sense of human connection, through the power of imaginative engagement between storyteller and listener, adds much to the mind's enrichment. To listen to the innocent prose of a children's tale is to hear a voice that speaks directly to us in its own distinctive and enthralling way. When reading to a child, as Hawthorne would do nightly with his own children, the parent's voice blends with that of the narrator, thus establishing a special bond between the teller and the listener.

Children exercise and develop their imagination and fashion a vision of the story from the words they hear.

Unpretentious and wise in equal measure, Hawthorne's narrative voice in the children's tales is beguiling. In its company, the child feels safe, encouraged, and consoled. In these stories, children are allowed to wonder, to pretend, to believe, and like so many of the characters in these tales, to come back home safely, just as I did decades ago when I lost my way in the forest.

But to describe Hawthorne's career as an author without discussing his wife, the former Sophia Peabody, would be like "trying to imagine," his son Julian (1884) wrote, "a sun without heat, or a day without a sun" (18). Along with his public declaration as an author, the refinement of his voice, and the encouraging reviews that followed the publication, the event that took him out of his haunted chamber into the world of readers and admirers, resulting in one of the happiest phases of his life, occurred 11 November 1838 when he visited the Peabody sisters at their Salem home.

There he met Sophia – a "small, graceful, intensely alive invalid, dressed in a simple white wrapper, who had come down from her room to meet him in the family parlor" (Woodberry 1902: 90). The Rev. Thomas Wentworth Higginson (1879) remembers her as looking "pensive and dreamy" (4). As Hawthorne rose to greet Sophia, looking at her with great intentness, her sister, Elizabeth, presciently knew that he would fall in love with her (Hawthorne 1884: I, 179). Thanks to one of my teachers, I came to appreciate what that meant for Hawthorne's creative life.

6

The Middle Years (1842–1849)

SOPHIA PEABODY HAWTHORNE
From a Portrait Painted in 1846

Sarah Peabody, etching by S.A. Schoff. Source: Bettmann/Getty Images.

[W]hat we have loved;
Others will love; and we may teach them how; . . .
　　—William Wordsworth, *The Prelude* (2012 [1850]): XIII, lines 443–444)

It has always been somewhat daring to enroll in a class or open a book and begin to read. Students never know what they will discover about themselves, or in what ways they will be challenged, or where the instruction will lead. What interesting stories must lie behind every lesson learned, lecture attended, consolation found, and career launched, because a friend was thoughtful enough to recommend a course, or by seeming coincidence a student discovered it in a promotional item, or for whatever reason, a student just decided to enroll in order to learn and refused to give up.

The Life of the Author: Nathaniel Hawthorne, First Edition. Dale Salwak.
© 2023 John Wiley & Sons Ltd. Published 2023 by John Wiley & Sons Ltd.

Isaac Stern and Chaim Potok (1999), for example, once remarked how it felt to experience the teaching of the great cellist, Pablo Casals: "Imagine yourself suddenly coming upon . . . a wall, not knowing that beyond it lay an exquisite garden. What Casals did was open a door into the garden; you entered and suddenly found yourself amid colors and scents you never dreamed existed. He revealed what might be accomplished once you were inside the garden. But how many of the colors and scents you could make your own, giving greater power to your musical imagination – that was your responsibility" (89).

I have never read a better description of a teacher's (or an author's) power to transform the lives of students. As a 10-year-old reading *The House of the Seven Gables*, I was granted a peek through that door. As I matured and advanced my understanding of Hawthorne's life and work, the door opened a bit wider. I read extensively, dreamed and mulled, and began to understand more about him. Fortunately, someone entered my life to lead me into the garden. While she suggested possibilities and hinted at layers of meaning, how far I took what I had been shown was my prerogative.

That someone happened to be my high school, senior year literature teacher, Mrs. Joanna Hayes. Up until then, what little I knew about Hawthorne came only from my own reading. But now, I enjoyed the benefit of hearing directly from a guide whose experience with literature surpassed mine by many years and who brought to the subject a verve and depth I could only admire. She was close to my favorite teacher – gentle, subtle, persuasive, rather than dominating and dogmatic, like the clerk in Chaucer's *The Canterbury Tales* 1961 (1837–1840) about whom the narrator writes in the General Prologue: "gladly wolde he lerne and gladly teche" (1961, line 308). Perhaps I owe more to her than to any other mentor I have encountered on my way to becoming a Hawthornean.

I can see her now, with her smooth white-gold hair, youthful face, and brilliant sky-blue eyes shining with intelligence and wit. Her class was a pure pleasure because she challenged us to put aside our youthful distractions and focus on what mattered. It simply never occurred to her that we were incapable of reading and understanding Hawthorne or his contemporaries. Sometimes, the pressure-cooker ambiance of the room was so intense that I expected the windows to shatter at any moment. I remember thinking: *This is the way all classes ought to be conducted.* Although a mere 6 feet separated me from where I was sitting in the front row to Mrs. Hayes, I knew it would be many years before I would have the privilege of standing where she stood.

I wrote down everything she said. When I re-visit the notes, as I am doing now, I am stunned at how generously and painstakingly Mrs. Hayes explored the authors. What she gave us was beyond anything I could have hoped to grasp at the time. Her expectations were exceedingly high.

We all know that a love for reading usually starts early in life. If my students come from homes filled with books, then I hope that from my experiences, they will hear an affirmation of their own. If, on the other hand, they were raised in homes in which books were rarely seen, never talked about, and seldom read, and if they feel betrayed (as many of them will) by this neglect, then perhaps stories such as Hawthorne's will pique their curiosity, encourage them, and give them more than a glimmer of hope. "Whichever group you find yourself in," I say, "you belong here." Then I add: "But there's one requirement – that you submit yourself fully to the authority of the text."

From Mrs. Hayes, and other teachers to come, I learned that an author's written words wait patiently until someone reads them – silently or aloud, alone or in company – and *honors* them as coming from someone who has greater insight and thinks more profoundly than we do. Suddenly, the words are wakened to life, as it were, and we enter into a silent contract with them.

"The author is calling us, through the text," she said, "and our response, if we are to glean all that he offers us, is to absorb the text as far as we are able." Some of what follows in this chapter, therefore, as I consider turning points in Hawthorne's life during the middle years 1842–1849, is the result of questions she planted in my mind.

1842 was truly transformational. For 12 years, he had remained in relative seclusion, a man as if under enchantment, living an "old life of shadows" (Woodberry 1902: 106). All of that was set to change. On 9 July, after a three-year engagement that was well-guarded, Nathaniel and Sophia Peabody, the daughter of a dentist, were married at her father's house in West Street, Boston. This wedding was witnessed by her parents, sisters, and Connie, a mesmerist (forerunner of a modern hypnotist). The Reverend James Freeman Clarke performed the service.

For their home (to which I will return in Chapter 7), Hawthorne rented the Old Manse (as he called the parsonage) in Concord, an ancestral property of the Emerson family. On the northwest edge of Concord, this two-story clapboard house, under a gambrel roof and faded to a sober grayish hue, still stands at the far end of a drive reaching to derelict posts at the public road. Poplar trees lined the avenue. In the side yard to the left, Thoreau had planted a vegetable garden as a wedding gift. At the back, there was an apple orchard and a short walk took one to the river. A previous owner, the Rev. Ezra Ripley, had lived there for 60 years before passing away in his nineties on Tuesday morning, 21 September 1811, while sitting downstairs in the front room. Rumor had it that his ghost hid during the daytime and stalked forth at night. On many occasions, both Nathaniel and Sophia reported hearing strange noises – paper crumpling in the kitchen, a breeze as if someone had just passed by, and thumps and pounding at night, as if somebody was at work in the study (McFarland 2004: 8, 10).

There they lived for the next three and a half years and associated, albeit skeptically on Nathaniel's part, with the Concord Transcendentalists Ralph Waldo Emerson, Henry David Thoreau, Margaret Fuller, Ellery Channing, and Bronson Alcott. Their life together was "one of village quiet and country happiness," a time of affection and security, a graceful dance surrounded by the harmony of trembling leaves and singing birds, proof of God's bounty, giving them a sense of intense sensuous delight (Woodberry 1902: 114). Milton's words in *Paradise Lost* (1909 [1667/1664]) – "The world was all before them, where to choose. / Their place of rest, and Providence their guide" – seems a fitting description of their early years of wedded Paradise (XII, lines 646–647).

On most afternoons, Hawthorne remained without interruption upstairs in his stove-warmed study, the same room where Emerson had composed *Nature* in 1834. He described his hideaway as "the most delightful little nook . . . that ever afforded its snug seclusion to a scholar" (*Works* X, 5). Sophia's presence, painting pictures downstairs as he wrote, meant the world to him, enabling him to concentrate on his own work. "Perhaps you will visit there someday," said Mrs. Hayes to our class, "and the experience will enlighten you."

She was right. I have often sat in the upper room where Hawthorne wrote at a small fold-down desk, listening to the ticking of the grandfather clock (acquired by the Rev. William Emerson in 1767 for $20), looking through the window to see the North Bridge, reflecting on the writing etched into the window-pane, and recalling how a sad event troubled their lives. On 1 February 1843, Sophia suffered a miscarriage after falling on the ice. In *The House of Hawthorne* Erika Robuck (2015) imagines Sophia's thoughts afterward:

> I slink around Nathaniel's study like our cat, aimless, distracting, unable to settle down to work or conversation. It was my fault. If I had never indulged in silly impulses – if I had not put our baby in harm's way – this would never have happened. Nathaniel grieves, but not as I do. He never felt the ripening, the quickening from the inside. The witness of an event has no access to the true emotion of the one who lives it, though he thinks himself capable of imagining all feeling. He scribbles in our common journal now, giving voice to our sufferings in a way he cannot compel his throat to do. (201)

"You don't forget this," my maternal grandmother told me years after she had experienced such a loss from falling off a stepladder. "It's with you every day," she said, "every moment." But then with typical New England resilience, she added, "But I shouldn't have been on that ladder." She felt the urgency to move on, and she did, and so did the Hawthornes. Within weeks, Sophia wrote reassuringly: "But dearest mother, does it not prove the vigorous state of my health that I have borne that extreme agony without any loss of force and rebound so instantly from it? . . . We are very happy, happier than ever" (Gaeddert 1980: 124). Nathaniel's journal entry from 31 March 1843 tells us that he too recovered quickly:

> One grief we have had . . . all else has been happiness. Nor did the grief penetrate to the reality of our life. We do not feel as if our promised child were taken from us forever; but only as if his coming had been delayed for a season; and that, by-and-by, we shall welcome that very same little stranger whom we had expected to gladden our home at an earlier period. The longer we live together – the deeper we penetrate into one another and become mutually interfused – the happier we are. God will surely crown our union with children because it fulfills [*sic*] the highest conditions of marriage. (Lawrence and Werner 2005: 153)

On occasion, we feel sure that something we want to happen will happen. As many of his characters would find out, the only way out of darkness is to walk straight through it.

One day in April, Nathaniel had borrowed Sophia's ring to etch one of the windows with these poignant words: "Nath Hawthorne / This is his study / 1843." Above his name, Sophia wrote, "Man's accidents are God's purposes," signing her name: Sophia A. Hawthorne. Underneath his inscription, a small prose poem declares: "The smallest twig / Leans clear against the sky" – to which Hawthorne added, "Composed by my wife / and written with her diamond." Sophia added also: "Inscribed by my / husband at sunset / April 3d 1843 / In the gold light SAH." Below this is *Sund* [Sunday], though technically, 3 April fell on a Monday that year. "The symbolic value of these inscriptions," wrote Carlos Baker (1996), "was to make the Manse and the study more their own than ever, as if they had now permanently superseded Emerson, and even exorcised by such an act the more elderly Emersonian ghosts" (228).

Just as Nathaniel had foreseen, the cloud lifted a year later. On 3 March 1844, after a ten-hour long, painful labor Sophia gave birth to their auburn-haired daughter. "Every morning when I wake and find the darling lying there," Sophia wrote to her mother on 5 April, "or hear the sound of her soft breathing, I am filled with joy and wonder and awe" (Gaeddert 1980: 132).

Both parents cultivated high hopes for their child, christening her Una after Edmund Spenser's heroine in *The Faerie Queene* (1590). In Book I, Canto X, Stanza 28, we learn about her coming to the aid of the Red Cross Knight:

> In which his torment often was so great,
> That like a Lyon, he would cry and rore,
> And rend his flesh, and his owne synewes eat.

> His owne deare *Vna* hearing evermore
> His ruefull shriekes and gronings, often tore
> Her guiltlesse garments, and her golden heare,
> For pitty of his paine and anguish sore;
> Yet all with patience wisely she did beare; . . .. (1909: 129)

Here she represents an ideal woman of truth, reverence, and humility. She remains loyal to the Red Cross Knight even under the most terrifying circumstances, rescuing him with her courage and tact and saving his life by snatching the dagger from his hand when he is in despair. A devoted daughter, she also makes valiant attempts to deliver her parents from the dragon that is scourging their land. She is the paragon of all things virtuous: meek and humble on the one hand, yet brave and fearless on the other. Innocent and wise, she finds no fault with others, even when they are in the wrong. On the contrary, she suffers and struggles for the greater good of others, completely subjugating her own interests and desires in the process, self-denial, and sacrifice incarnate. Whether or not Una Hawthorne would live up to her namesake is a matter of conjecture, but we will hear haunting echoes of this description in the woman known as Hester Prynne in *The Scarlet Letter*.

Names can be both informative and allegorical, sometimes bordering on self-fulfilling prophecy. In his writings (as with his own children), Hawthorne chose each character's name with great care, not only because it suited the tone of the story but also because of what it foreshadowed about his or her future. Social scientists refer to this as the Dorian Gray effect after Oscar Wilde's novel, *The Picture of Dorian Gray* (1890), in which the dissolute protagonist never ages while his portrait reveals the ravages of a life of excess. In story after story, Hawthorne uses an interplay between the names of characters, their physical traits, and how others perceive them – all of which, in turn, affect how they feel about and see themselves.

Hawthorne's view of Una's childhood behavior, with unambiguous references to Spenser's incarnation, will influence his portraits, for example, of Violet ("modesty" or "humility") and Penny (a diminutive of Penelope, meaning "weaver") in "The Snow Image" (1851) and the precocious Pearl (of great price, purchased with all she had, her mother's only treasure) in *The Scarlet Letter*, published seven years after Una's birth. On 22 June 1846, upon the birth of their son, they named him Julian (young at heart) after the Roman centurion Julius, who saved St. Paul's life during a hazardous voyage recounted in the Book of Acts, Chapter 27. Hawthorne loved this reference: If a pagan soldier who purportedly did not know God could demonstrate such a great act of kindness, then how much more God's people should be moved to do so. Meanwhile, on 20 May 1851, Rose (passion and sacrifice) was born. Hawthorne never stopped thinking about his children's education from the time they were born. What concerned him most was how their imagination and intellectual powers could or should be shaped. In 1863, to his father's great satisfaction, Julian would be admitted to Harvard.

Just as Sophia transformed her husband's life, so did the publication of *Mosses from an Old Manse* (1846, 1854), a book that brought him closer to self-confidence and fame. Yes, loneliness nourishes art, and he guarded his loneliness as a saint does his wounds, but he also recognized the importance of striking a balance between idealism and pragmatism.

In class, we focus on six representative magical and mystical tales for their variety of form, subject, and themes: "The Birth-mark" (1843), "Rappaccini's Daughter" (1844), "The Artist of the Beautiful" (1844), "Egotism; or, The Bosom Serpent" (1843), "The Celestial Rail-road" (1843), and "Earth's Holocaust" (1844). I have seen firsthand how easily students become engaged with the plots and characters even as Hawthorne confronts the fundamental moral concerns of art and artists, death and immortality, crisis of maturity, and guilt.

"Why so few?" someone might ask. Early in my career, a dean advised me to cut everything by two-thirds for one of my classes. "Imposing an excessive workload on your students," he said, "is a symptom of inexperience." Time proved him right. From eighteen tales, I cut to six. I would rather keep my students involved with a close study of a few texts spread over the semester than haplessly see their impressionable minds drift away by rushing through twenty or more. Quality and not quantity encourages deeper, clearer thinking. Although I wouldn't recommend this in practice, theoretically one could focus on just one tale or one novel and teach from that one text just about everything a student might be expected to learn about a particular literary period. Individual works are almost infinitely layered. The more we look at a specific work, the more we see.

Following Mrs. Hayes's lead, I try to encourage a new generation of readers by creating a subtext of larger questions that Hawthorne's passion for books addresses. How do stories shape and nourish our inner lives? What will happen to us as a people if we become a nation of nonreaders? By shepherding us through the answers to these questions, along with many others, she was offering us an alternative voice to the apathetic ones we heard much too often in society. And as our minds grew, we were able to help others grow along the way, just as I hope I am now doing with my own students. The Chinese put it best: "A book is like a garden carried in the pocket."

"The Birth-mark," Hawthorne's first work of fiction after marrying Sophia and set in the latter part of the eighteenth century, is one of his most anthologized. Why? It reminds us that the capacity to perceive the consequences of our actions before we take them is one of the most important lessons we can learn. "Whenever we are about to do or say something that goes against our better judgment," Mrs. Hayes said, "we suffer the consequences."

Hawthorne probably had been thinking of this theme long before he composed the tale. In a notebook entry dated 25 October 1836, he hinted: "Those who are very difficult in choosing wives seem as if they would take none of Nature's ready-made works, but want a woman manufactured particularly to their order." Then, on 16 October 1837, he wrote: "A person to be in the possession of something as perfect as mortal man has a right to demand; he tries to make it better, and ruins it entirely," and another gem: "A person to spend all his life and splendid talents in trying to achieve something naturally impossible, – as to make a conquest over Nature." This was followed by a word of caution on 4 January 1839: "A person to be the death of his beloved in trying to raise her to be more than mortal perfection; yet this should be a comfort to him for having aimed so highly and holily" (*Works* VIII, 20, 165, 184).

"The Birth-mark" tells of a devoted alchemist, Aylmer (as we soon discover, he truly *ails*), who, like the author, is also a newlywed. After his wedding, he becomes obsessed with correcting the one flaw in his otherwise beautiful wife, Georgiana (meaning "farmer," therefore innocent, unworldly): a birthmark on her left cheek, shaped like a small crimson hand, which changes color based on her moods. To him, this hand has become "the symbol of his wife's liability to sin, sorrow, decay, and death" (*Works* X, 39).

He leads Georgiana to his laboratory, where amidst its ominously fiery furnace and soot, its machines and oppressive odors, its unadorned walls, he gives her a crystal goblet full of a colorless liquid. Misguidedly devoted to her husband, she drinks it. As the birthmark fades, so does her life, but she urges him not to feel guilty, for he has "aimed loftily" and "done nobly! Do not repent," she says with a hint of irony, "that, with so high and pure a feeling, you have rejected the best that earth could offer" (*Works* X, 55). Then she dies.

Aylmer fails to weigh the haunting consequences of his obsession, "to look beyond the shadowy scope of Time" and "find the perfect Future in the present" (*Works* X, 56). In rejecting Georgiana because of her imperfection, in allowing his love for science to take precedence over his love for his wife, he succumbs to self-conceit.

There wasn't a student in Mrs. Hayes's class who didn't connect with the story, and that continues to be true in my own classes. It teaches the moral that striving for perfection at all costs can end in futility. But the story also warns us against falling into the trap that preoccupied Hawthorne for a lifetime: sacrificing one's emotions/feelings in pursuit of an intellectual ideal. At some point in their academic lives, many students feel tempted to sacrifice the heart on the altar of the intellect. The heart shrinks, the student becomes cold and indifferent to others. The danger is that it can happen in any realm of study, often sneaking up over a period of years. Once the golden cord that ties us to our humanity snaps, we become less human and less connected with others.

Walt Whitman warned against this in his poem, "When I Heard the Learn'd Astronomer" (1867), written from the perspective of a student sitting in an astronomy class as the professor drones on about measuring the heavens. He reduces everything to observable, measurable phenomena, devoid of spirit, soul, or even emotion. Disenchanted, the student steps outside and looks up, awed by the sheer majesty of nature.

Considering this, it is heartening that Whitman, like Hawthorne, wanted us to remember to *leave time for wonder.* Celebrate the imagination. Embrace the unknown. Break free from preconceived notions. Although some students' arms might be crossed in defiance, the humanities can encourage them to un-cross them lest they become impervious to feelings and mystery. Such negative consequences are the subject of Hawthorne's next story.

"Rappaccini's Daughter," written a few months after Una's birth, is a tale of Beatrice, a young and beautiful woman who becomes an unsuspecting victim of a misguided horticulturist. Signor Giacomo Rappaccini (connoting "rapacious"), ostensibly in love with his wife, is said to transform plants into highly potent medicines.

When the story begins, Giovanni Guasconti, a young man who has traveled from the south of Italy to study at the University of Padua, takes lodgings in a high chamber which looks down on the doctor's neighboring garden. He watches as the doctor, who prefers science to human beings, examines flowers and shrubbery with detached curiosity. He is "a tall, emaciated, sallow, and sickly-looking man," dressed in black, with a face "marked with intellect and cultivation," but lacking "warmth of heart" (*Works* X, 95). He instructs his daughter to care for one magnificent purple blooming plant, which is poisonous to the touch and fatal to inhale. Even though the townspeople are aware of Rappaccini's malevolent experiments, they are powerless to protect Beatrice from her father, who would sacrifice human life "or whatever else was dearest to him" for the sake of knowledge (*Works* X, 99).

As the tale unfolds, the vain and facile Giovanni is lured into the garden, only to realize that he has fallen under her influence. To him, she is like an infant as she leads a life of such seclusion that she knows nothing of the world beyond the garden walls. Her father's "fatal love of science" has "estranged" her from all society (*Works* X, 123). She has no friends or companions – only a poisonous shrub that she calls "sister." Raised on a diet of poisonous plants, she has become as "poisonous as she is beautiful" (*Works* X, 97, 118). Giovanni realizes that he, too, is part of Rappaccini's experiment and that now he shares her powers. When he breathes on a swarm of insects, for example, many of them perish. Baglioni, a rival scientist, attempts to save Beatrice with a special potion, but after sipping it, she dies at his feet, saying that for her, "poison had been life, so the powerful antidote was death" (*Works* X, 127–128).

Like Georgiana in "The Birth-mark," it is inconceivable for Beatrice to live without her flaw. She realizes the situation is deadly but is unable to revert to her own self. Although her name derives from Dante's Beatrice in *The Divine Comedy* (1472), the similarity ends there. Unlike Dante's agent of grace, whose intercession in Heaven helps him find his way through the dark wood of error, Hawthorne's character ironically needs redemption herself. "[T]hough my body be nourished with poison," she cries, "my spirit is God's creature, and craves love as its daily food" (*Works* X, 125).

She is a prototype for the temptresses Hester Prynne (*The Scarlet Letter*), Zenobia (*The Blithedale Romance*), and Miriam (*The Marble Faun*). Rappaccini looks forward to the demonic Roger Chillingworth, whereas Giovanni anticipates the weak, self-righteous Arthur Dimmesdale. In each of these characters, their sins and the ensuing consequences dominate the tales. These concerns haunted Hawthorne for his entire creative life.

Every generation worries about the decline of human society, and Hawthorne's was no exception. He lived in an era when civilization was witnessing a paradigm shift, a major turning point in history when the assumptions on which society was structured were being analyzed, sharply challenged, and profoundly changed. We think, for example, of the controversy surrounding Sir Charles Lyell's proofs of the vast extent of geologic time, and Charles Darwin's theory of evolution through natural selection in *The Origin of Species* (1859). In political philosophy, the mid-century saw the rise of uncompromising materialism and the nihilism of Friedrich Nietzsche and Karl Marx. As a result, complacent atheism became common, about which A.N. Wilson (1999) wrote in *God's Funeral*: "The closing decades of the 19th century were the true era of 'the death of God'" (49).

It should not surprise us, therefore, to find this concern emerge in one of Hawthorne's processional tales, in which a large group of people embark on a collective journey. In "The Celestial Rail-road" he selectively exaggerates current aspects of social change and uses Bunyan's *Pilgrim's Progress* to structure his satire. The story haunts us because it evokes so powerfully what we all feel at times – the unnerving conviction that things are better elsewhere if only we can get there.

The naïve narrator takes a trip on the new railroad, recently established between the City of Destruction and the Celestial City. He discovers that many of the things he held sacred have been destroyed or devalued: books and learning; pure and sincere young women; the church. The engine, looking like a "mechanical demon," is driven by Apollyon, the enemy of Christian, the hero of *Pilgrim's Progress* (*Works* X, 190). The coach rattles over a rickety bridge; a quagmire, called the Slough of Despond, lies far below. His companion, a gentleman named Mr. Smooth-it-away, points out that many fruitless efforts have been made to convert the quagmire to firm ground. People have, without success, thrown in "books of morality, volumes of French philosophy and German rationalism, tracts, sermons, and essays of modern clergymen, extracts from Plato, Confucius, and various Hindoo sages" along with commentaries on Scripture (*Works* X, 187). After reaching Hill Difficulty and the Valley of Humiliation, the narrator expresses his desire to visit the Palace Beautiful and meet charming young ladies such as Miss Prudence, Miss Piety, and Miss Charity. But Mr. Smooth-it-all dismisses this idea with a laugh, remarking that they are now all old maids and barely recognizable.

Next, the train reaches Vanity Fair, the "great capital of human business and pleasure," where the narrator finds an "unlimited range of society," including the wise, powerful, and witty (*Works* X, 199). Every street has its church with an assortment of clergy: the Reverend Mr. Shallow-deep, the Reverend Mr. Stumble-at-truth, the Reverend Mr. Throw-to-day, the Reverend Mr. That-to-morrow, the Reverend Mr. Clog-the-spirit, and the Reverend Dr. Wind-of-doctrine (although a man of faith, Hawthorne was not a churchgoer). Finally, they arrive at the Celestial gates. The narrator hurries to board a steam ferryboat, his luggage lost, while Mr. Smooth-it-away remains on the shore, waving, only to be transformed (to the narrator's horror) into an apparition of the Devil or Fiend. The narrator then wakes "with a shiver and a heart-quake," extremely grateful to realize all of it has just been a dream (*Works* X, 206). He has been deluded. His journey has taken him to Hades, not the Celestial City, a journey to death, not life.

Throughout his career, Hawthorne made significant use of dreams, the dubious hinterland between sleeping and waking, in many instances invoking the classical conception of the experience as a medium of supernatural powers or as a premonition of future events. Dreams capture, at once, the terrors of the irrational (as may be the case in "Young Goodman Brown") and the creative powers of the imagination, of one's deepest fears and highest aspirations. Used in the early tales as a verbal or structural device, dreams become in the later romances a transforming experience that guides the dreamer toward a moment of catharsis and self-awareness. Whether or not something actually occurred isn't the point, but how it affects the dreamer.

As "The Celestial Rail-road" implies, the core of humanity's problem is spiritual, and therefore the antidote must be spiritual as well. "Egotism; or, The Bosom Serpent," written during Sophia's first pregnancy and miscarriage, carries this theme forward. Ever since he separated from his wife Rosina four years earlier, Roderick Elliston believes that he is harboring a serpent in his chest. He is now a "wretched being" who, with his lean body, glittering eyes, "sickly white" complexion with a "greenish tinge," long black hair, and undulating walk, reminds us of a menacing serpent (*Works* X, 269). Eventually, he retreats from the mystified townspeople and exhibits signs of insanity on account of his continued suffering. Hawthorne's theme is that "All persons, chronically diseased, are egotists, whether the disease be of the mind or body" (*Works* X, 273).

An old friend, George Herkimer, an American sculptor, returns after spending five years in Europe, shocked to find Elliston mad and recently released from an insane asylum. Having a snake in one's bosom, Elliston reassures him, is the "commonest thing in the world." Only the very "pure and wholesome" are exempt (*Works* X, 270). In his case, it seems to stem from jealousy of his wife.

Herkimer has come to rescue Elliston and brings along a "sad and tremulous" companion who remains hidden in the arbor. In the garden, Herkimer finds Elliston who, while reading a book on the natural history of serpents, has now realized that the serpent was engendered by his own psyche. "[T]here is poisonous stuff in any man's heart," he says, "sufficient to generate a brood of serpents" (*Works* X, 282).

The companion, revealed to be Rosina, now enters the garden with a countenance marked by "hope and unselfish love" and bends over him. "[F]orget yourself, my husband," she gently advises, "in the idea of another!" As she touches Elliston, he begs her forgiveness, causing her to shed "happy tears." They are now reconciled even as the serpent retreats with a "waving motion through the grass" (*Works* X, 283). The story is not without some comic elements, as when Elliston accosts the townspeople, and some say he simply has dyspepsia. But its chief theme is the way ordinary resentments can amount to madness, and a woman's patience and love can forgive.

As Hawthorne knew all too well, the practical and useful can be the enemy of art. "The Artist of the Beautiful," a parable of art and artistry written within three months of Una's birth, tells us the story of a young man, Owen Warland, an "irregular genius" who works on delicate objects rather than on ordinary tasks to make a living. (*Works* X, 448). A retired watchmaker, the unimaginative and utilitarian Peter Hovenden, walking along a village street with his daughter, Annie, gaze through the window of a small watch shop and observe Owen, Hovenden's former apprentice, at work. Then they pass the shop of a blacksmith, the manly and strong Robert Danforth, whom Hovenden hopes his daughter will marry, and of whom he speaks highly as one who, unlike the watchmaker, "spends his labor upon a reality" (*Works* X, 449). Although Owen is in love with Annie, the latter cannot possibly live up to his vision of her. He has connected "all his dreams of artistical success with Annie's image." Unfortunately though, the "real" Annie is "representative of the world" (*Works* X, 472). She marries the blacksmith.

After a spell of despair and heavy drinking, Owen regains the love of his art. He is happiest when, like a poet, painter, sculptor or the author himself, he wanders through the countryside, searching for wondrous beauty. He specializes in tiny exquisite objects and makes an ingeniously wrought mechanical butterfly, which he takes to Annie as a belated wedding gift. Annie's toddler son crushes the butterfly obliterating its "spiritual essence," but Owen remains happy as he fantasizes about putting "the very spirit of Beauty into form" (*Works* X, 452, 473). Owen is content to live in his own world, even though he has been rejected by the pragmatic, unimaginative, materialistic society around him.

Finally, looking ahead to *The Blithedale Romance* and its satire of utopian aspirations, Hawthorne's following tale reminds us that the success of any reform is predicated on the purity of the human heart. In that context, the apocalyptic "Earth's Holocaust" commences with an announcement: at some unspecified time, the world has been so burdened with "worn-out trumpery" that its inhabitants have decided to purge the world of folly in a general bonfire (*Works* X, 381). Articles judged "fit for nothing but to be burnt" are to be thrown into the fire, including family pedigrees and such "earthly distinctions" as the French Legion of Honor and English orders of nobility (*Works* X, 382, 383).

Suddenly, a gray-haired nobleman hurriedly protests the burning of such signs, which in his view mark the advance from "barbarism" to the "privileged orders" of patrons who were and continue to be the upholders of fine art, literature, and creativity in general (*Works* X, 383). But he shrinks back before the contemptuous crowd, which continues to toss in their prized possessions, both literal and metaphorical. The "playthings of wax" melt in flames, as do a guillotine, marriage certificates, and paper money; books and pamphlets are shoved into the blaze to rid the world of "dead men's thoughts" (*Works* X, 390, 395). A similar fate awaits ecclesiastical accouterments and even Bibles.

Soon, "a dark-complexioned personage" appears and objects, "[t]here is one thing that these wiseacres have forgotten to throw into the fire, and without which all the rest of the conflagration is just nothing at all" (*Works* X, 403). Because they have not thrown "the human heart itself" into the flames, it cannot be purified and thus, will "re-issue all the shapes of wrong and misery – the same old shapes, or worse ones – which they have taken such a vast deal of trouble" to burn (*Works* X, 403). The old world will find a way to survive, and the narrator concurs. Humans' cherished endeavor to attain perfection is doomed to failure, since only the intellect has been reformed, and not the recalcitrant human heart.

The release of *Mosses from an Old Manse* occasioned two of the most memorable statements in nineteenth-century American literary criticism. In his anonymous review in the 17 and 24 August 1850 issues of the *Literary World*, Melville said, "[W]hatever Nathaniel Hawthorne may hereafter write, 'The Mosses from an Old Manse' will be ultimately accounted his master-piece." Poe hailed Hawthorne as "*the* example, *par excellence*, in this country, of the privately-admired and publicly-unappreciated man of genius." Other reviewers were equally generous in their assessments: Charles Wilkins Webber in the *American Whig Review* for September 1846 (his Life has deepened); Samuel W.S. Dutton in the *New Englander* for January 1847 (decidedly superior); E.P. Whipple in *Graham's Magazine* for May 1850 (as few living men could write); and Amory

Dwight Mayo in the *Universalist Quarterly* for July 1851 (greater maturity of development). In short, most reviewers preferred this volume over *Twice-Told Tales* (Crowley 1970: 125, 134, 140, 141, 160, 222).

Two years after the publication of *Mosses from the Old Manse*, the Hawthornes's tenancy at the Old Manse ended in the spring of 1845. They had not paid any rent in a long while, and the owners needed the house. Thus, Nathaniel and Sophia returned to Salem and moved in with his mother and sisters. Here he was again, in the old, familiar bedroom where he had spent the formative years of his life.

In March 1846, the political influence of Bridge and Pierce and other friends in the Democratic Party helped to secure Hawthorne an appointment as Surveyor in the Salem Custom House, where he worked each morning. The position paid $1200 annually plus incidental fees. In 1849, with the election of General Andrew Jackson and the return of the Whigs to office, however, Democratic officials were removed from their assignments, resulting in Hawthorne's dismissal. From this experience, as we will see in Chapter 8, he went on to write the semi-autobiographical introductory essay to *The Scarlet Letter* where he chronicles his tumultuous relationship with his forefathers and Salem's Puritan legacy. While he did harbor resentment about this loss of employment, he directed his energies to the writing of his new novel – spurred on by the death of his mother.

She died on 30 July 1849 after a brief illness in the Mall Street house, Salem, where all the Hawthornes had been living. In a journal entry from the day before, her son wrote: "[T]he death of old age is the consummation of life, and yet there is so much gloom and ambiguity about it, that it opens no vista for us into Heaven" (*Works* VIII, 425). Distressed by the circumstances related to this event, Sophia wrote, "My husband came near a brain fever after seeing her for an hour" (Woodberry 1902: 180). Of that time, he added in his journal,

> Louisa [his sister] pointed to a chair near the bed; but I was moved to kneel down close by my mother, and take her hand. She knew me, but could only murmur a few indistinct words – among which I understood an injunction to take care of my sisters. Mrs. Dike [the aunt] left the chamber, and then I found the tears slowly gathering in my eyes. I tried to keep them down; but it would not be – I kept filling up, till, for a few moments, I shook with sobs. For a long time, I knelt there, holding her hand; and surely it is the darkest hour I ever lived. (*Works* VIII, 429)

The raw sorrow and loss that this passage conveys as he cried like a child always speaks to my students, many of whom have also lost one or both of their own parents or have had a close encounter with death which made them aware of time's inevitable constraints. They are buoyed when he expressed, almost immediately, what he yearned to believe:

> But God would not have made the close so dark and wretched, if there were nothing beyond; for then it would have been a fiend that created us, and measured out our existence, and not God. It would be something beyond wrong – it would be an insult – to be thrust out of life into annihilation in this miserable way. So, out of the very bitterness of death, I gather the sweet assurance of a better state of being. (*Works* VIII, 429)

Ironically, his mother's death set him free to write. Along with the memories – no day will go by that she won't enter his mind – she left him with the immeasurable gift of storytelling. When he had come to terms with her passing, he resumed writing with greater fervor.

Looking back over all we have covered so far, we see that Hawthorne used death as a plot device not merely to awaken terror in the reader but to underline a moral. To his credit, he resisted the temptation of sentimentalizing the greatest reality of life. In "Lady Eleanor's Mantle" or "The Ambitious Guest," in "The Wives of the Dead" or "The Wedding Knell," as we have seen, death is cold, real, indiscriminate. In "The Birth-mark" and "Rappaccini's Daughter," it is the awful consequence of some egregious choices. In "The Minister's Black Veil," it is the great mystery, "The undiscovered country," says Hamlet, "from whose bourn / No traveller returns . . ." (III.i.80–81).

As in all memento mori, Hawthorne's tales open our eyes to the truth by revealing a number of reasons we avoid grappling with death and its effects on our lives. Like Roger Malvin ("Roger Malvin's Burial"), if we think about our end, we are forced to evaluate the worth of how we are living; and if we have been less than judicious about spending our years, as seen in "The Hollow of the Three Hills," we fear the guilt and regret that might accompany our death. Or, we fear not so much the prospect of death but what may lead up to it – dependence, loss of dignity, mental deterioration, pain – as depicted in "The Wedding Knell" and "Lady Eleanore's Mantle."

Some people may dread what they believe to be an entry into nonbeing, insignificance, a perpetual blankness, bereft of spirit, as in "The Celestial Rail-road." The fearful prospect of forgetting or being forgotten, being unheard of and unnoticed in an indifferent universe, is another reason some characters (such as Aylmer in "The Birth-mark," Dr. Rappaccini in "Rappaccini's Daughter") are eager to avoid thoughts of death: I will cease to exist; there will be nothing – and yet the world will go on, the sun will continue to rise, the wind will blow, and people will go on without me. Perhaps, like Fanshawe or Hawthorne himself, the greatest fear for some people arises from the conviction that dying is inseparable from the act of divine judgment. As a result, the physical pain associated with dying pales in comparison to this colossal fear.

However, I suspect that none of these explanations applies personally to Hawthorne as much as something else: He was trying to reconcile the truth about mortality with his unwavering need to complete his good and useful work. He had devoted almost half of his life to bring him to this point. He knew his purpose, and when once this clarity of mind is achieved, there is little patience for the distractions that come from people who do not know theirs. The key is in not to delay. To do so is to become helplessly haunted by what might have been. Time is in short supply, his inner voice was saying. *Carpe diem.*

Looking ahead, we will continue to see how mature and settled Hawthorne's mind on the subject of mortality and immortality was by the time he produced his most accomplished longer works. In "The Old Manse": "[O]ur Creator would never have made such lovely days, and have given us the deep hearts to enjoy them, above and beyond all thought, unless we were meant to be immortal" (*Works* X, 27). In *The Scarlet Letter*: "By bringing me hither, to die this death of triumphant ignominy before the people! Had either of these agonies been wanting, I had been lost for ever! Praised be his name! His will be done! Farewell!" (*Works* I, 257) In *The House of the Seven Gables*: "Death is so genuine a fact that it excludes falsehood, or betrays its emptiness; it is a touch-stone that proves the gold, and dishonors the baser metal" (*Works* II, 310). In *The Marble Faun*: "Thank Heaven for its blue sky; it needs a long, upward gaze, to give us back our faith! Not here can we feel ourselves immortal, where the very altars . . . are heaps of human bones!" (*Works* IV, 194). Eternity, Hawthorne reminds us, does offer some compensation for our mortal limits and losses.

In 1849, like Christian in Bunyan's *Pilgrim's Progress*, he "bid farewell forever to this abominable city [Salem]" to become "a citizen of somewhere else" by accepting an offer to live in a handyman's cottage on the Tanglewood estate in the Berkshires (Woodberry 1902: 177, 204). We will return there in Chapter 8.

In the meantime, thinking back to Mrs. Hayes's class in nineteenth-century American literature, and all that I learned, I often wonder what would have happened if I had been absent and not heard her speak six memorable words that would go on to change my life. Would I be writing this book?

It was late in May, toward the end of the semester, when she said to our class, "To one of you I am giving an 'A' for the semester. You have earned a 'B+', but I'm giving you an 'A' because [and here are the six words] I think you have the potential." In hindsight, it's quite possible (and probable) that she was speaking to several students, but at the time, I believed that she was speaking only to me, and that made all the difference.

Those simple yet meaningful words for that impressionable schoolboy helped solidify the commitment that carried me through high school, university, graduate school, and throughout my career. Sure, there have been times when my dedication flagged, and it would have been easy to skip a class or abandon a project and do something else. But whenever I felt reluctant about completing an assignment, unsure about something said in class, fearful of taking an examination, or doubtful of my abilities, there arose within me, like a divine benediction, the soothing words of Mrs. Hayes: *I think you have the potential.*

In a sense, Sophia communicated the same message to Nathaniel as she went on to play a vital role in her husband's life. What does it mean to live with a writer? What makes the arrangement work? How does life at home contribute to the creative process? Does it contribute, and if yes, why? At what cost does a masterpiece come into existence? In one way or another, I suspect that most writers have probed these questions at some point in their careers, and so shall we. We will dive deeper into them, and others, in the next chapters as we witness the literary and personal evolution of Hawthorne when he approached the most productive years of his creative life under the watchful, protective eyes of his beloved wife.

7

Nathaniel and Sophia (1837–1860)

The Old Manse, Concord, Massachusetts. Source: Claire/Adobe Stock Photos.

What greater thing is there for two human souls, than to feel that
they are joined for life – to strengthen each other in all labour,
to rest on each other in all sorrow, to minister to each other in all pain,
to be one with each other in silent unspeakable memories
at the moment of last parting?

—George Eliot, *Adam Bede* (2008 [1859]: 475)

The Life of the Author: Nathaniel Hawthorne, First Edition. Dale Salwak.
© 2023 John Wiley & Sons Ltd. Published 2023 by John Wiley & Sons Ltd.

Given what is revealed about Sophia Peabody from her letters and journals, as well as the observations of those who knew her well, it's easy to imagine that on 10 July 1842, the morning after the wedding, Sophia promised Nathaniel that his writing would come first in their life together.

"Dearest husband, thou must be free," I can hear her saying, "to devote thyself to thy work."

With those words, she would help prevent the rancor that can develop between partners when one is struggling for literary success, and the other is not. I can also imagine Nathaniel taking those words as a confirmation of the depth of her love and returning them in full measure. On 21 August 1839, he had written to her: "Oh, beloved, if we had but a cottage, somewhere . . . and have a place to *be* in . . . And you should draw, and paint, and sculpture, and make music, and poetry too, and your husband would admire and criticize; and I, being pervaded with your spirit, would write beautifully, and make myself famous for your sake, because perhaps you would like to have the world acknowledge me" (*Works* XV, 339).

The compulsion to produce art, for whatever reason, is not an indulgence or a hobby that can be easily dismissed. It is a precious gift ingrained deep in the soul. It is this compulsion that makes the artist complete. Throughout their 22 years of married life, Sophia was Nathaniel's single greatest source of support as she set aside, without bitterness or regret, her own professional aspirations to nurture their children and create a home of extraordinary marital love. Because she had an intuitive understanding of her husband's doubts and worries, she could foresee the unrest he would feel if anyone were to undermine his inner world. The part she was to play in his life was greater than he could have possibly imagined. She went on to become his muse.

How she helped him shape his work, and why – and what we can learn from their example – is the subject to which we now turn. What emerges is the portrait of a brilliant woman of limitless devotion and affection, a marriage of sustained happiness, and a pathway into the genesis and allegories in Nathaniel's novels and tales since 1841.

We begin in 1822 when Sophia was 13 years old. Recognizing her spark of genius as an artist, both her mother and her older sister, Elizabeth, warned her of the perils that lay in wait should she pursue the traditional roles of marriage and motherhood. "[T]here is no more sombre enemy of good art," I can imagine them saying (to borrow from Cyril Connolly's *Enemies of Promise* 2008 [1938]), "than the pram in the hall" (116). In *The House of Hawthorne*, Erika Robuck (2015) has Margaret Fuller advising Sophia, "For you do not want to end up the little marker at the side of the grand headstone, where future writers and readers will lay their offerings, honoring only the man published and not the woman who supported and even made his work possible" (211). If you must marry, so the argument went, do not neglect your gifts or you will end up resenting your husband and becoming a bitter person. Distractions, after all, are the enemy of the imagination.

Because no colleges at the time were open to women, Elizabeth took responsibility for her sister's education. Under her tutelage, Sophia read widely across the fields of history, theology, literature, astronomy, chemistry, and philosophy, thus cultivating a lifelong habit of self-education. She studied with ease Greek, French, Latin, Hebrew, and some German, read the classics, and steeped herself in Shakespeare.

Then, from June 1830 onward, she focused on drawing and painting and was mentored by some of the most gifted artists of the time, including Thomas Doughty, Chester Harding, the illustrator Francis Graeter, and the then dean of American painters, Washington Allston (who was appreciative of her landscape in imitation of Salvator Rosa). She learned to create by copying powerful masters with pencils and paints – an experience she called "almost intoxication" (Gaeddert 1980: 58). According to Emerson, her exceptional copies of landscapes in oils, illustrations, and decorative work reflected a formidably penetrating mind, a highly refined taste, and a "beauty making eye, which transfigures landscapes & the heads it looks upon" (Valenti 2004: 143).

Sophia was also gifted with words. In 1833, she had been unwell and went with her younger sister Mary to spend 17 months in Cuba to restore her health, while Mary worked as a governess for a wealthy coffee plantation owner. Her mother advised Sophia to record in letters all that she saw in vivid sensory detail so that she might produce original art upon returning home. The fresh air, exercise, fellowship, and relaxation were just what she needed. She returned home in the spring of 1835 not just restored for a time but glowing.

The resulting three volumes of her widely circulated but never published Cuban journal justified her mother's confidence in her talent. Elizabeth referred to Sophia's "word paintings" of landscapes and cultural activities as "gentle masterpieces" (*Works* XV, 27). Her written words and the accompanying illustrations reveal, according to Patricia Valenti (2004), "a thinking and sensual woman, enlivened with the warmth of passion and unafraid to document the minutest reflection or to expose the most intense emotion on paper" (117).

Thus, the desire to resist the confines of marriage must have been strong, as she went on quietly drawing, painting, and modeling busts and bas-reliefs from her bedroom's art studio, earning what she could and struggling to find her own little space in the world. She rarely talked about her work, never felt impelled to compare herself to others, and never sought reassurance from friends or the public, which most artists need to be sure of their calling. Both family members and teachers expected her to continue. Indeed, Sophia was a young woman of real ability whose career pathway appeared to be fairly clear before her.

But her physical health was a serious concern. First, there was pain. When she was an infant, her dentist father had prescribed mercury as a treatment for teething, a decision that probably affected her entire life. Since 13, she had suffered from severe migraines and nervous disorders accompanied by dreadful nightmares and sporadic bouts of complete physical and emotional collapse. Sometimes, her painting left her with "the unalloyed agony of overstretched nerves," she wrote in her journal (dated 10 January and 15 February 1832). "I wonder if there are many people who live life thus as it were by drawing up buckets of life with hard labor from the well of the mind" (Valenti 1990: 7).

Her possessive mother explained to her that suffering was a woman's peculiar lot, having something to do with the sin of Eve. Cheerful suffering, she advised, would please God. Her ineffectual father allowed Boston doctors to prescribe, among other remedies, laudanum, more mercury, arsenic, hyoscyamus, homeopathy, leeches, bloodletting, morphine, outdoor exercise, and hypnotism (mesmerism) – yet the headaches persisted. Prayer did not seem to lessen the agony.

Given her ill-health, the stresses of Boston life, the suffocating attentions of her anxious family, and the inherent insecurity of an artist's profession (especially for a woman) at that time, she must have wondered how she could possibly defeat these ordeals. Her family thought she would remain bed-ridden forever, unable to marry or bear children, unable to experience love.

She also felt a gnawing loneliness. While her ebullient spirit allowed her to make friends with ease, Sophia did not come across many people who shared the depth and detail of her thinking and feeling, other than the talk of her intellectual family and their friends, the premier minds of the time (notably Emerson, Fuller, Alcott, and Thoreau). "[The trouble is] not that I am *single* woman and likely to remain a *single* woman," revealed Charlotte Brontë, one of Sophia's contemporaries with whom she identified, "– but because I am a *lonely* woman and likely to be *lonely*" (Wise and Alexander Symington 1932: III, 216).

In her love poem of 1830, "To the Unknown Yet Known" (a continuation of Coleridge's unfinished poem "Christabel" [1816]), Sophia addressed the imaginary lover or soul mate who is waiting for her presence, "an artist & a poet too" with whom she could live in blissful co-creation:

> . . .Though thou find not the way
> To me, this truth we'll rest content to know.
> This truth: All good I do
> For others or myself is done for thee;
> All good thou worked too . . . is done for me. (Marshall 2005: 211;
> Valenti 1987: 14–16)

In her journal from that time, she recorded reports of weddings and births as her friends assumed the accepted roles for young women of that bygone era, causing Sophia to languish in her own company. Although she dreamed of a home of her own, she had been taught to dread marriage.

Enter Nathaniel. According to Elizabeth, Sophia's first meeting with him on 11 November 1837 exercised such a strong "magnetic attraction" upon her that she was alarmed; she didn't understand what it meant and felt that she must draw back in self-defense (Hawthorne 1884: I, 180). She felt a palpable soul-level connection, yet was reticent about her emotions. This was the first time she had encountered someone who drained her nerve power so much.

But "people are only influenced," T.S. Eliot reminds us, "in the direction in which they already want to go" (Thwaite 1996: xviii). She shared her Cuban journal with Nathaniel, and as his fascination with her and her descriptions grew (he called her the "Queen of Journalizers" [Valenti 2011: 48]), so did their relationship. He said that he "could make a great many stories" from her work (*Works* XV, 28). He even copied passages. Unsurprisingly, Sophia's resistance weakened. Listening to her heart, she fell in love, and almost four years later and against her family's wishes, married him. She took seriously the role of what she understood to be an "inmost wife" (Lawrence and Werner 2005: 12).

That understanding came in part from the Hebrew Scriptures which she had studied in the original language. Genesis 1:18 tells the story of how the first woman was created. God says that He will make for man an 'ezer (meaning "helper," or "to rescue and save," or "strength") kenegdo (meaning "suitable") – which, when taken in unison, means "an aid alongside him," "a suitable helper," "the complement of one's exact counterpart" or, most interestingly, "a helper opposed to him." Sophia realized, perhaps unconsciously, that a wife is called to be a supporter and protector when her husband is on the right path and to be in opposition to him when he is in the wrong. In the Hebrew Bible, 'ezer is never used to denote a woman's subordination or inferiority; on the contrary, it refers to someone who is superior or at least an equal. How different is this understanding from the nineteenth century's timeworn expectation of women as passive and subservient entities.

As for Nathaniel, it must have been difficult for a reclusive, shy bachelor of 38 to enter into the life of a pampered, semi-invalid five years younger with no financial prospects. Despite being attracted to her, Nathaniel was understandably worried that any news of their January 1839 engagement would shock his sisters, especially his collaborator, Elizabeth, and his ailing mother. He knew how hard it would be for the three of them to survive financially without him. Thus, he insisted that Sophia keep it a secret until just before the wedding three years later. None of his family members attended the ceremony – citing insufficient time to prepare themselves emotionally for the occasion.

But marriage was precisely what they both needed. They complemented, completed, and humanized each other with their enduring love. She took him out of his "unsubstantial loneliness" and got him closer to the reality of the world he was living in. He once remarked that his love for Sophia was his only warm, flesh-and-blood contact with the world. He was able to provide the love she yearned for (Matthiessen 1941: 255). On 28 June 1839, she wrote to her sister, Elizabeth, "*Now* I am indeed made deeply conscious of what it is to be loved" (Valenti 2015: 28). Never could she have foreseen the huge improvement in her life this marriage would bring.

On their wedding day, when the newlyweds moved into the Manse (which their friend Elizabeth Hoar had filled with flowers), they called it their Eden, a tranquil place of intense and inescapable sensuous delight. They cast themselves as the new Adam and Eve redeemed from their mutual fallen state of solitude and single life (Lawrence and Werner 2005: 1). From his study, Sophia removed the "'grim prints of Puritan ministers that hung around' and replaced them with 'the sweet and lovely head of one of Raphael's Madonnas,'" along with her own "'two pleasant little pictures of the Lake of Como,'" thereby broadening her beloved husband's "imaginative horizons" beyond the guilt-ridden, darker inclinations that had preoccupied him thus far (Valenti 2004: 246, 252). Their time together was ceremonial and celebratory in equal measure, one of the most unmistakable signs of conjugal harmony.

Their common journal (July 1842–October 1843), a private chronicle of the intimate details of their life together that first year, confirmed the happiest understanding between them. "A rainy day – a rainy day," begins Nathaniel's first entry on 5 April 1842, "and I do verily believe there is no sunshine in this world, except what beams from my wife's eyes" (Lawrence and Werner 2005: 39). To his credit, he slipped into his new role as a husband without any trouble. "It is usually supposed that the cares of life come with matrimony," he wrote on 3 April; "but I seem to have cast off all care, and live on with as much easy trust in Providence, as Adam could possibly have felt, before he had learned that there was a world beyond his Paradise" (71).

Sophia, meanwhile, relished the physical pleasures of their union. When spring came, she compared nature's rebirth to her own awakening. "Oh lovely GOD!" she wrote. "I thank thee that I can rush into my sweet husband with all my many waters, & sing & thunder with all my waves in the vast expanse of his comprehensive bosom. How I exult there – how I foam & sparkle in the Sun of his love . . . I myself am Spring with all its birds, its rivers, its buds, singing, rushing, blooming in his arms. I feel new as the Earth which is just born again. I rejoice that I am, because I am his, wholly, unreservedly his" (183). The suggestiveness of Sophia's language and its latent eroticism is unmistakable here.

Trying to outdo each other with endearing names, Nathaniel called her "Dove," "Dearest Love," "Dearissima," "Phoebe," "Thou sinless Eve," "Belovedest," and most eloquent, "Wife." She called him "My soul's star," "Thine ownest truest Love and Dove," "my Phoebus Apollo," and "Oh King by divine right."

As the seasons passed, the Hawthornes observed them together. "This is Thanksgiving Day," Nathaniel wrote on 24 November – "a good old festival; and my wife and I have kept it with our hearts, and besides have made good cheer upon our turkey, and pudding, and pies, and custards, although none sat at our board but our two selves" (145). Similarly, both tried their hand in the garden that Thoreau had planted for them when summer beckoned. On 9 May, Sophia teased her artistic husband as she observed him with rake in hand. "Dearest husband," she wrote, "thou shouldst not have to labour, especially with the hands, & thou hatest it rightfully. Thou art a seraph come to observe Nature & men in a still repose, without being <u>obliged</u> to exert thyself in . . . clearing away old rubbish. Apollo among his herds could not have looked so out of place as thou with saw & axe & rake in hand" (203).

This organized, love-infused, and relaxing life at home gave Hawthorne the opportunity to further pursue his natural inclinations. Sophia made and maintained a safe haven for him. He could always count upon her when others let him down. As the years passed, through miscarriage and childbearing, financial strain, illness, deaths of family members and friends, European travel, and much more, theirs was a relationship – writer and artist, husband and wife, father and mother – of unbroken harmony, a minuet safe and secure.

But Sophia also became that most valued person in any writer's life, the first critic, the person with whom he gladly shared his creations. In the summer of 1839, Nathaniel wrote to her: "I shall always read my manuscripts to you, in the summer afternoons or winter evenings; and if they please you I shall expect a smile and kiss as my reward – and if they do not please, I must have a smile and kiss to comfort me" (*Works* XV, 339).

Their earliest collaboration occurred within a year after they had met. As we have seen, Sophia illustrated Hawthorne's story, "The Gentle Boy," which had originally appeared in 1832 in *The Token*. In his first public declaration of attachment, he dedicated the book thus: "Miss Sophia Amelia Peabody, This Little Tale, To which Her Kindred Art has Given Value, is respectfully inscribed." The story was also published in a separate volume, with Sophia's illustration as the frontispiece, by Weeks & Jordan in Boston and by Wiley & Putnam in New York and London in 1839.

Following his marriage, Hawthorne's words were written because Sophia was there to read them. He trusted her judgment in all its aspects, rightly, I believe, even though she had never ventured into his fictional terrain herself. She could hear when he was at his best and worst. If something he had written was not ready to publish, she would let him know. She knew her husband, and though she couldn't write as well as Nathaniel, she could tell him how to write more like himself. In a letter dated 1 April 1860 to John Lothrop Motley, he wrote, "[Sophia] speaks so near me that I cannot tell her voice from my own" (*Works* XVIII, 256).

Works of art, which figured so prominently in Sophia's life, naturally found their way into their life together. She filled their residence with copies of paintings, busts, and statuary, including Madonnas and Sibyls by Michelangelo, Leonardo da Vinci, and Raphael; landscapes by Claude Gellé and Rosa Bonheur; statues by Bertel Thorvaldsen, Antonio Canova, and Thomas Crawford. She wanted their children to grow up in an atmosphere suffused with culture and artistic sensibilities. They also discussed literature and painting and the relationship between the two.

Under her watch, she helped her husband see from the perspective of an artist, to introduce an idea without spoiling the mood. She adjusted his writing to become a more accurate representation of the real world. Under her influence, too, Nathaniel mastered the art of insightful, often engaging accounts of daily experiences. In her drawing, painting, and sculpture, wrote Julian (1884), "she was able to meet at all points her husband's meditative and theoretic needs with substantial and practical gratification" (I, 41).

Her influence hovers, for example, over forty-nine of the fifty chapters of *The Marble Faun*, as meticulously traced by Patricia Valenti (2015). Drawing upon her greater familiarity with Italian culture and art, Sophia corrected the Italian "contadina" (peasant girl or woman) to the plural "contadine," made the writing more accurate with "*white*-wash" on a building becoming "a coat of stucco and yellow-wash," replaced the description of a cross as "black" with the more realistic "iron," and changed the name of a sculptor from Graydon to Kenyon. For practical purposes, most of her well-intended suggestions adjusted "his writing to a more accurate representation of the real world" (195–196). Edmund Wilson (1977) did not miss this change. In a letter to Newton Arvin, dated 24 May 1946, he said that in the later books – that is, those written after Hawthorne had married – "the backgrounds become less shadowy and the characters live with an intense life" (443).

"To paint is not to represent," Balthus (2001) would say 160 years later, "but to penetrate, to go to the heart of the secret, to work in a way to reflect the interior language. The painter is also a mirror; he reflects the mind, the line of interior light" (70). The same may be said for an author's words. On 11 December 1839, Nathaniel wrote the following about the Daguerrotype, an early form of a photograph that produced accurate, detailed, and sharp images on a silvered copper plate: "I wish there was something in the intellectual world analagous [*sic*] to the Daguerrotype (is that the name of it?) in the visible – something which should print off our deepest, and subtlest, and delicatest thoughts and feelings, as minutely and accurately as the . . . instrument paints the various aspects of

Nature" (*Works* XV, 384). In another passage from 3 January 1840, he acknowledged the pleasure he derived from visual arts: "I have often felt as if I could be a painter, only I am sure that I could never handle a brush; – now my Dove will show me the images of my inward eye, beautified and etherealized by the mixture of her own spirit" (*Works* XV, 398).

His domestic bliss emboldened him to attempt more ambitious projects. His love letters reveal drafts of female characters that would go on to dominate his later works. Sympathetic depictions of those who would become Hester Prynne in *The Scarlet Letter*, Zenobia in *The Blithedale Romance*, and Hilda in *The Marble Faun* all remind us of the social subjugation of women in the nineteenth century and earlier, against which Hawthorne (like his characters) rebelled.

Further evidence of Sophia's impact on his thinking and writing is provided in some of his tales. Her elucidation of restoring a painting inspired, for instance, his "Edward Randolph's Portrait" (1838). Possibly he was referring to Sophia when he described the heroine, Alice Vane, as "a pale, ethereal creature, who, though a native of New England, had been educated abroad, and seemed not merely a stranger from another clime, but almost a being from another world . . . It was said that the early productions of her own pencil exhibited no inferior genius, though, perhaps, the rude atmosphere of New England had cramped her hand, and dimmed the glowing colors of her fancy" (*Works* IX, 259). Sophia's journal entries fed his imagination, "laying the groundwork for both the recurring figure of the dark, sensuous woman and the rich, exotic landscapes" in some of his later fiction, including *The House of the Seven Gables* and *The Marble Faun* (Valenti 2004: 119).

Out of Sophia, he formed two kinds of women – one the ethereal, spiritual, ideal entity who might elicit the highest potential from a man; the other an earthy, practical, willful being which could threaten his sense of manliness. Hawthorne might have explored these two dimensions of a woman without having married Sophia, but his female characters would have been much less profound and certainly more theoretical than experiential (Valenti 2004: 168).

So, what do my students learn from the example of Hawthorne and Sophia?

They learn the importance of marrying or entering into a partnership with someone who respects their work and lets them pursue their cherished passion without necessarily understanding it. They learn that, with a few obvious exceptions, the words "sacrifice" and "compromise" do not belong in the marital vocabulary. If they are constantly sacrificing or compromising, then they are probably married to the wrong person. They learn that their relationship with their spouse (or partner) has everything to do with how they feel supported in their respective endeavors. That takes a lot of understanding, compassion, and real love.

Because Sophia allowed Hawthorne to approach his art with the sole idea of serving it sincerely and earnestly and assisted him in whatever way she could to reach that desired end, the result was mutually gratifying. She shielded him from disturbances, admired him, provided innumerable touches to his creations, and preserved his work. In every respect, Sophia lived up to the Hebrew origin of her name, meaning "watchman or guard." She ensured his well-being.

Some students with whom I share these insights find the idyllic scenes hard to believe. It's true that Hawthorne sometimes actively discouraged his wife from her artistic pursuits and urged her not to publish her journals out of concern for her health. I am sure that at times, Sophia imagined, as she does in *The House of Hawthorne*, what her life would have been if she had never entered the parlor that November day in 1837 to meet Nathaniel:

> Such thoughts come on the difficult nights, when Nathaniel is cross, the children needy, and the blank sketch pad seems to accuse me of neglect from across the room. Would I be a world-famous painter by now if I had not chosen domesticity? Would I want such a thing, when the pressure and act of creation often brought me such physical misery? I do sometimes mourn the death of my single artist's existence, but almost never (Robuck 2015: 330).

Some others who met them may have felt as did Emily Tennyson after encountering the Hawthornes at Manchester's Great Exhibition in 1857. In an unfair observation, she wrote that Sophia was not "the angel of the house," and noted, "her pose of submission repressing overt rage" (Thwaite 1996: 332). But Tennyson was mistaken, which has also been the case with other critics who have since then played fast and loose with the facts.

At this stage, it is important to mention T. Walter Herbert's speculation in his book, *Dearest Beloved: The Hawthornes and the Making of the Middle-Class Family* (1993) that the Hawthorne marriage was not as happy as it appeared to be. (One reviewer of the book called the marriage "a glittering edifice on shaky foundations" indicative of more deep-rooted challenges with relations between the genders in American culture [Reynolds 1993: 25]). Their professions of love, Herbert argued, masked deeper anxieties as they aimed to dominate each other, fueling in Sophia a perennial tug-of-war between fulfilling her domestic duties and pursuing her own desires as an artist.

But everything that the Hawthornes left behind, including their journals and letters, testifies to a marriage that was, in contrast to the critics' opinion, a model and (in Julian's words) a vindication of "true love and married happiness" (1884: 1). To those who have expressed the belief that Sophia's artistic skills were wasted in marriage and motherhood, they may want to refer to what she said in a letter to her friend, Caroline Sturgis Tappan, that her children had become her works of art (Gaeddert 1980: 133; Robuck 2015: 223). After the arrival of their first child, Una, on 3 March 1844, Sophia wrote to Elizabeth: "It was great happiness to be able to put her to my breast immediately, & I thanked Heaven I was to have the privilege of nursing her" (Valenti 2004: 207).

Had I the opportunity to interview Sophia, I would have asked her, "Were you ever resentful of your husband's devotion to his work?" Her answer, as I imagine, would be this: "I was proud of what he was doing, and I was just too busy to be resentful. I never felt neglected, never even gave it a thought. He was busy and I was busy. To put it simply, I worked alongside him, but in a different way."

Indeed, work was the constant through their lives together. The nature and contour of their tasks may have differed, but the goal of their separate labors was a shared one: a happy, financially stable, productive life for their family and themselves. They had not married because of societal pressures or personal insecurities. They had married because they found in one another a kindred spirit. "Loving to work" became their nature.

8

The Scarlet Letter (1850)

> *I think that the power of art is the power to wake us up,*
> *strike us to our depths, change us . . . We are searching,*
> *through a work of art, for something that alters us, that we*
> *weren't aware of before. We want to transform ourselves . . .*
>
> —Jhumpa Lahiri (2015: 36)

Widely regarded as Hawthorne's masterpiece, *The Scarlet Letter* is America's first psychological novel (or romance, as he preferred to call it) – a dark story set in mid-seventeenth century colonial New England. He wrote it at the age of 45, with 22 years' experience of authorship behind him. His lifelong, brooding concern with distinctly American themes – sin, punishment, penitence, and penance; the clash between our private and public selves; and the oft-neglected spiritual and psychological hardships of living as a social outcast – finds its perfect expression in this fateful tale. Hester Prynne's and the Reverend Arthur Dimmesdale's struggle to recover from disgrace and regain their honor and dignity has the directness and simplicity of classic Greek tragedy.

"To tell you the truth," he confided to his friend Horatio Bridge on 4 February 1850, "– it is positively a h-ll-fired story, into which I found it almost impossible to throw any cheering light" (*Works* XVI, 311–312). After listening to her husband read the conclusion aloud, Sophia went to bed with a terrible headache. "[L]ightning writing," she wrote later to her sister Elizabeth. "I really thought an ocean was trying to pour out of my heart & eyes" (Valenti 2015: 37). Hawthorne is at the pinnacle of his powers. Not a line is wasted; not a moment lags in this perfectly pitched performance. There is nothing else quite like it. This is the book that fixed him in the public mind at the time as America's pre-eminent novelist.

One autumn morning in 1985, when I was 12 years into my teaching career, I was leading my class through the opening scenes. It suddenly dawned on me that I was not relying on my carefully prepared lecture notes. I was not thinking about

The Life of the Author: Nathaniel Hawthorne, First Edition. Dale Salwak.
© 2023 John Wiley & Sons Ltd. Published 2023 by John Wiley & Sons Ltd.

what ideas or questions should come next. For the first time in my career, I felt, with utter calm and clarity, that I "owned" the material, that I had become one with the novel. Who among us has no fear of revealing our own hypocrisy? Would we tell the whole truth even if it might destroy our hard-earned reputation? Are we hiding secrets about our past? Are we as ready as Hawthorne's Puritans to judge the sins of others? What do our desires reveal about who we are?

Whatever questions the novel posed to its characters, it seemed to be posing to me as well, perhaps telling me more than I might like to hear about myself and my neighbors. I had achieved an intimacy with the text and the author's meaning that I did not have before, and that continues to this day. I felt a growing sense of confidence in myself as a teacher, confirming what one of my professors had said years earlier: "You will begin to truly teach when you have matured emotionally, when you begin to feel what you understand intellectually."

My transformation did not come early. It could not be forced or hastened. As an avid reader since childhood, and long before I had begun to teach, I always seemed to have a predilection for words and what could be done with them. But, like many teachers at the beginning of their career, I was an outsider looking in. I could communicate my appreciation for the texts and their creators, but knew I was teaching very little that was genuinely original about what my students and I were reading. Put succinctly, I could address the words, but not the spirit of the piece.

Graduate school at the University of Southern California had taught me what to say about Hawthorne's work and how to say it. I had become well-versed in the subject matter, the social and cultural contexts, and most of the theoretical approaches to reading deeply. In the classroom, however, I rarely trusted my own insights or spoke my own words; instead, I was imitating my wise and considerate professors. No matter how much I studied, I felt stymied and relegated to enjoy and admire, but only from a distance.

All this, I now realize, seemed false to me. More importantly, my students may also have found it superficial. There is a difference between reading the material and knowing it, between understanding the written word and living inside it. Much to my chagrin, I could sense the difference, but not overcome it. As I reflect on that period, it seems that my awareness that I was missing something made me look harder. As my familiarity with the text and its creator deepened, and as my confidence in the classroom grew, I sought out nuances in the novel, to free my mind from the bonds of "standard interpretation" and be open to all its possibilities.

I began to take intellectual chances by approaching *The Scarlet Letter* on the author's terms and allowing myself to be drawn into his world as if I were born to it. I put myself in his shoes. What would it be like to be him? How would it feel to embrace his beliefs? What qualities of him do I find in myself? In other words,

I found ways to befriend the text, and discovered that, as is the case with all good friendships, getting rid of my short-sighted expectations was both liberating and fulfilling in equal measure. I heard and understood more than ever before. The more I looked, the more I saw.

The highest goal of teaching is personal transformation. The best teachers, through their knowledge, enthusiasm, insight, encouragement, and high expectations, engender in their students an insatiable quest to seek answers and, in the famous words of Marcel Proust (1982 [1923]) from *The Captive*, "to possess other eyes" (13). After sharing my epiphany with the students, therefore, I suggest how to prepare for the golden moment when they, too, will step beyond self-imposed boundaries and tap into the passion that drove the author to create the novel we're privileged to be studying.

What are we going to talk about? Not about what we think the text says, not what we hope it says, not even necessarily what we have been told it says. Instead, we are going to discuss what it *does* say. "Trust the text," I say, thinking back to my high school teacher, Mrs. Hayes. "That is our authority." This means trying to see every word, every sentence from a nineteenth-century perspective; otherwise, we risk distorting the creative process and the created product. So we start with what the author says of his own work.

In "The Custom-House," the preface (or framing chapter) preceding the novel, Hawthorne tells us how his story will combine elements of romance and realism and draws us into its mystery. He aims to depict a world "somewhere between the real world and fairy-land, where the Actual and the Imaginary may meet, and each imbue itself with the nature of the other" (*Works* I, 36). He beautifully explicates this idea in a famous, poignant passage, that is worth quoting in full:

> Moonlight, in a familiar room, falling so white upon the carpet, and showing all its figures so distinctly, – making every object so minutely visible, yet so unlike a morning or noontide visibility, – is a medium the most suitable for a romance-writer to get acquainted with his illusive guests. There is the little domestic scenery of the well-known apartment; the chairs, with each its separate individuality; the centre-table, sustaining a work-basket, a volume or two, and an extinguished lamp; the sofa; the book-case; the picture on the wall; – all these details, so completely seen, are so spiritualized by the unusual light, that they seem to lose their actual substance, and become things of intellect. Nothing is too small or too trifling to undergo this change, and acquire dignity thereby. A child's shoe; the doll, seated in her little wicker carriage; the hobby-horse; – whatever, in a word, has been used or played, with during the day, is now invested with a quality of strangeness and remoteness, though still almost as vividly present as by daylight . . . The somewhat dim coal-fire has an essential influence in

producing the effect which I would describe. It throws its unobtrusive tinge throughout the room, with a faint ruddiness upon the walls and ceiling, and a reflected gleam from the polish of the furniture. This warmer light mingles itself with the cold spirituality of the moonbeams, and communicates, as it were, a heart and sensibilities of human tenderness to the forms which fancy summons up. It converts them from snow-images into men and women. Glancing at the looking-glass, we behold – deep within its haunted verge – the smouldering glow of the half-extinguished anthracite, the white moonbeams on the floor, and a repetition of all the gleam and shadow of the picture, with one remove farther from the actual, and nearer to the imaginative. Then, at such an hour, and with this scene before him, if a man, sitting all alone, cannot dream strange things, and make them look like truth, he need never try to write romances. (*Works* I, 35–36)

It is noteworthy that Hawthorne always felt the pull of romance with its emphasis on an authentic long-ago, an uncanny combination of fancy and fact. Here, the moon-beams (that is, the natural world which he loved) become the means by which the author can access the past. Characters, even objects as small or trifling as a child's shoe or doll, are endowed with an aura of mystery. The form is that of a struggle between personified abstractions. All visible objects are emblems of a larger reality. We are asked to suspend our disbelief, and we do.

In a romance, the social background is abstract at best, and a striking, otherworldly plot serves as a vehicle for an overarching allegorical truth. The characters are symbolic of heroism, goodness, chastity, or evil, malice, lies. Hawthorne wants to "dream strange things, and make them look like truth," to blend romance and realism. He manages to suggest a distinct past: he assigns specific dates to the action of the story (from June 1642 to late May or early June 1649), invents documentary evidence for the story, and makes his two central characters recognizable human beings. He combines historical realism with mysterious and magical elements that derive from the romance tradition.

"What is Past is Prologue" proclaims Antonio in Shakespeare's *The Tempest* (II.i.253–254). Using this rich precept as both framework and guide, we can understand why Hawthorne uses a combination of autobiography and magic to get his story going. His conscientious narrator relates how he has found a mysterious package in the dusty attic of the Salem Custom House. Inside, he discovers the capital letter "A" made "of fine red cloth, much worn and faded" and measuring precisely three inches and a quarter in length. The narrator speculates, "Certainly, there was some deep meaning in it, most worthy of interpretation" (*Works* I, 31). He clutches the "A" to his own breast, but the red letter scorches him, "as if the letter were not of red cloth, but red-hot iron," and he drops it on the floor. Sometimes the past comes back to burn us (*Works* I, 32).

He also discovers the eighteenth-century Surveyor Jonathan Pue's scrolled manuscript chronicling the life of Mistress Hester Prynne, whose adultery in Puritan Boston two centuries earlier had led to her public shaming. For three hours she had to stand on the town scaffold and wear the red "A" on her bosom forever after. Do right by this woman's tale, admonishes Pue, echoing the ghost's command in *Hamlet* (1603). The narrator complies, and thus Hester Prynne is born.

Fearing that the story would be too bleak for public taste, Hawthorne intended to make his new work only one of a series of a half-dozen stories (including recent titles like "The Great Stone Face" and "Ethan Brand" as well as some uncollected pieces) in a book titled *Old-Time Legends: Together with Sketches, Experimental and Ideal.* Not that this should surprise us. Many masterpieces have risen Phoenix-like from the gap between a writer's frustrated intentions and the resultant book. We think of *Moby-Dick.* As Melville first conceived it, this was supposed to be a commercial whaling story; then Hawthorne suggested he might want to steer toward the deeper waters of metaphysical blackness. As a result, Melville went on to write the great symbolic masterpiece that we know.

Similarly, it is one of the ironies of literary history that were it not for the intervention of Hawthorne's publisher, James T. Fields (who was since 1843 a partner in the Boston firm of Ticknor, Reed & Fields), along with the literary critic, Edwin P. Whipple (who recommended publication), his work might never have become the standalone, spellbinding novel it eventually became.

The publisher and author first met in the spring of 1849 when Hawthorne (as secretary) invited Fields to lecture at the Salem Lyceum. Later, Fields, who had faith in his work when he was unknown and advanced his career whenever he could, asked for a story for *The Boston Book.* In response, the author gave him "Drowne's Wooden Image" (1844), based on the Pygmalion myth that proposes (as does "The Artist of the Beautiful," 1844) passion as the source of truly great art.

Apparently, they got along well at that first meeting. Upon hearing that Hawthorne had been dismissed from the Custom House, Fields tried to help him by seeking support from several political acquaintances on his behalf, but his efforts came to nothing. In December 1849, the commercially astute publisher took the train to Salem to flush more stories out of the author, promising to print two thousand copies of anything he gave him. Disenchanted and discouraged, Hawthorne murmured there was none. But Fields saw a chest of drawers in the room and made a prescient guess that Hawthorne had a story hidden away in it. He said so. Taken aback, Hawthorne shook his head. However, as Fields clomped down the wooden stairs to catch his train, Hawthorne called after him with a roll of manuscript in his hand. "How in Heaven's name did you know this thing was there?" he asked. "It is either very good or very bad, – I don't know which" (Fields 1872: 50).

Fields read the manuscript on the train. He was astounded and returned to Salem the next day "like a bullet, having realized he possessed something more spellbinding, and salable, than just another tale about the Puritans" (Wineapple 2003: 209). Sophia told her sister that Fields had "exploded & gone off like a sky-rocket" after reading the manuscript (Valenti 2015: 38).

He told Hawthorne to elaborate on the story and extend it into a single book rather than as one tale among several (an account later disputed by Sophia). Hawthorne replied on 20 January 1850: "Is it safe, then, to stake the fate of the book entirely on this one chance? A hunter loads his gun with a bullet and several buck-shot; and, following his sagacious example, it was my purpose to conjoin the one long story with half a dozen shorter ones; so that, failing to kill the public outright with my biggest and heaviest lump of lead, I might have other chances with the smaller bits, individually and in the aggregate" (*Works* XVI, 307). Fields assured him that this was the best way to publish it.

On 15 January 1850, therefore, Hawthorne sent the bulk of the novel to his publisher ("at least fourteen miles long" he wrote to Bridge on 4 February 1850 [*Works* XVI, 311]), followed by the final three chapters on 3 February. (Because *The Scarlet Letter* was rushed into print, the passages in which Hawthorne refers in the preface to the nonexistent other stories in the volume could not be corrected.) It is worth pausing to consider what might have happened had Fields not asked for a new work in the first place. It might have lingered in Hawthorne's drawer, awaiting revival as a literary curiosity, perhaps after the author's demise; and who knows what reception it would have had then.

The novel came out on 16 March 1850 in the first edition of 2500 copies which sold out in 10 days. One thousand five hundred copies of the second edition of 2000 were sold out in three days. Consider what this implies. In 1850, the population of the United States was close to 23 million, so *The Scarlet Letter*'s sale of more than 6000 copies can be multiplied by at least ten to give us a modern equivalent; a sale of 60 000 hardbound copies today would find the author a place on a best-seller list. We can multiply the dollar amounts in the same way. At a time when a clothbound book cost a dollar, his sales did not make Hawthorne rich but gave him a comfortable income. He also received a proposal from the Leipzig publisher, Bernhard Tauchnitz, to publish the novel. In a letter to Louisa on 1 December 1851, Sophia noted this, along with the pirated British editions (for which he was never paid) and the translation from Prussia: "all the world is on its knees at his feet & he is fast becoming Crowned King in the realm of Letters & Genius" (*Works* XVI, 511). Since then, it has never been out of print.

With the exception of a few critics who were disparaging of the novel's unrelieved gloom and corrupting influence – Orestes Brownson called the subject "not fit . . . for popular literature" in the October 1850 issue of *Brownson's Quarterly Review*; Arthur Cleveland Coxe complained about the novel's "running undertide of filth" in the January 1851 issue of the *Church Review* – the reviewers hailed the occasion as marking Hawthorne's arrival, and the book received widespread appreciation (Crowley 1970: 176, 182). Henry James (1984 [1879]) would later look upon it as a landmark event in American literature: "the best of it was that the thing was absolutely America; it belonged to the soil, to the air; it came out of the very heart of New England" (88). Longfellow (1864), in his memorial poem "Hawthorne," that appeared in the August issue of the Atlantic (under the title "Concord") wrote of his friend: "wand of magic power" – with obvious echoes of the self-taught sorcerer Prospero in Shakespeare's *The Tempest* (170).

Let's see how the author works his magic on his readers.

In a manner characteristic of his artistic control and attention to detail, Hawthorne structured the novel in 24 chapters resembling the scenes in a three-act play. Each act contains a key episode which takes place on the town's pillory scaffold – symbolic of both the stern Puritan code and the honest confession of personal sin. Thus in Chapter 1, at midday, Hester with her infant daughter Pearl is exposed and censured in public by more than 500 citizens. In Chapter 12, seven years later, at midnight, her lover, Arthur Dimmesdale, goes to the scaffold stealthily to proclaim his guilt while almost everyone is sleeping. In Chapter 23, at noon, after Dimmesdale delivers his Election Day sermon at the church, he walks to the scaffold, climbs the stairs, confesses to the paternity of the child with Hester and Pearl standing next to him, and gives up the ghost. The narrative alternates between describing Hester's and Dimmesdale's interior sorrow and anguish and the exterior dramatic exchanges between the characters and the townspeople, revealing how the private and public worlds are so often at tragic odds.

The novel traces the effects of adultery on the lives of four people, all of whom are carrying their own well-guarded secrets: Hester Prynne (whose prototype appears in "Mrs. Hutchinson," 1830), Arthur Dimmesdale (first seen as Roderick Elliston in "Egotism; or the Bosom Serpent," 1843), her husband, Roger Chillingworth (reminiscent of Ethan Brand, Dr. Rappaccini as well as the protagonist in "Edward Fane's Rosebud" published anonymously in 1837), and Pearl (modeled after Hawthorne's eldest daughter, Una).

All this is held together by an unnamed, third-person omniscient narrator speaking for Hawthorne (who remains hidden behind a veil of sorts) as the conscientious voice of reason that we recognize from prior tales. As a character in his own right, he speaks directly to the reader, comments on the actions, withholds knowledge, and sometimes is intentionally nebulous. He takes us on a quest from the "A" in the attic of the Custom House to the "A" on Hester's breast to the "A" carved on a tombstone in the Boston graveyard (Hansen 1991: 160).

Hawthorne gradually reveals what has occurred before Hester mounts the scaffold in Chapter 2. Seven years prior to the novel's opening, a beautiful and virtuous young English woman named Hester Prynne, while living in Amsterdam, marries in obedience to the will of her poverty-stricken parents, an older, partially crippled scientist whom she does not love. We do not know why he married her, but we are led to understand that he has sinned against Nature by taking such a young wife whom he does not love or care for.

Deciding to immigrate to the New World, he sends her on ahead while he stays behind to look after some necessary affairs, promising to soon follow her. After not hearing from her husband, she assumes that he has died at sea. (This was not an unusual occurrence. We remember the fate of Hawthorne's father.) Only later do we learn that her husband's ship had been wrecked on the coast and that he had been captive among the Indians for many months. In the meantime, she has fallen in love with a handsome and deeply spiritual bachelor, the minister Arthur Dimmesdale, who is the opposite of her husband in every respect. The duo embark on a secret love affair that results in her pregnancy. D.H. Lawrence (1977 [1923]) assumed Hester seduced Dimmesdale, but the text never confirms this (171).

To his congregation, Dimmesdale appears as a saint in pursuit of his community's welfare, but his secret sin torments his spirit and betrays his body. "While thus suffering under bodily disease, and gnawed and tortured by some black trouble of the soul, and given over to the machinations of his deadliest enemy, the Reverend Dimmesdale [echoing the minister with the black veil] had achieved a brilliant popularity in his sacred office. He won it, indeed, in great part, by his sorrows" (*Works* I, 141). Thus, he repeatedly finds himself in the pulpit or on the balcony and a scaffold, speaking and preaching to the people of Boston, but he is not to be confused, as some critics have done, with the fraudulent holy man, the Pardoner in Chaucer's *The Canterbury Tales* (1392). When Dimmesdale preaches against adultery, for example, he is speaking with the voice of authority – more so than his listeners imagine.

The plot begins one June day in Boston, as Hester Prynne emerges from prison. The year is 1642, when fornication and adultery are considered capital crimes according to the moral and legal code of the Massachusetts Bay Colony. Given the unusual circumstances of her husband's disappearance, however, a panel of magistrates, "in their great mercy and tenderness of heart," spares Hester's life and sentences her to stand with her three-month-old child, Pearl, for three hours on the town scaffold, exposed to the scornful gaze of the crowd, as a reproach and warning to all who see her. Thereafter, for the remainder of her "natural life," she is "to wear [as] a mark of shame upon her bosom" the scarlet letter "A" (*Works* I, 63). However, the villagers' perspective on her crime says more about themselves than about the adulteress. "There is always a taint of hypocrisy in the air," observed Laurence Goldstein (1988), "when people with guilty secrets of their own decry the wickedness of those who happen to be caught" (1).

To Hester, however, the "A" means something quite different. To try to escape the situation would be to admit that she has sinned. She wears it triumphantly rather than penitently, as both a defiant refusal to be disgraced and an ironic testimony to her secret lover (we may also read "A" for Arthur). In another irony, it is Arthur Dimmesdale ("AD" for adultery), the sinner, renowned for his eloquence, religious fervor, and theological expertise, who calls upon Hester to reveal the truth on the scaffold: "Hester Prynne . . . thou hearest what this good man says, and seest the accountability under which I labor. If thou feelest it to be for thy soul's peace . . . I charge thee to speak out the name of thy fellow-sinner and fellow-sufferer!" (*Works* I, 67) Alluding to the biblical Peter who denied Jesus three times, Hester looks into his cowardly eyes and vows three times *never* to betray her lover – preferring to bear the burden of the sin by herself. "The world's law was no law for her mind," the narrator tells us later. "She assumed a freedom of speculation, then common enough on the other side of the Atlantic, but which our forefathers, had they known of it, would have held to be a deadlier crime than that stigmatized by the scarlet letter" (*Works* I, 164). Had she divulged her lover's name, life might have been easier for her. She bears a social burden, but not a moral burden, since she does not accept that she has sinned. Dimmesdale carries a moral burden because he lives a lie; Hester is shunned but inwardly proud and free.

A symbol of severe enforcement of the harsh Puritanical law, the prison itself is old, dark, and formidable. The arresting metaphors – "weather-stains," "gloomy front," "rust on the ponderous iron-work of its oaken door" – make vividly concrete the sustained image of tradition as an organism wherein growth has become decay (*Works* I, 47). Weeds suggest that the ground upon which the prison is built, like tradition itself, is choked and dying. The Puritanical codes are not as noble in practice as they were once conceived to be. The prison door opens and the guilty woman steps forth. The narrator then invites us to compare her with the sainted Anne Hutchinson, an Englishwoman who traveled to the North American colonies in the 1630s to practice what she believed was the true form of Christianity but was put on trial for heresy. Thus, the narrator establishes a connection between the fictional Hester Prynne and a real-life woman also punished for defying society.

Throughout this scene, we experience with the narrator an unnerving chill as we read of the prison, the pillory, the scarlet letter, and then the terrifying moment when she recognizes her husband (who conceals his identity with the name, Roger Chillingworth) standing in the crowd. He raises his finger to his lips, signaling her to keep quiet. Later, when he demands that she reveal her lover in private, Hester refuses. From his viewpoint, this becomes therefore a story of vengeance and hate. He suspects the truth and passes himself off as a physician, thus enabling him to treat Dimmesdale's physical symptoms while tormenting the guilt-stricken, self-loathing young man.

Chillingworth, the erudite doctor, is remote and misshapen, with one shoulder higher than the other, a diabolical force reminiscent of Mephistopheles, Rappaccini, Ethan Brand, even Shakespeare's Iago with eyes that are "keen and penetrative"

(*Works* I, 61). He delights in seeing into and through the eyes of others, and in the process, manipulating those people. Thus Chillingworth is guilty of what Hawthorne refers to in a 27 July 1844 entry in his *American Notebooks* as "The Unpardonable Sin," committed when a person who represents unfeeling intellect "prie[s] into [the] dark depths" of the human soul, "not with a hope or purpose of making it better, but from a cold philosophical curiosity, – content that it should be wicked in whatever kind or degree, and only desiring to study it out" (*Works* VIII, 251). His ultimate failure to enslave the soul of Dimmesdale is his own personal failure, which then kills him. Hawthorne holds out no hope for him in the next world.

Once her term of imprisonment is over, Hester and Pearl live alone in a small cottage at the edge of the settlement for the next seven years, earning her living from needlework, and still wearing the scarlet emblem on her breast. However, she is anything but a typical seventeenth-century woman. She is as tough and practical and self-reliant as she can be, a model of dignified defiance, of stoicism, "a woman . . . lofty, pure, and beautiful; and wise, moreover, not through dusky grief, but the ethereal medium of joy; and showing how sacred love should make us happy, by the truest test of a life successful to such an end!" (*Works* I, 263) Mark Van Doren (1949) described her as New England's "most heroic creature," a heroine who is "almost a goddess" (147, 151). Nina Auerbach (1982) called her "a solitary icon," "a feminist saint, the vehicle for 'a new truth' of empowered and transfigured womanhood" (166, 176). "[She is] struggling for her soul, in a male world," wrote John Updike (2007), "which heavily favors those who would dominate, exploit, and numb her" (146).

In yet another act of defiance, Hester clothes Pearl (her name suggesting one of great value, a great prize) in bright, almost incandescently decorative clothing. She is willful and wild. Some self-righteous townspeople view her as a demon's child, but the novel depicts her more like a child of Nature. She is the truth-sayer. She sees what the adults are trying to hide and reacts to it. She identifies Chillingworth as the "old Black Man" (*Works* I, 134). She develops an attachment to her mother's scarlet letter. She refuses to allow Dimmesdale to behave in a fatherly way as long as he hides his identity from the public. She objects when Hester tries to remove the "A."

Midway in the novel, Hester and Pearl encounter Dimmesdale for a second time at the scaffold. He attempts to expiate his crime in public, but it is late at night when everyone is asleep, and so his spoken words go unheard – except to Chillingworth, who watches the scene from the shadows, and possibly Mistress Gibbons, the village witch. The symbol of Dimmesdale's guilt, however, seems to appear in the sky as a meteor in the shape of the letter "A." Hester is so shocked by Dimmesdale's feeble and unhealthy condition that she decides to reveal Chillingworth's identity to him and warn him of his malicious plans when they are reunited in the forest.

For Hester, in the book's gentlest scene, there is an outpouring of passion she has continued to feel since the time of their affair. She is desperate to release her former lover from his misery, not only out of concern for his well-being but also because she wants him to accept her and their child into his life. "What we did had a consecration of its own," she says. "We felt it so! . . . Hast thou forgotten it?" (*Works* I, 195) After chastising Hester (unfairly) for having caused him to stray and blaming Chillingworth for his confused emotional state, he finally agrees to her plan that the three of them leave Boston to live together in Europe as a family.

However, their happy plans fail. After Dimmesdale's Election Day Sermon, she learns that Chillingworth has booked passage aboard the same ship. Father, mother, and child are never destined to leave together. After delivering his final climactic sermon on adultery, Dimmesdale takes Hester and Pearl with him onto the scaffold for the third time. There, before a crowd, he seems to expose a mark in the shape of the letter "A" that has broken out on his breast. He then dies, having atoned for his sin, with his head resting on the scarlet letter and the kiss of his daughter upon his lips. "A spell was broken" (*Works* I, 256). He is at last free from Chillingworth (much to the latter's exasperation).

Years later, Hester returns alone, still wearing the scarlet letter, to live in her old cottage and resume her charitable work. She receives occasional letters from Pearl, who has married a European aristocrat and established a family of her own. Upon her death, Hester is buried near the minister, and they share the same gravestone marked with the scarlet "A."

In the penultimate chapter, with distant echoes of the Greek Chorus, the moral of Dimmesdale's life is given: "Be true! Be true! Be true! Show freely to the world, if not your worst, yet some trait whereby the worst may be inferred!" (*Works* I, 260). Or as the Chorus says in Sophocles's *Oedipus Tyrannos* (2021 [429 BC]): "Time, who sees all things, he hath found thee out" (line 1264). Hawthorne makes the point that time has all the power attributed to it in Greek tragedy – the power to damage and even ruin a career when a youthful folly or transgression becomes known.

The creative genesis of most of Hawthorne's works can be traced back to some key idea or intense emotional need. Knowing what we know of his life up to now, it is clear that the desire for revenge was partially the passion fueling the writing of this novel. Hawthorne had some scores to settle, and none weightier than his shame over his ancestors' bigoted, intolerant Puritan ways and his anger about his unceremonious dismissal from the Custom House. The grief caused by his mother's death (for whom he created Hester Prynne as a memorial) and his constant struggle for money exacerbated his misery. But once again, Hawthorne's traumas became his strength, reworked in the characters in the novel. He had it in mind for many years.

In the preface, he meditates on his Puritan ancestors and the martyrdom of the witches whose blood may fairly be said to have left a stain upon them all. Taking their shame upon himself, Hawthorne views his work as "sufficient retribution" for their sins: "[L]et them scorn me as they will," he says, referring to his ancestors' probable attitude toward his profession; "strong traits of their nature have intertwined themselves with mine." He must live with and make art out of his race's guilt, although he hopes that his children "shall strike their roots into unaccustomed earth" (*Works* I, 10, 12).

In the preface, Hawthorne also takes the opportunity to lighten the serious tone of the story to come by venting his anger about his time at work in the Custom House. In 1846, he was back in Salem as Surveyor of the Revenue, a job he desperately wanted to keep in order to support his family, yet loathed doing. He felt it sapped his energy for writing and stunted his imagination. While he was enslaved to the drudgery of the Surveyorship, his characters "retained all the rigidity of dead corpses." He imagines his fictional characters resisting and mocking him: "The little power you might once have possessed over the tribe of unrealities is gone! . . . Go, then, and earn your wages!" (*Works* I, 34–35) We can hardly imagine more challenging circumstances under which to produce an exemplary work of fiction than this assignment from hell.

Then the Whigs defeated the Democrats in an election, promptly named one of their supporters to the office, and dismissed Hawthorne on 8 June 1849. This rejection further embittered him, so much so that at the conclusion of the preface, he refers to himself as "A DECAPITATED SURVEYOR" (*Works* I, 43). In his satirical portrait of unproductive government coworkers, he says that none of them "had ever read a page of my inditing" [*sic*] (*Works* I, 26). No wonder he detests this town so much that he hates to go out into the streets or to have people see him. Yet the narrator perseveres. Once he is released from his work, he can force the "rag of scarlet cloth" to open into the exotic blossom of *The Scarlet Letter* (*Works* I, 31). This "corpse of dead activity," he opines, requires only his magic touch to be resuscitated, and he finds it (*Works* I, 29).

Hawthorne's wife emerged as a competent assistant in this situation. When he lost his job in June 1849, he had come home from the docks early and shared with her the bleak news. "Oh, then, you can write your book!" Sophia exclaimed happily (Hawthorne 1884: II, 340). She opened a drawer and displayed a collection of gold pieces she had saved from some of his wages. Added to this sum was what she had earned painting parchment lampshades and fine screens, which Elizabeth sold for $5 and $10 each. They would live off this money which she had been saving for such emergencies while he wrote. That very midsummer afternoon of 1849, he began work on the story, which grew to become *The Scarlet Letter*.

It is clear from the appearance of an adulteress with the capital "A" embroidered on her gray gown in his tale, "Endicott and the Red Cross" (1837), and from a number of notable entries in his *American Notebooks* (which he kept irregularly from 1835 to 1853) that the idea for the novel had been germinating in his mind for many years. In an entry from 27 July 1844, for example, he referred to "The life of a woman, who, by the old colony law, was condemned always to wear the letter A, sewed on her garment, in token of her having committed adultery" (*Works* VIII, 254). On 17 November 1847, he wrote, "A story of the effects of revenge, in diabolizing him who indulges in it" (*Works* VIII, 278).

Other notes help us understand his purpose. They suggest, for instance, that Hawthorne sincerely scrutinized the motives of his characters as if he were looking at himself in a mirror. Of Dimmesdale, he wrote on 6 December 1837: "Insincerity in a man's own heart must make all his enjoyments, all that concerns him, unreal; so that his whole life must seem like a merely dramatic representation," and "A man living a wicked life in one place, and simultaneously a virtuous and religious one in another" (*Works* VIII, 166, 167). On 27 July 1844: "To represent a man in the midst of all sorts of cares and annoyances – with impossibilities to perform – and almost driven distracted by his inadequacy. Then quietly comes Death, and releases him from all his troubles; and at his last gasp, he smiles, and congratulates himself on escaping so easily" (*Works* VIII, 253).

He recorded a pertinent thought on 6 December 1837: "The influence of a peculiar mind, in close communion with another, to drive the latter to insanity" (*Works* I, 170), which suggests Chillingworth's relationship with Dimmesdale – "Men of cold passions have quick eyes" – and another on 4 January 1839: "The situation of a man in the midst of a crowd, yet as completely in the power of another, life and all, as if they two were in the deepest solitude"; and "The strange sensation of a person who feels himself an object of deep interest, and close observation, and various construction of all his actions, by another person" (*Works* I, 169, 183). He was fascinated by the corrupting influence of power, as in this note of 27 July 1844: "Sketch of a person, who, by strength of character, or assistant circumstances, has reduced another to absolute slavery and dependence on him. Then show, that the person who appears to be the master, must inevitably be at least as much a slave, if not more, than the other. All slavery is reciprocal, on the supposition most favorable to the rulers" (*Works* I, 253).

Evidently, Pearl also developed at an early stage of his thinking. On 1 June 1842: "Pearl – the English of Margaret – a pretty name for a girl in a story" (*Works* I, 242). 9 August 1845: "In the eyes of a young child, or other innocent person, the image of a cherub or an angel to be seen peeping out; – in those of a vicious person, a devil" (*Works* I, 270). On the basis of observations made of his daughter, Una, he wrote on 30 July 1849: "I now and then catch an aspect of her, in which I cannot believe her to be my own human child, but a spirit strangely mingled with good and evil, haunting the house where I dwell" (*Works* VIII, 430–431).

Each of these profound and suggestive notes inspired continued thought in Hawthorne, and I offer several of them to my students as ideas for essay thesis statements. Judging by these entries, when he began to write, Hawthorne knew what he was doing every step of the way. Once free of the Custom House and after mourning his mother's passing, he speedily composed *The Scarlet Letter* (initially as a story), working for nine hours a day, "with an intensity he had not experienced since he had written *Seven Tales of My Native Land*" (Cantwell 1948: 427). On 3 November 1850, he wrote to Fields, "The Scarlet Letter being all in one tone, I had only to get my pitch, and then could go on interminably. Many passages of this book ought to be finished with the minuteness of a Dutch picture, in order to give them their proper effect" (*Works* XVI, 371). Words poured out of him with white-hot speed as the new book eventually began to assume shape. Sophia admitted to being "almost frightened about it . . . he has written vehemently morning & afternoon & has not walked as much as he used to do. He has become tender from confinement & brain work" (Risjord 2001: 139).

The best time to get a glimpse into how a society or a culture works is at times of dissolution. If we stand overlooking the Great Barrier Reef, only when there is a gap and the tide recedes can we see what lies underneath. Similarly, we get a hint of how a culture works only when it is in the process of disintegrating, and we see how its parts are used to fit together.

When we consider once again the opening chapter, "The Prison Door," for example, we should ask: What is the reason for this scene? How can we understand what it means to the era in which it was written, and how can we relate this idea to our own time? In a somber atmosphere Hawthorne introduces the theme that he will develop throughout the novel. The scene is completely in black, gray, and white – drab, harsh, ugly – but for the surprising sight of a wild rose-bush "with its delicate gems" in front of the prison door (*Works* I, 48).

This contrast is not random; it is deliberate. This splash of color comes to be associated with the beauty and persistence of untamed, passionate nature – that of Hester herself. It represents a pure and colorful spot of relief in this woeful tale of "human frailty and sorrow" (*Works* I, 48). To the criminal or sinner, it is a "fragran[t] and fragile" reminder that beauty still exists. Every prisoner who goes in or out must see it. "[To the] condemned criminal as he [comes] forth to his doom," it is a reminder of Nature's pity or sympathy for him. The narrator says, "Finding it so directly on the threshold of our narrative . . . we could hardly do otherwise than pluck one of its flowers and present it to the reader" (*Works* I, 48).

Hawthorne adroitly uses the color red throughout the novel to create images of both life and death and to portray the injustices perpetrated during Puritan times. He sums up the era in its prison, a crumbling institution, thus setting the stage for the remainder of the book. A red-on-black image is repeated at the end of the novel when the narrator describes in heraldic terms the carving on the gravestone, "ON A FIELD, SABLE, THE LETTER A, GULES [in red]" (*Works* I, 264).

"The whole secret of the teacher's force," wrote Emerson in his journal on 20 April 1834, "lies in the conviction that men [and women] are convertible.

And they are. They want awakening" (*Complete Works* IV, 278). No student remains the same after *truly reading* this novel. Most of them experience some of the sharp chill and pervasive awfulness that Hawthorne himself must have felt while writing it. One student said, "Why are we reading something so depressing by somebody so unpleasant?" I responded by quoting one of my former professors (who was quoting Anton Chekhov): "Great art is never depressing."

We can understand why Hawthorne himself, upon completing the work, felt unwell and exhausted. Indubitably, part of his intention was to unnerve the reader as he created a supernatural and indeed paranormal atmosphere. On reading it, one would have to be dull and unimaginative not to feel an Aristotelian cathartic combination of pity and fear. Such a book pierces our soul and keeps us awake at night. We come away feeling not only pity for Hester and Arthur but also fear for ourselves. Given the right circumstances, this could very well be us if we allow our culture to descend into hatred and injustice. The narrator concludes:

> And be the stern and sad truth spoken, that the breach which guilt has once made into the human soul is never, in this mortal state, repaired. It may be watched and guarded; so that the enemy shall not force his way again into the citadel, and might even, in his subsequent assaults, select some other avenue, in preference to that where he had formerly succeeded. But there is still the ruined wall, and, near it, the stealthy tread of the foe that would win over again his unforgotten triumph. (*Works* I, 200–201)

The past is always more ambiguous than we think it is. Although the book's sexual content pales in comparison to what is available in modern fiction, the story of Hester's and Dimmesdale's suffering makes us think about the social implications of sex and love. Beneath the façade of normal life, we share an awareness of sin symbolized by the scarlet letter. For we, also, are admonished to be true.

Like all great works of art, *The Scarlet Letter* remains relevant, and transcends place and time. Great work lasts beyond the social context in which it is written. Hawthorne's novel doesn't feel time-bound. It is the work of a mature artist, way ahead of his time.

9

Hawthorne and Melville (1850–1860)

Herman Melville (Library of Congress).

> *No matter what the writer may say, the work is always written to*
> *someone, for someone, against someone.*
>
> —Walker Percy (Elie 2003: xiii)

Perhaps it was as much an indication of his rising popularity and ambition as it was of the small size of the literary world that, within the course of his 59 years, Hawthorne encountered nearly every prominent writer of his time, with the notable exceptions of Henry James, Dickens, and Thackeray. One of them happened to be Herman Melville. The two had an instinctive kinship and mutual respect and encouraged each other in their literary aspirations. "If we don't know Melville," I say to my students, "then we don't know Hawthorne."

The Life of the Author: Nathaniel Hawthorne, First Edition. Dale Salwak.
© 2023 John Wiley & Sons Ltd. Published 2023 by John Wiley & Sons Ltd.

Having published *The Scarlet Letter* in March, Hawthorne was now living with Sophia and the children in the Little Red Farmhouse at Tanglewood, in Lenox (rented from the affluent Caroline Sturgis Tappan), and making preparations to commence work on *The House of the Seven Gables*. Melville, who had established himself with the popular sea-faring adventure *Typee: A Peep at Polynesian Life* (1846), which Hawthorne had read and reviewed for the Salem *Advertiser*, was staying with his wife, Lizzie, and three of his sisters at his aunt's house in nearby Pittsfield, while working on what would go on to become his most ambitious work, *Moby-Dick* (1851). Both men craved literary companionship, a soul mate of sorts.

That opportunity presented itself on Monday, 5 August 1850, the kind of day in history upon which legends are created. Their mutual acquaintance David Dudley Field, a resident of the area and the author of local history, organized a picnic and hike for a number of literary personalities in the Berkshire Mountain country. Together with the two novelists, the group included: Field's wife, Harriet, and daughter, Jenny; poet and essayist Dr. Oliver Wendell Holmes; Hawthorne's publisher James T. Fields and his wife, Eliza; poet James Russell Lowell; Evert A. Duyckinck, the editor of the New York-based *Literary World* and a friend of Melville; attorney Henry Sedgwick, nephew of local novelist Catharine Maria Sedgwick; and poet Cornelius Mathews. Everyone seems to have accepted the invitation in their earnest longing for intelligent, cultivated companionship along with high-spirited fun and frolic, which is what they had.

In the morning, the group climbed the picturesque Monument Mountain at Stockbridge, Massachusetts, a two-hour pilgrimage that I have retraced at the peak of summer, as do hundreds of visitors annually. I, too, traveled by train from Pittsfield to the still-standing Little Station, just south of Stockbridge's Main Street. From there, I was conveyed by coach to the mountain and rode halfway up on a carriage before hiking the remaining distance to the 1642-foot high summit, Squaw Peak. To say that it is not an easy climb would be an understatement.

It is not difficult to decipher why this area has been nothing short of an inspiration for artists, musicians, and writers, ranging from Jonathan Edwards to William Cullen Bryant to Henry Wadsworth Longfellow. As someone who has always been besotted with the mountains, I was awestruck by its bucolic majesty and splendor. The air was redolent with the fragrance of mint, pine, and clover. A breeze fluttered the leaves overhead; the trees were comfortingly full and verdant. I could hear the mellifluous singing of small birds. Suddenly, I became aware of an immense silence, as if time itself had stopped. Inured to artificial and commercial surroundings, I found tranquility here, elusive in my everyday life, conducive to thinking and reflecting, just as it must have been in Hawthorne's day.

In my mind's eye, I can see them as they scrambled along the path, everyone in a positive frame of mind, when "a black thunder cloud from the south dragged its ragged skirts [toward them], the thunder rolling in the distance" (Parker 1996: 745). They sheltered from the imminent shower beneath overhanging rocks. Holmes cut tree branches for an umbrella to protect the ladies and then took out bottles of champagne and silver mugs from his medical bag. He drank so much that he almost lost his footing and could have tumbled straight down a thousand feet. Melville was also intoxicated with the height and had a predilection for flaunting his maritime past, certainly fancying himself among the whalers of the Pacific, for he "bestrode a peaked rock, which ran out like a bowsprit, and pulled and hauled imaginary ropes for our delectation" (Fields 1872: 52).

At some point, Hawthorne and Melville settled down to talk in a cave. Although the author of *The Scarlet Letter* was 15 years older, and the two were quite different in temperament (Melville tense and highly emotional, Hawthorne reticent and aloof), they seemed to bond well. In his account of the outing, local poet and journalist J. E. A. [Joseph Edward Adams] Smith (1820) put their interaction this way: "Two hours of enforced intercourse settled the matter. They learned so much of each other's character, and found that they held so much of thought, feeling and opinion in common, that the most intimate friendship for the future was inevitable" (Parker 1996: 748).

Both men knew what it meant to lose early in life a mariner father who was, for the lack of a better word, indifferent to his son. Both were profound thinkers and ambitious writers who found in each other a shared obsession with history, guilt, and endless speculations about the universe. Both guarded their privacy, worried about the weight of mounting personal debt, endured troubles with publishers, lacked public recognition, and struggled to reconcile family duties with the sacredness of a writing routine. As wanderers longing for a permanent home, both relished strange tales of the high seas, although the landlocked Hawthorne could only dream of the life Melville had lived as a longtime sailor and vagabond in the South Pacific.

Melville, enthralled by the breadth of his learning, concluded that the Byronically handsome Hawthorne was "the most fascinating American he had ever met" (Fields 1872: 13). Hawthorne, jolted out of his reserve, was equally impressed by the fertile imagination of the red-bearded and bronzed Melville to the point that he would invite him, along with Mathews and Duyckinck, to call at his home three days after the picnic. Clearly, something had taken hold of both men's spirits.

After drinks, the party struggled to the summit, where they rested and gazed across the landscape of the Housatonic River Valley as Mathews concluded the reading aloud of William Cullen Bryant's lyrical ode, "Monument Mountain" (2009 [1824]). According to the legend that gave the place its name, a lovesick Mohican maiden threw herself off a ledge after she was forbidden to marry her cousin. Her body was then covered with stones as a monument to the event.

The first three lines urge: "Thou who wouldst see the lovely and the wild / Mingled in harmony on Nature's face / Ascend our rocky mountains."

I have visited the purported site and read the poem aloud, although I can't be sure a Mohican is indeed buried beneath the mound of rocks visible from where I stood. I remember thinking that it would take little imagination to connect the summit with what the ancient Greeks believed Olympus to be – the home of their most important gods – which Melville would visit in 1856 and about which Hawthorne would write in his retelling of classical myths, *A Wonder Book for Boys and Girls* (1851). "Just think," I tell my students as they view my photographs of the area. "Here had stood with godlike eminence two of America's greatest novelists."

By midday, back at his spacious cottage, Field supplied dry clothes, a three-hour dinner, and lots of wine. A heated debate ensued on the merits of English and American authors, fueled by a question the Rev. Sydney Smith (1820) had posed in the January issue of the *Edinburgh Review:* "In the four corners of the globe, who reads an American book?" (79; Spiller 1929: 3–11) Understandably, the nation and the press were furious at this sneering remark, but it pointed to a legitimate concern. American writers were battling over a question of national identity while struggling to establish themselves and prove that their literature could rival that of Great Britain. Up to then, only James Fenimore Cooper (1789–1851) and Washington Irving (1783–1859) had earned an international readership and respect back home. Hawthorne sat quietly, listening and watching, eventually taking the side of the Americans.

Afterward, popular historian Joel Tyler Headley led the intoxicated revelers to the nearby Icy-Glen. Sophia said in a letter to her sister, Elizabeth, that the formation of massive glacial rocks looked to her husband "as if the Devil had torn his way through a rock & left it all jagged behind him" (Parker 1996: 747). In this setting, the group skidded about like children. According to Fields (1872), Hawthorne "was among the most enterprising of the merry-maker; and being in the dark much of the time, he ventured to call out lustily and pretend that certain destruction was inevitable to all of us" (53).

We don't know what the two men discussed privately on that occasion, but we do have the result of Melville's thoughts in a laudatory essay that he dashed off about *Mosses from an Old Manse* (1846) just a few days later. "Hawthorne and His Mosses" was published in the 17 and 24 August 1850 issues of the highly regarded *Literary World* under the self-protecting anonymous byline, "By a Virginian Spending July in Vermont." In it, we are given an illuminating portrait of Hawthorne's achievement through the eyes of a fellow writer and genuine admirer.

To much of the world, he began, Hawthorne seems at first "a pleasant writer, with a pleasant style, – a sequestered, harmless man, from whom any deep and weighty thing would hardly be anticipated – a man who means no meanings," but the world is mistaken; in reality, he possesses "a great, deep intellect, which drops down into the universe like a plummet" (Crowley 1970: 115).

The "hither side of Hawthorne's soul," noted Melville, "like the dark half of the physical sphere – is shrouded in a blackness, ten times black" (115). He referred to this as Hawthorne's "Calvinistic sense of Innate Depravity and Original sin, from whose visitations, in some shape or other, no deeply thinking mind is always and wholly free. For, in certain moods, no man can weigh this world without throwing in something, somehow like Original Sin, to strike the uneven balance" (116). Hawthorne was aware of some of the mysteries of that sphere, but unlike Melville, he didn't know what it was to be immersed in it.

Many great artists have aimed for a popular audience while conveying a vision of darker truth. Shakespeare, for example, is a crowd-pleasing dramatist who created tortured souls like Hamlet, Lear, Timon, and Iago to embody his belief in a universe where evil reigns. He must conceal these ideas, Melville argued, because "in this world of lies, Truth is forced to fly like a sacred white doe in the woodlands; and only by cunning glimpses will she reveal herself, as in Shakespeare and other masters of the great Art of Telling the Truth, – even though it be covertly, and by snatches" (117).

Hawthorne, continued Melville, comes close to being another Shakespeare. His insights match the "short, quick probings at the very axis of reality" in the greatest of plays. He possesses "the largest brain with the largest heart" in American literature (116, 125). "Believe me, my friends," he urged, "that men, not very much inferior to Shakespeare, are this day being born on the banks of the Ohio" (118). Native writers must stop aping the English, for the Bard "is sure to be surpassed" by an American born now or yet to be born (119). This necessitates originality, which poses the risk of failure. So be it. "Failure," proclaimed Melville, "is the true test of greatness . . . For genius, all over the world, stands hand in hand, and one shock of recognition runs the whole circle round" (120, 121).

He concluded his essay with some frankly suggestive imagery. "The soft ravishments of the man spun me roundabout in a web of dreams, and when the book was closed, when the spell was over, this wizard 'dismissed me with but reminiscences, as if I had been dreaming of him.' . . . To what infinite height of loving wonder and admiration I may yet be borne, when by repeatedly banqueting on these Mosses I shall have thoroughly incorporated their whole stuff into my being, – that, I cannot tell. But already I feel that this Hawthorne has dropped germinous seeds into my soul. He expands and deepens down, the more I contemplate him; and further and further, shoots his strong New England roots into the hot soil in my Southern soul" (113, 122–123).

How do we begin to explain such intensity? The standard narrative is that Melville had fallen in love with Hawthorne. But as many of my students recognize, this connection is deeper and more complex than infatuation, something far removed from the possibility of homoerotic love that recent scholars have pushed with the thinnest of circumstantial evidence – as seen, for example, in Mark Beauregard's *The Whale: A Love Story* (2016).

For Melville, nothing was felt or done half-heartedly. He poured himself into the work he did, the books he read, the opinions he held, and the friends he made. Smoldering beneath this essay is an undiminished fury over the odious reviews he had received for his work since *Typee* (1846). It is difficult not to separate the tone of the essay from the relief of meeting Hawthorne days earlier. It seems plausible that his rhetoric, not unique among reviewers at the time, was so effusive in gratitude for Hawthorne's gift of understanding and appreciating his work at a time when few readers seemed to care. Hawthorne had left an indelible and critical impression on Melville's artistic sensibility. That is clear.

The idealization in his review of *Mosses* strongly suggests that Melville was assigning to Hawthorne, the role of mentor. The fact that Melville's subsequent revisions to *Moby-Dick* – darker, apocalyptic – evolved in part from his discussions with Hawthorne suggests that during his re-writing, he was editing and selecting the impressions that he hoped would most engage and please his friend. He later dedicated the book, "To Nathaniel Hawthorne: In token of my admiration for his genius."

Although Melville yearned for a close relationship with the older writer, there is no evidence to suggest that he thought of making it physical. To argue otherwise would be a great disservice to both men and surely reveals more about the emotional and psychological state of the writer proposing such a claim than it does of the subjects themselves. Hawthorne couldn't bear the idea, as he made clear, for example, in his 1851 essay critical of the men he saw living in close intimacy at a Shaker dormitory that he visited with Melville in the Berkshires. He deplored "their utter and systematic lack of privacy; their close junction of man with man, and supervision of one man over another – it is hateful and disgusting to think of; and the sooner the sect is extinct the better – a consummation which, I am happy to hear, is thought to be not a great many years distant" (*Works* VIII, 465). Nowhere in his journals or letters is there even a modicum of homoerotic desire.

When recent scholars show such mistaken prurient interest in the lives of Hawthorne and Melville, they might be conflating two parallel stories – Melville's intellectual bond with Hawthorne and his passionate love for a married woman, his neighbor Sarah Anne Morehead. Michael Shelden said that it had taken 150 years to unravel this secret when he came upon evidence that had apparently managed to escape the attention of scholars until then.

If Shelden's *Melville in Love: The Secret Life of Herman Melville and the Muse of Moby-Dick* (2016) is to be believed, during the time Melville forged a bond of mutual admiration with Hawthorne, he also fell in love with Sarah Morehead, "a woman both bookish and beautiful, intelligent and inquisitive, creative and compassionate," married to a businessman who cared little for art or adventure, literature or indulgence (8). Melville risked his reputation and even his life for her during fun-filled picnics, serious conversations about books and poems, flirtations, and an overnight camp out on Mount Greylock. Shelden conjectured that she was also at the heart of inspiration for *Moby-Dick* and the subsequent novel, *Pierre* (1852). "[I]n the grip of his own obsession," said Shelden (2016); he wrote excitedly about the obsessed Captain Ahab's hunt for an elusive whale (99). The novel, Shelden argued, "is the result of the author's own extended dive into the depths of his life" (100).

To Shelden, the affair helps to explain Melville's fascination with Hawthorne who, in *The Scarlet Letter*, had plunged into the mysteries of the sin of adultery, about which Melville was curious to know more. There is no evidence to suggest that Hawthorne guessed anything. If he did, he chose to remain quiet about it out of respect for his friend.

Whether or not Shelden is correct may be reasonably disputed. Prominent Melville scholars, including Andrew Delbanco and Newton Arvin, barely mentioned her at all; the 16 contributors to *The New Cambridge Companion to Herman Melville* (2013) included nothing about her; and Hershel Parker dismissed (as Shelden acknowledges) the possibility of such a romance. Nevertheless, the mystery remains, and Shelden's argument makes for a tantalizing story that I give to my students to consider and research.

While we know a great deal of what Melville thought of Hawthorne from his ten surviving letters, barring brief journal entries, no one knows much of what Hawthorne thought of him. Like many scholars, I have spent years hunting in vain, for all but one of his letters to Melville (27 March 1851) have been lost or destroyed, quite possibly by the recipient himself at his friend's request, thus suggesting a desire for concealment. This is understandable. In writing them, I am sure, Hawthorne revealed his heart as a writer. He lifted the veil to share with Melville more than he wanted the world to know: the words of the muse were solely intended for his intellectual companion. Hawthorne may have feared that they would be published for an audience that had no business with them; he wanted his books alone to speak for him.

What we do know is that when the anonymous review of *Mosses* appeared in print, both Nathaniel and Sophia were moved powerfully by the writer's praise. In a letter to Duyckinck (dated 29 August), Sophia referred to the anonymous reviewer as the "first person who has ever in *Print* apprehended Mr Hawthorne" (*Works* XVI, 361). She elaborated rhapsodically in another letter to her sister, Elizabeth: "At last someone speaks the right word of him. I have not before heard it. I have been wearied & annoyed hitherto with hearing him *compared* to Washington Irving & other American writers – & put generally *second*. At last someone dares to say what in my secret mind I have often thought – that he is only to be mentioned with the Swan of Avon – The Great Heart and the Grand Intellect combined" (Parker 1996: 769).

From the perspective of Hawthorne, the essay on *Mosses* was indeed the "shock of recognition" that he needed to experience from a worthy reader if he were to ascertain that he was appreciated in his own country (Crowley 1970: 121). He was grateful that such an accomplished writer would praise him more than he deserved. As Melville wrote, he hoped that such generous recognition might prompt Hawthorne "to the full flower of some still greater achievement" (Crowley 1970: 121). Indeed, their close association released him from the sorrow, self-doubt, and disappointment of his Salem years: the death of his mother, the loss of his Custom House job, his consequent and constant worry about money, his deteriorating health, and a growing concern that he was steadily losing the powers that enabled him to attain the recognition that he did garner for himself.

Some early critics (see, for example, Lewis Mumford in *Herman Melville* [1929] and Newton Arvin in *Hawthorne* [1930]) concluded that the inspiration behind "Ethan Brand" (1850) was a spiritual portrait of Melville himself and the perils of hubris and solitude. As a case in point, they noted that Brand's language parodies Ahab's in *Moby-Dick*, with its theme of moral enslavement of one person by another. This theme took center stage in some of Hawthorne's work, including Chillingworth's psychological manipulation (bordering on the demonic) of Dimmesdale (*The Scarlet Letter*), Matthew Maule's of Alice Pyncheon (*The House of the Seven Gables*), Westervelt's of Zenobia (*The Blithedale Romance*), and now, Brand's of Esther – all of whom violate the sanctity of another individual's soul.

"Ethan Brand" conveys the story of a lime-burner named Bartram and his son who hear a disconcerting roar of laughter echo through the twilight in the hills. Soon thereafter, Brand arrives at the kiln and is questioned by the lime-burner. Brand points out that he used to keep the very same kiln before he went off in search of the "Unpardonable Sin," which he claims to have found. He explains, "It is a sin that grew within my own breast . . . A sin that grew nowhere else! The sin of an intellect that triumphed over the sense of brotherhood with man, and reverence for God, and sacrificed everything to its own mighty claims! The only sin that deserves a recompense of immortal agony! Freely, were it to do again, would I incur the guilt. Unshrinkingly, I accept the retribution!" (*Works* XI, 90) At the end of the tale, he commits suicide.

To equate Brand with Melville would be a fascinating proposal. Given Melville's ambition, anxiety, and deep probings into the interior of others' lives, it is not difficult to understand how one might make such a connection. But there is one serious disproof, as E.K. Brown discussed in "Hawthorne, Melville, and 'Ethan Brand'" (*American Literature*, March 1931). Hawthorne had finished the tale before the end of 1848, and it was published (without his consent or approval) in the 5 January 1850 issue of the *Boston Weekly Museum* as "The Unpardonable Sin.

From an Unpublished Work" under Hawthorne's own name – seven months before he and Melville met. It was then re-published (with his approval) as "Ethan Brand; or, The Unpardonable Sin" in *The Dollar Magazine* for May 1851, when Melville read it and wrote in a letter in early May:

> He was a sad fellow, that Ethan Brand . . . It is a frightful poetical creed that the cultivation of the brain eats out the heart. But it's my *prose* opinion that in most cases, in those men who have fine brains and work them well, the heart extends down to hams. And though you smoke them with the fire of tribulation, yet like veritable hams, the head only gives the richer and the better flavor. I stand for the heart. To the dogs with the head! I had rather be a fool with a heart than Jupiter Olympus with his head! (Niemeyer 2016:46)

Moreover, Hawthorne had thought of the theme as early as 1838, taking notes for its development during an inspirational trip to North Adams, Massachusetts from 26 July to 11 September 1838, when he saw a lime kiln burning while climbing Mount Greylock. Also, Julian Hawthorne interprets as a reference to "Ethan Brand" a passage from a letter that Sophia writes to her mother in early December 1848: "It is a tremendous truth, written, as he often writes truth, with characters of fire, upon an infinite gloom, – softened so as not wholly to terrify, by divine touches of beauty, – revealing pictures of nature, and also the tender spirit of a child" (*Works* XI, 381; Hawthorne 1884: II, 330–331).

Without revealing the author of the *Mosses* review, Duyckinck, ever the promoter, shipped copies of all Melville's books to Hawthorne. He read through them "with a progressive appreciation of the author," he wrote Duyckinck on 20 August 1850. "No writer ever put the reality before his reader more unflinchingly." *Mardi*, for example, he called "a rich book, with depths here and there that compel a man to swim for his life" (*Works* XVI, 362). On the strength of these books and what he knew of the man from their earlier encounter, the otherwise reclusive Hawthorne asked Melville to spend 3 to 7 September 1850 with him and his family.

Sometimes when we develop admiration for an author through his or her works, our expectations are disappointed when we actually meet in person. However, this wasn't the case with Melville. Sophia confirmed how happy she was that meeting him only enhanced her regard for him as a person. At some time during this period, the Hawthornes became aware of the reviewer's identity. Sophia wrote to Elizabeth, "He is all on fire with the subject that interests him. It rings through his frame like a cathedral bell. His truth & honesty shine out at every point" (Parker 1996: 775).

Of great significance is that within a week of meeting Hawthorne, Melville looked to purchase a property nearby. Melville's father-in-law, Lemuel Shaw, Chief Justice of the Massachusetts Supreme Court, had been subsidizing the former's income ever since his writing career had faltered with the publication of *Omoo* (1847). Melville borrowed $3000 (raising the other necessary $3500 on his own), this time against his wife's inheritance, to buy on 14 September an eighteenth-century farmhouse in Pittsfield on 160 acres of land. He lived here with his wife Elizabeth and son Malcolm, his widowed mother and three of his four grown sisters. He was where he needed to be: next door to his lover, Sarah, and only six miles from his mentor, Hawthorne. This explains his urgency to make the purchase.

I have visited the re-created two-story house, dating from the Revolutionary War when it had been a tavern. Yellow with red trim, atop a hill, it includes a workshop, animal pens, and a Shaker-style barn where the two authors spent hours in the loft talking – away from the noises of the family. The land includes a forest, streams, grazing pastures, berry patches, and bean fields with chestnut and maple trees. He raised his four children, and grew corn, turnips, potatoes, and pumpkins. There, too, he found the solace, inspiration, and cool weather that he needed to proceed with his work. He named it Arrowhead for the Indian relics his plow turned over.

During the next 16 months, Hawthorne and Melville saw each other at least six times as they worked on their respective novels. They discussed "the Universe with a bottle of brandy & cigars," as Melville put it, and engaged in profound conversations about "time and eternity, things of this world and of the next, and books, and publishers, and all possible and impossible matters," as Hawthorne recounted in his notebook for 1 August 1851 (*Works* XIV, 180; VIII, 448). Usually, Melville did most of the talking as Hawthorne sat acutely attentive and listened, clear-eyed, to long tales of the high seas. Sophia wrote: "Nothing pleases me better than to sit & hear this growing man dash his tumultuous waves of thought up against Mr Hawthorne's great, genial, comprehending silences . . . [s]uch a love & reverence & admiration for Mr Hawthorne . . . is really beautiful to witness" (Parker 1996: 834).

On 14 November, the two men met again for a late midday dinner at the Little Red Inn in Lenox. In order to celebrate the publication of *Moby-Dick*, Melville presented an inscribed copy dedicated to his friend, saying in a letter three days later, that he had "written a wicked book, and feel spotless as the lamb" (Niemeyer 2016: 53). We don't need to look any further than Hawthorne's response to appreciate the immensity of the intellectual effort that it cost the author. After he had speedily read the novel, he shared his views on it in a letter to Duyckinck: "What a book Melville has written! It gives me an idea of much greater power than his preceding ones" (*Works* XVI, 508).

He also wrote to the author a now lost "joy-giving and exultation-breeding letter," as Melville called it, showering praises on *Moby-Dick* (Niemeyer 2016: 52). Although we do not have the letter, we do have Melville's brief references to it when he later wrote to Sophia on 8 January 1852, saying that Hawthorne had been able to decipher the novel's latent meanings and deeper interpretations. Hawthorne's reading was to influence *The House of the Seven Gables*, which he was writing at the time.

"A sense of unspeakable security is in me this moment," Melville wrote to Hawthorne on 17 [?] November 1851, "on account of your having understood the book . . . I am content and can be happy. I shall leave the world, I feel, with more satisfaction for having come to know you. Knowing you persuades me more than the Bible of our immortality" (Niemeyer 2016: 53, 54). Here, it is evident that he felt a transcendent oneness with Hawthorne: "Whence come you, Hawthorne? By what right do you drink from my flagon of life? And when I put it to my lips – lo, they are yours and not mine. I feel that the Godhead is broken up like the bread at the Supper, and that we are the pieces. Hence this infinite fraternity of feeling . . . The divine magnet is in you, and my magnet responds" (Niemeyer 2016: 53, 54). He ended the letter "Herman" – the only time he signed a letter with his first name for someone who was not a family member.

In Hawthorne, Melville had found someone to accept him on his own terms, someone with a literary temperament he could respect and rely on. What began as an acquaintance metamorphosed into an intense friendship, having as its bedrock Melville's absolute trust in Hawthorne's judgment and boundless faith in his work. This was certainly Sophia's understanding: Adoringly obsessed with her husband, Sophia "saw nothing excessive in Melville's own enthusiasm" (Parker 1996: 775). Theirs was "a spiritual communion embodied in Hawthorne's perfect understanding of his masterpiece" (Lingeman 2006: 43). Had there developed simmering competitiveness (as some critics have alleged) beneath the tranquil surface of their friendship? In the surviving letters, I don't hear that.

When Melville wrote of the "divine magnet" in [17?] November 1851, he knew that Hawthorne would be leaving the Berkshires just a few days later, moving to West Newton, Massachusetts (Niemeyer 2016: 52). Many reasons influenced this decision, but, contrary to the theories propounded by some scholars, none concerned a desire to distance himself from Melville. Hawthorne left because he hated the bitter cold which was unfavorable for Sophia's health. Besides, the cottage in Lenox was very small, and now he was offered the opportunity to stay at the actress Fanny Kemble's home in West Newton relatively rent-free but declined. Discordant neighbors, financial stress, opportunities elsewhere, loneliness for his friends, a dispute with the Tappans about fruit picking – these circumstances, too, may help explain why he stormed in his diary on 29 July 1851: "I detest it! I detest it! I detest it! I hate Berkshire with my whole soul, and would joyfully see its mountains laid flat" (*Works* VIII, 439).

Melville, however, chose to stay at Arrowhead for another 12 years – as we now suspect, to be close to Sarah. After the departure, he and Hawthorne corresponded, albeit infrequently, and they saw each other only three more times, once in Concord in November 1853; and twice in Liverpool in 1856 and during the winter of 1856–1857. By then, Hawthorne's place as a major figure in American letters seemed secure. In contrast, Melville's popularity was on the decline, which may help explain their infrequent communication and visits.

On an extended trip to Europe and the Holy Land, partly in an effort to improve his health, in November 1856, Melville visited Hawthorne, who was serving as the United States consul in Liverpool and living in nearby Southport. Hawthorne had attempted half-heartedly and unsuccessfully to secure Melville a post in President Pierce's administration, something that he later felt guilty about. They spent a week together, conversing. They walked along the beach, sat down in "a hollow among the sand hills," smoked cigars, and visited the area, including an excursion to the town of Chester (*Works* XXII, 162–163). Hawthorne's comments from his notebook on Melville at the time offer a rare and poignant portrait of Melville (and of the writer himself) that also suggests why it was Melville (not Hawthorne) who distanced himself. On this point, nothing can replace his incomparable journal entries written after Melville's visit.

On Thursday, 10 November, after a two-night stay, Hawthorne wrote of Melville and reflected that he looked "a little paler, and perhaps a little sadder" with the same "gravity and reserve of manner." They soon found themselves "on pretty much our former terms of sociability and confidence" and, as he always did, he began "to reason of Providence and futurity, and of everything that lies beyond human ken, and informed me that he had 'pretty much made up his mind to be annihilated'; but still he does not seem to rest in that anticipation; and, I think, will never rest until he gets hold of a definite belief. It is strange how he persists – and has persisted ever since I knew him, and probably long before – in wandering to-and-fro over these deserts, as dismal and monotonous as the sand hills amid which we were sitting. He can neither believe, nor be comfortable in his unbelief; and he is too honest and courageous not to try to do one or the other. If he were a religious man, he would be one of the most truly religious and reverential; he has a very high and noble nature, and better worth immortality than most of us" (*Works* XXII, 162, 163).

On a return leg of his trip, on 4 May 1857, Melville stopped again at the consulate in Liverpool to pick up a trunk he had left there and saw Hawthorne, albeit briefly. It would be their last meeting. We sense the end of something. What every aspiring writer yearns for is the sincere approval of an older, more established counterpart. Hawthorne gave him that. While that says a lot about Melville, it says as much about Hawthorne as a man, as a fellow writer, as a friend – "two 'big hearts' striking together" (Lingeman 2006: 43). Years later, upon hearing the news of his friend's passing, Melville was left in a state of prolonged shock. "Herman was much attached to him," his mother Maria wrote to her brother, Peter Gansevoort, "& will mourn his loss" (Argersinger and Person 2008: 48).

10

The House of the Seven Gables (1851)

The House of the Seven Gables, 54 Turner Street, Salem.
Source: Library of Congress.

> *Look back, and the past becomes a story.*
> *The fixed shadowy shapes begin to move again,*
> *and make new patterns in the memory,*
> *some familiar, some strange.*
>
> —Richard Holmes (2000: 3)

Before I turn to *The House of the Seven Gables* with my students, I describe one of my favorite scenes from Shakespeare's *The Merchant of Venice* (2015 [1598]), when Lorenzo speaks to Jessica about the power of music to transform human lives. He alludes to the image of a herd of untrained, unrestrained colts that leap around wildly, neighing shrilly and with great abandon because it is "the hot condition of their blood." But if the wild young beasts happen to hear "a trumpet sound / Or any air of music," Lorenzo goes on, they all stand still, "Their savage eyes turn'd to a modest gaze / By the sweet power of music." Any person who can't be likewise moved by harmonious melodies, any man who "hath no music in himself,"

The Life of the Author: Nathaniel Hawthorne, First Edition. Dale Salwak.

Lorenzo concludes, "Is fit for treasons, stratagems and spoils; / . . . Let no such man be trusted. Mark the music" (V.i.79–93).

When we listen to sublime melodies, gaze upon an inspiring painting, or when we immerse ourselves in a novel, we develop our minds and hearts in subtle ways. If we understand the sufferings, emotions, and joys of others, we can diminish our feelings of separateness and find commonalities of the human condition. Surely Hawthorne had this sentiment in mind when he wrote in the preface to his next romance:

> [T]he Author has provided himself with a moral; – the truth, namely, that the wrong-doing of one generation lives into the successive ones, and, divesting itself of every temporary advantage, becomes a pure and uncontrollable mischief; – and he would feel it a singular gratification, if this Romance might effectually convince mankind . . . of the folly of tumbling down an avalanche of ill-gotten gold, or real estate, on the heads of an unfortunate posterity, thereby to maim or crush them, until the accumulated mass shall be shattered abroad in its original atoms. (*Works* II, 2)

Arguments can convince the head but can rarely win the heart. We understand that. But through the magic of allegory Hawthorne entertains us, persuades us to accept his "hospitality" and enter into his narrative willingly.

Hawthorne first uses the theme of the transformative power of art for both the creator and observer in his "Drowne's Wooden Image" (1844), based on an enchanting Greek myth. The Roman poet Ovid in Book X of his *Metamorphoses* (which Hawthorne had read in Latin as a schoolboy), tells of Pygmalion, King of Cyprus and a sculptor who carves his ideal woman in ivory. After seeing the daughters of Propoetus prostituting themselves, he had declared himself uninterested in women. He finds his ivory statue increasingly beautiful and realistic, however, and falls in love with it as if it were an actual woman. Responding to his prayer, the goddess Venus intervenes, brings the statue to life, and they marry and have a daughter. Although the transformation is the work of a goddess, it is the result of human passion.

In his own version, almost 1800 years later, Hawthorne moves the setting to America and makes the sculptor, Drowne, a wood-carver of ship figureheads. He is a practical, stolid man, a mechanic, with no aesthetic sense, no apparent feeling for beauty or spirituality. He needs a powerful emotion to make him shake off his overall begrudging disposition. However, his art is transformed when he falls in love with the figurehead of a beautiful woman he has been asked to carve. "The face was still imperfect; but, gradually, by a magic touch, intelligence and sensibility brightened through the features, with all the effect of light gleaming forth from within the solid oak. The face became alive" (*Works* X, 312–313).

To the discerning reader, both versions of the Pygmalion myth suggest that Hawthorne himself, like a sculptor or painter, brings to life the characters in his own masterpieces – *The Scarlet Letter*, as we have seen, and now *The House of the Seven Gables*. The ideal becomes real through the creative power and love of the artist.

On 25 March 1840, long before he began writing the book, he visited a gabled house (whose core dates to 1668) at No. 54 Turner Street, Salem. This was the same waterfront house he had frequented as a child, owned by his wealthy second cousin, Susannah Ingersoll (c. 1785–1868). This time, he went there to see how she and the structure had weathered the great storm that had struck Salem the day before.

Once inside, he found the house gave him a powerful sense of the past and its former inhabitants. Afterwards, in May 1840, he wrote to her adopted son, Horace Conolly, also a resident and close friend of Hawthorne's: "I had a more than ordinary pleasant visit, and among other things, in speaking of the old house, she said it has had in the history of its changes and alterations Seven Gables. The expression was new and struck me very forcibly; I think I shall make something of it. I expressed a wish to go all over the house; she assented and I repaired to the Attic, and there was no corner or dark hole I did not peep into" (*Works* XV, 456).

Low-ceilinged, gas-lamplit rooms, steep stairs, whispers, shadows, closets explored in solitude, distant noises of creaking floors and gurgling pipes, and the sounds of gentle wind flowing under the cedar shingles – all this, and more, captured Hawthorne's imagination. He knew that he would have to set a novel here. "It was itself like a great human heart, with a life of its own, and full of rich and sombre reminiscences," he would write in the novel. "The deep projection of the second story gave the house such a meditative look, that you could not pass it without the idea that it had secrets to keep, and an eventful history to moralize upon" (*Works* II, 27).

I can imagine how he would have felt. It is an alive and haunting place that I have thought about since the age of ten when I first went there. Years later, during one of my return visits, the guide left me alone to explore room by room. An enigmatic door in the dining room led to a narrow staircase (probably built in the early 1690s during the Salem trials as a hiding place from witch hunters) that twisted and turned up to the second floor. This secret staircase was just wide enough for my shoulders to fit between the brick walls. The words "eerily fascinating" come to mind now as I remember entering the attic. It was as if I were being observed by a ghostly presence of other people who had lived here and had never gone away. I wondered aloud, "Is there anyone there?" and immediately thought of the stirring lines from Walter de la Mare's poem, "The Listeners" (1969 [1912]): "And he felt in his heart their strangeness / Their stillness answering his cry" (lines 21–22). Once seen, the house stays lodged in the mind's eye. Like Hawthorne, I experienced something emotionally deep and lasting that day. I wanted to know more.

Along with the house, Hawthorne was fascinated with an elaborately carved oak chair in the parlor. Over tea, after he lamented having nothing to write about, Ingersoll suggested that he write a story around it. "[I]t is an old Puritan relict," she told him, "and you can make a biographical sketch of each old Puritan who became in succession the owner of the chair" (*Works* XV, 456). Hawthorne immediately went on to write a children's book and publish it in time for Christmas 1840: *Grandfather's Chair: A History for Youth*. This was followed by two more volumes in January (*Famous Old People*) and March (*Liberty Tree*). The series offers captivating glimpses of life from the beginning of the Massachusetts Bay Colony through the period of the Revolutionary War. Young readers follow the chair, starting with its arrival in America aboard the ship *Arbella*, through the various vagaries and vicissitudes of life, until many years later, when grandfather buys it at an auction. Hawthorne drops famous and infamous names and shares brief histories of those figures who once sat in it and ruminated on how their actions affected the country.

Sir William Phips searches for sunken treasure. Betsy Hull is given her weight in silver on her marriage day. Governor Hutchinson escapes the wrath of a Boston mob. Other momentous events include the tragedy of the great Acadian exile, the Salem witch trials, the Boston Massacre, and the plague in New England. The chair, however, becomes more than a mere seat, for it talks back to the narrator and his grandchildren, concluding with the message, "JUSTICE, TRUTH, and LOVE, are the chief ingredients of every happy life" – the same theme that will emerge by the end of his new novel as well (*Works* VI, 209).

Besides the house and the chair, an equally powerful inspiration was Hawthorne's family history. Ingersoll told him about Sarah Good's curse on his great-grandfather John Hathorne, the hanging judge, after the Rev. Nicholas Noyes had called her a witch: "I'm no more a witch than you're a wizard! And if you take my life God will give you blood to drink!" (Loggins 1951: 133) Hawthorne linked this event with the legend that a curse had robbed the judge's descendants of 9000 acres of land in Waldo County, eastern Maine. The sins of the fathers harm their children's children. Hawthorne believed that although we are not responsible for those sins, we must learn from our ancestors' mistakes and come to terms with our guilty inheritance.

As we read the novel, we can feel him trying to shake off his own dismal ancestral past as Holgrave, one of the characters, cries out (as perhaps many of us have done): "Shall we never, never get rid of this Past? . . . It lies upon the Present like a giant's dead body! . . . [W]hat slaves we are to by-gone times" (*Works* II, 182–183). The writing of the novel was Hawthorne's way of coming to terms with the unforgiving grip of ancestral guilt, to see it for what it is, and not to be frightened or oppressed by it. All this and more lies behind the spirit of *The House of the Seven Gables*.

For the next 10 years after his visit, he kept turning over in his mind what he had discovered. Slowly, the shadows of a new story began to hover about him. He wondered, *How do people react when they find themselves influenced by secret histories that they feel in their hearts more than they understand with their minds?* We see him address this question as early as in *Fanshawe*, with its story of the seclusion caused by youthful ambition, and "Alice Doane's Appeal," with its picture of isolated old age.

Not until early in August 1850 – awash with the success of *The Scarlet Letter*, free of the drudgery and tedium of working at the Custom House, and living away from Salem, temporarily in the Berkshires with the precious time to work – was Hawthorne ready to commence. "I am never good for anything in the literary way till after the first autumnal frost," he explained to his publisher, Fields, on 1 October 1850, "which has somewhat such an effect on my imagination that it does on the foliage here about me, multiplying and brightening its hues" (*Works* XVI, 369). Good reviews of his prior work, a regular flow of income to support his family, undiminished imaginative powers, and the impending arrival of their third child, Rose, had raised his spirits. Hawthorne felt that he had the whole book in his head; it was now a matter of getting it down.

During the next five months, he secluded himself "religiously" each morning at his upstairs desk (*Works* XVI, 359). This was, by no means, an easy time for him. The tone of *The Scarlet Letter* had been uniformly gloomy, and he had found it impossible to introduce even one ray of cheering light. Once Hawthorne had found his "pitch," he explained to Fields on 1 November, the writing progressed smoothly (*Works* XVI, 371). In his new novel, he wanted to explore a gamut of emotions from somber to humorous, from realistic to romantic, from shade to sunshine, to convey, as he wrote to Duyckinck on 27 April 1851, "a more natural and healthy product of my mind" (*Works* XVI, 421).

Needless to say, writing the novel involved a great deal of care, thought, and precision as he labored sentence-by-sentence, page-by-page. He felt a responsibility to his talent, to Sophia, to his friends, and to the general reading public which, with its genteel taste, had regrettably grown to perceive him as melancholy (*Works* XVI, 407). He didn't want to acquiesce again to the darkness of his imagination that Melville had written about in his review of *Mosses from the Old Manse*.

As he worked, the tone continued to concern him. "It darkens damnably towards the close," he told Fields on 29 November 1850, "but I shall try hard to pour some setting sunshine over it" (*Works* XVI, 376). On 9 December 1850, he wrote again to Fields, "I have been in a Slough of Despond, for some days past – having written so fiercely that I came to a stand still." He was "bewildered," not knowing "what he has done" and "what to do next," determined to "keep quiet" until he did (*Works* XVI, 378).

Although he concluded the novel by mid-January, he devoted another ten days to revising the final pages until he was convinced that he had found the right words – a testament to him as a writer and how hard he worked at his craft to achieve perfection. He wrote to Duyckinck on 27 April 1851: "[I]n writing it, I suppose I was illuminated by my purpose to bring it to a prosperous close; while the gloom of the past threw its shadow along the reader's pathway" (*Works* XVI, 421).

On account of its light-hearted, happy ending – there is a marriage, the family is redeemed from its evil past and virtue is rewarded – he felt more confident about publishing it as compared to the relatively darker *Scarlet Letter*. In writing to Fields on 27 January 1851, he stated: "[The book] has met with extraordinary success from that portion of the public to whose judgment it has been submitted; – viz, from my wife. I likewise prefer it to the Scarlet Letter" (*Works* XVI, 386). Indeed, Sophia loved his work. "There is unspeakable grace and beauty," she wrote of the conclusion, "[throwing back] upon the sterner tragedy of the commencement an ethereal light, and a dear home-loveliness and satisfaction – [with] the flowers of Paradise scattered over all the dark places, the sweet wall-flower scent of Phoebe's character" (Argersinger and Person 2008: 257). Finally, he sent the manuscript to his publisher.

Fields published the book on 9 April and the outcome was beyond positive. It quickly outstripped *The Scarlet Letter* in its success, with 6710 copies in print by September, 710 more than *Scarlet* by August 1851, 18 months after its publication. The early reviews confirmed Sophia's reaction. "The impression which it leaves on the reader's mind," wrote *The Christian Examiner* for May 1851, "is, indeed, much pleasanter than that produced by its predecessor." The *Southern Quarterly Review* in July called it "a more truthful book" for similar reasons. Noting a "tendency to disease" in Hawthorne's nature, "a sort of unnaturalness in his world," Unitarian minister Amory Dwight Mayo, while writing for the July *Universalist Quarterly*, saw the author "struggling out of its grasp, with a vigor which we believe ensures a final recovery" and concluded: "as a whole, it is nearer actual life, and more comprehensively true to human nature, than any former work of its author." Others, such as Henry T. Tuckerman in the June *Southern Literary Messenger,* praised the book's "local authenticity" and ascribed its success to Hawthorne's "fidelity to local characteristics" of New England life and leaving behind the melodramatic in favor of realism and humor. In the May 1851 issue of *Graham's Magazine*, Whipple stated that the novel was "sure of immediate popularity and permanent fame" (Crowley 1970: 195, 198, 203, 217, 220, 224).

Melville, to whom Sophia had presented a signed copy on 11 April, also believed that the novel surpassed the earlier work. In a letter dated 16 April [?], he compared it to "a fine old chamber, abundantly, but still judiciously, furnished with precisely that sort of furniture best fitted to furnish it." In this chamber, he said, there is an "admirable sideboard, plentifully stored with good viands [and] a smell as of old wine in the pantry . . . The curtains are more drawn; the sun comes in more; genialities peep out more [and] in one corner [of the chamber] a dark little black-letter volume in golden clasps, entitled 'Hawthorne: A Problem'" (Crowley 1970: 189, 190).

He continued with his incisive insights: In his narrative, Hawthorne had also managed to embody "a certain tragic phase of humanity [meaning] the tragical-ness of human thought in its own unbiassed [*sic*], native, and profounder work-ings . . . the visable [*sic*] truth . . . of the absolute condition of present things as they strike the eye of the man who fears them not, though they do their worst to him." Here, Melville declares, he discovered a grand truth about Nathaniel Hawthorne. "He says NO! in thunder; but the Devil himself cannot make him say *yes*" (Crowley 1970: 190).

Why did the novel fortify his reputation? What impelled many critics on the strength of this evidence to hail him as the finest writer the Republic had yet pro-duced? To answer these questions, we turn first to Hawthorne's preface, in which he concedes that he has chosen to write another Romance – permitting "a certain latitude," especially with respect to incorporating "the Marvelous" – rather than a Novel – requiring "a very minute fidelity, not merely to the possible, but to the probable and ordinary course of man's experience." He describes his story as "a Legend, prolonging itself, from an epoch now gray in the distance, down into our own broad daylight, and bringing along with it some of its legendary mist" (*Works* II, 1, 2).

In a manner reminiscent of the gothic romance popularized in England by Ann Radcliffe in the 1790s, Hawthorne uses hereditary curses, ghosts, fated out-comes, a desolate bedchamber, disturbing family histories, a mysterious lost-land deed, three deaths that look like murder, and a creaky history-haunted house to explore the dark side of the psyche. At the end, however, the book surprises as it turns into realistic, domestic fiction. There is at last harmony and unity within the house and, as is customary for a gothic story, all mysteries are explained naturally.

To heighten the mystery of the family drama, Hawthorne withholds informa-tion about the characters and only gradually explains their relationships to the past and to each other. Part of the satisfaction the novel gives is that of a puzzle; the mysteries are satisfactorily resolved at the end. The first-person narrator starts in the heart of commercial Salem during the late 1600s, revealing that from the beginning, the family is cursed with greed. A commoner named Matthew Maule builds a humble thatched hut on a plot of land that is otherwise notable for its freshwater spring. The aristocratic Colonel Pyncheon, a rich, powerful, "iron-hearted Puritan" who covets the site and believes he has a legitimate right to the land, orchestrates a death sentence for Maule during the 1692–1693 dreaded witch hunts and trials. On the scaffold, the plebeian Maule curses him and prophesizes: "God hath given him blood to drink!" (*Works* II, 15, 16)

After the hanging, the undaunted Pyncheon takes possession of the land and, with the help of Maule's carpenter-son Thomas, ironically builds "over an unquiet grave" a fine, seven-gabled mansion for his family as a monument to his own fame and wealth. But the water, as if issuing a premonition, grows "hard and brackish," and the land seethes with memories of guilt and revenge (*Works* II, 10). When the guests arrive for the house's dedication, they find the colonel bloodied and dead in a great oak chair in his study beneath his portrait, fixing forever "[t]hose stern, immitigable features [that] seemed to symbolize an evil influence, and so darkly to mingle the shadow of their presence with the sunshine of the passing hour, that no good thoughts or purposes could ever spring up and blossom there" (*Works* II, 21). Although the doctors attribute his death to apoplexy, the guests whisper about a curse.

From this point on, the chair becomes a symbol of the aristocratic pretensions of the ancient Pyncheon line: "a very antique elbow-chair, with a high back, carved elaborately in oak, and a roomy depth within its arms." The details – antique, high back, carved elaborately, roomy depth – set the chair in contrast to the other modern chairs in the room: "straight and stiff," "ingeniously contrived for the discomfort of the human person," "irksome even to sight," lacking "artistic curves," conveying "the ugliest possible idea of the state of society to which they could have been adapted" (*Works* II, 33). This one comfortable chair assumes significance not only because two characters (Colonel Pyncheon and Judge Jaffrey Pyncheon) die in it but also because it becomes their impoverished relative Clifford's favorite place for relaxation and an afternoon nap.

The damning repercussions of the curse and the Colonel's death reverberate down through the centuries as seven generations of the Pyncheon family persist in pride and greed. Each commits "anew the great guilt of his ancestor, and incur[s] all its original responsibilities" (*Works* II, 20). Too often, those victimized react by imitating their oppressors. Now, 160 years later, the house has become run-down, its timbers rotting, while the furniture is old and decrepit. The family's wealth has dwindled. Judge Jaffrey Puncheon is now the villain, who comes to the house to look in vain for the deed to vast estates in Maine. All that remain of the family are the Judge's poor cousins, Hepzibah and her brother Clifford, and their niece Phoebe. Upstairs in the attic is a tenant, a young man called Holgrave.

Judge Jaffrey Pyncheon dies and his wife, daughter, son, and nephew Jaffrey also die mysteriously and hideously as if under the same curse as that pronounced on the Colonel by the condemned "wizard." The now worthless title deed is revealed to be hidden behind the Colonel's portrait. Only after the youngest (and last) representatives of the two families, Holgrave, revealed to be a descendant of Maule, and Phoebe Pyncheon, fall in love and marry (in a model union founded upon the marriage of Nathaniel and Sophia) is the curse lifted. Their magical spell overpowers the evil spell. Vain illusions are eliminated; the old brutal separation of classes is transcended. Hepzibah, her brother Clifford (recently released from prison), and her niece Phoebe will inherit the Pyncheon country estate (thereby recovering the old Maule claim). The worthy members of the family inherit Judge Pyncheon's wealth. All is reconciled. Life goes on.

Part of the novel's power derives from an element of fiction that I wait to address until we are well into the course when my students are better acquainted with the author's strategies. It is this: None of Hawthorne's characters knows that either the narrator or we as readers are watching them and listening to them. We open the novel, the fourth wall drops, and then the pages begin to talk to us. We become voyeurs, eavesdroppers into the lives of others. As in drama, so in the novel, the appeal of the characters lies in their apparent unawareness that we are looking into their lives.

In some of Hawthorne's tales, the narrator tells the story to an ambiguous "someone." The fourth wall is never broken, and everything happens as if we are only watching. But here, the first-person narrator speaks directly to us, the readers, thus creating the illusion that we are listening to "our" story told by a good friend. He says, for example, that he mustn't "fail to direct the reader's eye" (*Works* II, 28). While acknowledging that the subject of Hepzibah's cent-shop is "disagreeably delicate to handle," the reader must be allowed into the secret of its history (*Works* II, 28). Sometimes he uses self-deprecating humor, as when he says, "Far from us be the indecorum of assisting, even in imagination, at a maiden lady's toilet!" (*Works* II, 30) He reminisces, confesses, admits his reticence to divulge what is about to transpire, expresses a need for "great faith [in the] reader's sympathy," and philosophizes, at one point exclaiming, when Clifford asks Phoebe to stop reading from a melancholy story (perhaps a witty reference to Hawthorne's own reputation for gloom): "And wisely, too! Is not the world sad enough, in genuine earnest, without making a pastime of mock-sorrows?" (*Works* II, 146, 150) The storyteller carries the plot forward and becomes a character, almost a part of the narrative. He engages the audience by appearing to take his readers into his confidence.

Here I find it helpful to connect students with modes of perception that are familiar to them. Given that we now live in an image-driven society, one effective exercise is to compare scenes from the novel with the wordless art of photography. Unless taken with a trained eye, most photographs are devoid of meaning; they merely capture the immediate impression of scenes and faces. Photographs never tell us as much as we want to know about what is going on inside the subject or what is behind the shot itself. They do provide an image but lack context; we don't quite know what led up to their taking or what ensued after they were taken. In addition, when subjects know they are being photographed, the image may memorialize the artificial or the superficial rather than capture the true or the essential.

Hawthorne's genius, and a key to the timelessness of his characters, is precisely the opposite. The "pictures" he creates are dynamic and multidimensional, the context fully established and thoroughly explored. I know of few nineteenth-century authors that can explicate an event, a room, a thought, a person, with such precision-laden detail, paying utmost attention to the treatment of ordinary people and the necessaries of life. "In spite of the supernatural drapery in which they are enveloped," wrote the reviewer for the May 1851 issue of *Harper's New Monthly Magazine*, "they have such a genuine expression of flesh and blood, that we can not [*sic*] doubt we have known them all our days. They have the air of old acquaintance – only we wonder how the artist got them to sit for their likenesses" (Crowley 1970: 196).

Through Holgrave's captivating thoughts and dialogue, for instance, the novelist portrays his innermost heart, captures the dynamic tensions in him, and reveals his discoveries truthfully. He also helps us to understand other distinct, lively characters such as Hepzibah Pyncheon or Matthew Maule. We follow the evolution of the relationship between Holgrave and Phoebe, the sequences of the house's decline, and more. We suddenly sit up and even experience a shiver down our spine on reaching Chapter 11, "The Arched Window," which deals with Clifford's decision to contemplate suicide. Hawthorne's ability to put himself into the character's shoes at this crucial moment is both convincing and frightful as Clifford, half-hidden behind a curtain, peers out of the "uncommonly large" upstairs arched window (suggestive of a draped theater box) at the "mighty river of life," glimpses into "the rush and roar of the human tide," and imagines "plunging into the surging stream" of humanity below to escape the oppressive interior of the house (*Works* II, 159, 165).

The scene conjures memories of George Eliot's treatment of the young, pregnant farm girl, Hetty Sorrel, in *Adam Bede*. In Chapter 37, she considers suicide while sitting by a dark shrouded pool under a great oak. "There was no need to hurry – there was all the night to drown herself in" (2008 [1859]: 378). Fortunately, unlike Hetty, Clifford is rescued when Hepzibah and Phoebe grab his garment to pull him back.

Here and throughout the novel, Hawthorne presents scenes that seem like fingerprints of the soul, and the imagined people come across not as posed or static, as in photographs, but fully realized. In Hawthorne's hands, a thousand words are worth a picture. His art trumps and triumphs over time.

How do we explain this? Like an artist, Hawthorne used literary techniques to transform everyday life into allegory. In his preface, he says that the romancer is similar to a painter. "If he think fit, also, he may so manage his atmospherical medium as to bring out or mellow the lights and deepen and enrich the shadows of the picture" (*Works* II, 1). It is not surprising, therefore, that he recognized the symbolic potential in the realistic works of the Dutch Masters. In meticulous detail, combined with truth and endearing simplicity, Hawthorne deliberately crafted his novel in the style of the Dutch realists he admired, notably Gerrit Dou (1613–1675), who is famous for his candlelit night-scenes. The novel is a succession of pictures, done in words, not oils – pictures of the street life, the house, the chair, the gables, and the Pyncheon Elm overhanging them, Alice's Posies growing on them, the abandoned garden, Old Maule's Well, the fountain whose waters had turned brackish and, like the Pyncheon's themselves, the "ancient and dilapidated" chickens (Hartley 1967: 97). We know how it feels to live there.

Hawthorne devotes considerable effort to explicate not only the house and its interior and exterior but also its characters, which he obviously felt deeply about. Hepzibah Pyncheon, who has been residing there, alone, for 30 years, is marvelously portrayed as the embodiment of decayed gentility obsessed with dreams of finding the long-lost deed. When she runs out of money, she must open a cent-shop and take in her niece Phoebe as a boarder to make ends meet. Penury-stricken, solitary, friendless, a disgrace upon her family when we first meet Hepzibah, her only sustaining hope is that she may yet provide help and succor to her unfortunate brother, Clifford. "I am too old . . . feeble . . . hopeless . . . I am a woman" (*Works* II, 44).

Clifford Pyncheon, her brother, is now a frail old man returning from 30 years spent in jail for the alleged murder of his Uncle Jaffrey (who actually died of an apoplectic seizure). He is so stunted by his sufferings that he has "grown accustomed to a sad monotony of life" with a soul like a "dark and ruinous mansion" (*Works* II, 105, 111). Only later, with the sunshine of Phoebe, is he transported back to his pre-prison youth, but his great release comes when he sees that the Judge, his jailer, his tormentor, has died.

Judge Jaffrey Pyncheon is well off, but when he offers to help out his cousin, Phoebe, she refuses, believing rightly that he had framed Clifford. As a candidate for the governorship, he is a confidence man, modeled in revenge on Reverend Charles Wentworth Uphill (1802–1875) for the role he played in Hawthorne's dismissal from the custom house: outwardly respectful, a do-gooder, faithful churchgoer, lover of flowers, but sinister, the living embodiment of the worst in the exploitative Pyncheon, who tries to seize the property of his cousins, Hepzibah and Clifford, with the same ruthless unscrupulousness that had motivated the original Colonel. He is convinced that Clifford knows the location of the hidden Pyncheon real-estate deed. While sitting inside the parlor, on the same chair where Colonel Pyncheon had sat, he dies suddenly of a stroke as he waits for Clifford.

His and Hepzibah's niece, 17-year-old Phoebe (meaning "bright," one of Hawthorne's pet names for his wife) Pyncheon, free of Maule's curse, needs a place to stay, and Hepzibah agrees to house her in exchange for taking care of the shop and dwelling. She is demure, charming, and self-reliant. She is likened to the sunshine, a source of warmth and comforting ebullience, as well as to the rose, a traditional symbol of a woman's mystical purity and beauty. She is Hawthorne's ideal of simple human goodness, who refurbishes the old house, restoring its kitchen, garden, and chambers with her busy, cheerful presence, her "homely witchcraft" (*Works* II, 72).

The 21-year-old Holgrave is a social reformer who has mastered the science of mesmerism and captures people's images on the silver surface of his daguerreotype plates. The narrator says of him: "Altogether, in his culture and want of culture; in his crude, wild, and misty philosophy, and the practical experience that counteracted some of its tendencies; in his magnanimous zeal for man's welfare, and his recklessness of whatever the ages had established in man's behalf; in his faith, and in his infidelity; in what he had, and in what he lacked – the artist might fitly enough stand forth as the representative of many compeers in his native land" (*Works* II, 181).

Phoebe is spellbound as he narrates the story of Alice Pyncheon, her ancestor from 100 years ago, who was beguiled into serving Matthew Maule's grandson and whose flight from Maule caused her death. "He meant to humble Alice, not to kill her; – but he had taken a woman's delicate soul into his rude gripe [sic], to play with; – and she was dead!" (*Works* II, 210) Unlike the Maules, however, Holgrave abdicates his right to revenge. He is courageous, kindhearted, self-reliant, and sensitive. He has "never violated the inmost man," has "carried his conscience along with him," and combines inward fortitude with enthusiasm and warmth (*Works* II, 177). "Coming freshly, as he did, out of the morning light, he appeared to have brought some of its cheery influences into the shop along with him" (*Works* II, 43). Judge Pyncheon's duplicity is revealed to him by the medium of a daguerreotype. The camera never lies, it has been said. When he declares his love, he promises "to set out trees, to make fences – perhaps, even, in due time, to build a house for another generation" (*Works* II, 307).

Like the characters themselves, the background sketches are "so life-like in the minutiae," wrote Henry T. Tuckerman in the June 1851 *Southern Literary Messenger*, "that they are daguerreotyped in the reader's mind" (Crowley 1970: 217). From life on the little back street to the succession of morning carts, from the scissor-grinder or butcher's carts to the bucolic garden of flowers and vegetables, these elucidations impart an intrinsic glow to the narrative. We can hear life in the cent-shop with the string of customers jingling the bell. We can see Sunday afternoon in the ruinous arbor. We can savor the fragrance of a loaf of warm bread or a china bowl of currants. We can hear the hens transported from the great coop of Berkshire cottage. These and a hundred other trifles "make up a glamour of reality that grows over the whole book like the mosses on the house" (Woodberry 1902:

212–213). The local realism extends to the characters, too. Thus, in his essay, "The Hawthorne Aspect," T.S. Eliot (1918) noted the depth of moral atmosphere in which the characters are steeped and said it is "Hawthorne's best novel after all" (47). James (1984 [1879]) called it "a great work of fiction" (124). I cannot improve upon those judgments.

By the time we have closed the book, one question inevitably comes to mind: What *right* have we as readers to judge the characters' private lives as we have done? The answer, as always, is that we have no right. We have neither earned it nor do we deserve it. We are allowed entry into these private lives by the grace of the author, who remains invisible behind the voice of the first-person narrator. It is a gift from the author, and we receive it gladly and discover the splendors within.

11

The Blithedale Romance (1852)

Hawthorne, 1852, portrait by George P.A. Healy. Source: Art Collection 3/Alamy Images.

> *I believe that in all men's lives at certain periods, . . . one of the most dominant elements is the desire to be inside the local Ring and the terror of being left outside.*
>
> —C. S. Lewis, "The Inner Ring" (1965 [1944]a: 58)

In 1944, C.S. Lewis (1965 [1949]b) delivered one of his most memorable speeches, entitled "The Inner Ring," where he described the experience we commonly have at some stage in our lives – the desire to be accepted by a group we are interested in at the time. We want to be in the know, to be one of the essential people in that social circle.

The Life of the Author: Nathaniel Hawthorne, First Edition. Dale Salwak.
© 2023 John Wiley & Sons Ltd. Published 2023 by John Wiley & Sons Ltd.

But what happens if we do manage to enter the inner ring? Will it give us the satisfaction that we're seeking? We may not get what we wanted. For "once the novelty" has worn off, "[a]s soon as your new associates have been staled to you by custom," the members of this circle "will be no more interesting than your old friends." "Why should they be?" Lewis asked. "You were not looking for virtue or kindness or loyalty or humour or learning or wit or any of the things that can really be enjoyed. You merely wanted to be 'in'" (64).

On my fourth or fifth time teaching Hawthorne's next novel, the semi-autobiographical *The Blithedale Romance* (1852), I realized that when he joined the utopian colony, Brook Farm (on which the novel is based), the author was grasping for exactly what Lewis described.

What led Hawthorne to write the novel? To answer the question, we must return to 1841. At 37, as we have seen, Hawthorne felt harassed and perplexed. Dismissed on 1 January from his job at the Boston Custom House and disenchanted with his writing career, he was naturally worried about how he was going to raise the money to set up housekeeping with Sophia Peabody – to whom he had been secretly engaged for three years. How could he pull himself together? How could he revive his literary efforts? He needed a practical alternative to living under the suffocating pressures of Salem, a place where he could read, think, and write, all the while looking for a home where he could begin his married life.

Hawthorne, however, was not alone in his distress. The country's 23 million citizens found themselves in the midst of a cataclysmic depression that started with the global panic in 1837 and lasted until 1843. The economy of New England was in shambles. Businesses and banks collapsed, affecting every class of society, and "the air became heavy with doubt and distress" (Rezneck 1935: 662). Political disagreement became sharp and embittered. The impoverished working class found itself ever more segregated from the middle and upper classes, and the threat of social disorder loomed large. The poor turned to alcohol, untaxed and cheap, as an escape. Its consumption had reached epidemic levels and led to massive violations of law. There were plenty of rumors of "riot, insurrection, and tumult" (Rezneck 1935: 676). As people lost faith in their social and political systems, a number of utopian movements were founded, seeking to replace existing social forms with smaller, idealistic communities.

Enter Unitarian Minister George Ripley. Feeling stifled by traditional religion, he gave his last sermon on 28 March 1841 and left the pulpit. With 20 other people, he started a socialistic community on 179 acres, the Brook Farm Institute of Agriculture and Education, eight miles southwest of Boston in West Roxbury. Inspired by the ideals of Transcendentalism (such as individual responsibility, free-thinking, rights of women) and the utopian writings of the French social scientist Charles Fourier (1772–1837). Ripley's plan, as formulated in his invitation (dated 9 November 1840) to Emerson, was to bring order and justice to the emerging industrial society and reform a church he considered "vicious in its foundations" (Richardson 1995: 337). He wrote:

> Our objects, as you know, are to insure a more natural union between intellectual and manual labor than now exists; to combine the thinker and the worker, as far as possible, in the same individual; to guarantee the highest mental freedom, by providing all with labor, adapted to their tastes and talents, and securing to them the fruits of their industry; to do away the necessity of menial services, by opening the benefits of education and the profits of labor to all; and thus to prepare a society of liberal, intelligent, and cultivated persons, whose relations with each other would permit a more simple and wholesome life, than can be led amidst the pressure of our competitive institutions. (Millington 2011: 174–175)

Ripley envisioned "a society of educated friends, working, thinking, and living together, with no strife, except that of each to contribute the most to the benefit of all" (Millington 2011: 176). Those who worked at Brook Farm would receive free room and board as well as a fixed salary regardless of their assignments. Education would be made available to any student. Members would earn 5% interest on their investment of $500 or more. Unlike other communities (such as the Shakers), it would not be mandatory for anyone to adhere to a religious belief. There would also be an open-door admission policy.

Emerson (1969 [1840]) did support the plan but emphatically declined the invitation. He didn't want to compromise his individuality, he explained; to join would contradict his theory of self-reliance – the "infinitude of the private man" – and his deep conviction "that a man is stronger than a city, that his solitude is more prevalent & beneficent than the concert of crowds" (*Journals* VII, 408). Although Hawthorne was also skeptical of reform movements and preferred solitude over society, he joined as a founding member, bought two shares, and invested another $500 toward the building of a house. "I quitted my cosey pair of bachelor-rooms – with a good fire burning in the grate," recalls Miles Coverdale, the narrator of *The Blithedale Romance*, "and plunged into the heart of the pitiless snowstorm, in quest of a better life" (*Works* III, 10). However, it is not surprising that Hawthorne should take this step. At no other stage in his life as yet was he so eager to live in a different setting. Brook Farm, he thought, might be just the place where he could save money while building a retreat for himself and his future wife from the cares of the world. The experience might also offer material for a new novel.

Hawthorne was sensitive but not naive. He knew that since 1800, America had been a haven for utopian and communal societies – 119, as a matter of fact, 60 of them during the 1840s. He had read about and openly admired, for example, the Scottish socialist Robert Owen and his followers in New Harmony, Indiana

(1825–1828). He was acquainted with Bronson Alcott's short-lived educational experiment, Fruitlands (in 1843). Hawthorne had even visited three of New England's Shaker communities: at Canterbury, New Hampshire in 1831 with his uncle, Samuel Manning; near Harvard in 1842 with Emerson; and at Hancock in 1851 with his son Julian, along with Melville, Evert and George Duyckinck. In a letter dated 17 August 1831, he shared his thoughts specifically on the Shakers with Louisa: "On the whole, they lead a good and comfortable life, and if it were not for their ridiculous ceremonies, a man could not do a wiser thing than to join them. Those whom I conversed with were intelligent, and appeared happy. I spoke to them about becoming a member of the Society, but have come to no decision on that point" (*Works* XV, 213). The project intrigued him to such an extent that it became the subject of two of his stories: "The Canterbury Pilgrims" (1832) and "The Shaker Bridal" (1837).

The community appeared to be a place where people lived and worked harmoniously while striving for a better society. Delving deeper, however, as he does in both stories, Hawthorne found that the cooperative spirit was actually a façade that hid deceit and selfishness. Once inside, his characters in "The Canterbury Pilgrims" discover, instead of high spirits, good food, and comfortable life, the settlement offers only "a cold and passionless security" much like "that other refuge of the world's weary outcasts, the grave" (*Works* XI, 131). Since his first visits, he had become far more critical of the Shakers. In a journal entry dated 8 August 1851, Hawthorne referred to the Shakers as "a filthy set . . . hateful and disgusting to think of" (*Works* VIII, 465). His sense of outrage about the disparity between romantic anticipation and harsh reality, between art and experience, foreshadowed his future disillusionment at Brook Farm and became a formula of sorts that he would employ to write his new novel.

Like his narrator, Hawthorne arrived at Brook Farm on a wintry day, 12 April 1841. Initially, his enthusiasm was apparent. "This is one of the most beautiful places I ever saw in my life, and as secluded as if it were a hundred miles from any city or village," he wrote to Louisa on 3 May. "There are woods, in which we can ramble all day, without meeting anybody, or scarcely seeing a house" (*Works* XV, 539). After a 10-hour workday, residents utilized their spare time for relaxing, writing, music-making, dancing, and dramatizations. An evening choir sang choruses of Mozart and Haydn. Lectures embraced a wide variety of subjects including literature, art, and philosophy. Masquerades featured impersonations, such as Hamlet, Shakespeare, Queen Elizabeth, and Sir Walter Raleigh. The alternation of work and pleasant company, with communal meals, prompted Hawthorne to express his optimism in a letter to Louisa: "such a delectable way of life has never been seen on earth, since the days of the early Christians" (*Works* XV, 540).

Life here seemed to be in stark contrast to the strait-laced, grim Puritan influence of his ancestry, the background to so much of his fiction. After Sophia visited him in late May, she wrote, "My life – how beautiful is Brook Farm! I was enchanted with it & it far surpassed my expectations. Most joyously could I dwell there for its own beauty's sake" (*Works* XV, 31).

Residents lived in communal houses, one of which was the farmhouse, also known as the Hive (because it was focal point of myriad activities). There were dining and sitting rooms downstairs. In a letter to Sophia dated 13 April, Hawthorne said that he believed the front room was "the best chamber in the house" due to its large size and location (*Works* XV, 527). From his solitary perch, Hawthorne was able to browse through the volumes of Ripley's library outside the bedroom while, like Miles Coverdale, he quietly observed the comings and goings of his housemates.

Hawthorne also took great delight at first in the daily chores on the farm: pitching hay, chopping, wood, forking manure, and milking cows, while the women tended to the domestic duties (an arrangement that soon changed to allow a more equitable division of labor). They hoed fervently, as he wrote in the novel, hoping that each stroke will "uncover some aromatic root of wisdom" (*Works* III, 65). They drank merrily out of earthen cups together with the laboring classes. During the early weeks of his participation, Ripley's wife wrote of Hawthorne: "He is our prince – our prince in everything – yet despising no labour and very athletic and able-bodied in the barnyard and field" (Updike 2007: 125). On 13 April, he wrote to Sophia: "I feel the original Adam reviving within me" (*Works* XV, 529).

By June, however, the glow was dimming. Farm work sounded noble in theory; he found it tiring and repetitive in practice. The long workdays now left Hawthorne feeling as uninspired to write as had his time in the Boston Custom House. In the evenings, small talk and the emptiness of sociability bored him. "The real Me was never an associate of the community," he wrote to Sophia on 3 September. His life had become "an unnatural and unsuitable, and therefore an unreal one" (*Works* XV, 566). He was unable to find "the sense of perfect seclusion," which had always been the hallmark of his creative power; although nobody intruded into his room, he continued to feel restless: "Nothing here is settled," he wrote to Sophia on 22 September. "My mind will not be abstracted" (*Works* XV, 575). He could not find the privacy so essential to his art.

After spending six months within this "inner ring" (other than a brief trip to Salem in September) and after being urged by his mother and sisters to return home, he officially resigned on 17 October 1841. In an earlier letter (25 May) to David Mack, he had alluded to his love of the domestic hearth to which he now yearned to return: "I can best attain the higher ends of life, by retaining the ordinary relation to society" (*Works* XV, 624). On 4 October 1841 [?], he had written to Sophia, "Thou art my only reality – all other people are but shadows to me; all events and actions, in which thou dost not mingle, are but dreams" (*Works* XV, 584). In saying no to others, he was saying yes to something deeper, something far more profound, within himself.

He left at the right time. By 1844, Brook Farm was in decline. Morale was low; members were drifting apart. The threat of smallpox loomed large a year later in November. Class antagonisms smoldered beneath the surface. Its central building (called the Phalanstery), constructed in honor of their socialist hero Fourier, burned to the ground on 3 March 1846, the day of its opening. It was not insured and the fire meant a total loss of $7000. Hawthorne brought suit against Ripley for $800 (including back wages) in the fall of 1845. The case was tried a year later, and he was awarded $585.70 on 7 March, but none of this was ever paid. By early 1846, Brook Farm was facing bankruptcy and was abandoned in 1847. In 1845, Mary Ann Dwight had summarized the community's fatal flaw when she wrote, "we have not had business men [sic] to conduct our affairs" (Delano 2004: 250–251). Coverdale reflects that "delectable visions of the spiritualization of labor" did not come to pass: "The clods of earth, which we so constantly belabored and turned over and over, were never etherealized into thought. Our thoughts, on the contrary, were fast becoming cloddish" (*Works* III, 65, 66). Later on, the farm served as a poorhouse, a Civil War Training camp (renamed Camp Andrew), as well as a Lutheran orphanage. For all concerned, the Blithedale experience did not have a happy end.

I'm not sure what I expected to see on a crisp autumn day in 2016 during my first pilgrimage there. On the one hand, the rolling meadows, mature pine forests, and wetlands were as visually stunning as Sophia Ripley (1840) had described them in a letter from 1840: "[I]n this tranquil retreat I have found that entire separation from worldly care and rest to the spirit which I knew was in waiting for me somewhere" (Burns 1982: 31).

On the other hand, the community site itself was disappointingly overgrown with scrubs and forest. A modern cemetery with asphalt roadways and headstones blanketed its center. A second cemetery covered another portion. Cellar holes served as mere reminders of what once was. I learned that the "Cottage" had survived until the 1980s when it was destroyed by an arsonist. Barring brief explanatory panels at the entrance, historical markers were absent. A residential trailer and a small cemetery office building replaced the formerly bucolic view that Hawthorne savored from the "Hive."

Unless acquainted with its history, a twenty-first-century visitor would never be able to guess that this once used to be the location for what Ripley envisioned as a model for a new America living in perfect harmony with nature, founded on the promises of women's rights and universal education. I thought, as Hawthorne must have thought when he departed: so much effort and expense, such high ideals and high hopes, for so little return.

For Hawthorne, the writer, however, all was not lost. The "no place" that was Brook Farm went on to become the illusionary Blithedale in his next successful novel. "When I write another romance, I shall take the Community for a subject," he wrote to his friend William B. Pike on 24 July 1851, "and shall give some of my experiences and observations at Brook Farm" (*Works* XVI, 465). He wrote it within a span of five months between late November 1851 and early 1852 while living in West Newton at the home of Horace Mann. It was published in mid-July.

In *Graham's Magazine* for September 1852, Whipple (to whom he had sent the manuscript on 2 May) called it "the most perfect in execution of any of Hawthorne's works, and as a work of art, hardly equalled by anything else which the country has produced" (Crowley 1970: 256). In 1879, Henry James called it "the lightest, the brightest, the liveliest" of his "unhumorous fictions" (1984 [1879]: 105). Three days after receiving a copy from Sophia, Melville wrote on 17 July: "As I am only just home, I have not yet got far into the book but enough to see that you have most admirably employed materials which are richer than I had fancied them. Especially at this day, the volume is welcome, as an antidote to the mooniness of some dreamers – who are merely dreamers – Yet who the devel [*sic*] aint [*sic*] a dreamer?" (Niemeyer 2016: 57)

In his preface, however, Hawthorne does not claim to attack such idealistic dreams and false hopes. He says that the aim of his romance (a term now included in the novel's title) is "to establish a theatre, a little removed from the highway of ordinary travel, where the creatures of his brain may play their phantasmagorical antics, without exposing them to too close a comparison with the actual events of real lives" (*Works* III, 1). Although he disclaims any direct connection between his life at Brook Farm and the events of the novel and asserts that his work is not intended to stake out a position on socialism, the book is clearly autobiographical.

The description of the discovery of Zenobia's body, for example, is based on his memory of finding the remains of a young woman who drowned in the Concord River in the summer of 1845, as well as the drowning of Margaret Fuller on 19 July 1850. He is also known to have drawn heavily from his journal kept toward the end of his stay at Brook Farm. The actual inspiration for Priscilla was a "little sempstress from Boston, about seventeen years old" who, he wrote on 9 October 1841, visited Brook Farm for a week. "[S]he is not a little girl, but really like a little woman, with all the prerogatives and liabilities of a woman." He added, "her intellect is very ordinary, and she never says anything worth hearing, or even laughing at, in itself" (*Works* VIII, 209, 210).

Also filtered through his imagination are the characters based on the intellectual personalities he knew. There are tantalizing allusions to Margaret Fuller (Zenobia), Emerson, Melville, or Alcott (Hollingsworth). The characters discuss a cross-section of New England cultural concerns and reform movements of the time: feminism and women's rights, progress and reform, the temperance movement, philanthropy, spiritualism and mesmerism, as well as what Arlin Turner (1958) called "the moral and psychological aspects of brotherhood" (14).

Although I invite my students to explore any of these topics, all of them seem peripheral compared to the one that most engages them, and me as well: the one with which I opened this chapter. The universal longing for community is deep and personal. At some point, all of us have felt like outsiders. If only we were in just the right place or knew just the right people, we believe, we could also belong to their group, and eventually, be contented. Instead of wondering what it might be like to live among a group, however, we only have eyes for the means of getting inside.

Like Hawthorne himself at Brook Farm, each of his characters is vulnerable to the allure of Blithedale's dream of social harmony. They desire to be at the center of a group that they believe is doing important work, but once inside, the sheen proves to be an illusion. Like all utopian societies, ultimately, Blithedale is revealed to be a mere masquerade, even a joke – what one critic called "a kind of *Walden* in reverse" (Male 1955: 279). It was D.H. Lawrence who first stated, in *Studies in Classic American Literature* (1977 [1923]), that the actual subject of the book is social and psychological disintegration (218).

The plot, beginning in the spring and ending in the fall, focuses on four principal characters. The first-person narrator, Miles Coverdale, a middle-aged bachelor and minor poet (whose poems we never see), tells his story in retrospect 12 years later. He arrives in a snowstorm (an unfavorable omen) one April night, to be greeted by the strong-willed Zenobia, a wealthy Boston woman and benefactress (each day wearing a fresh, exotic flower in her hair as a token of her aristocratic pride) whose money is being used to fund the operation and who devotes most of her time fighting for women's respect, dignity, and agency in the world. Hollingsworth, a blacksmith turned philanthropist and reformer, also arrives with Priscilla, a young seamstress entrusted to his care by the drifter, Old Moodie, revealed to be the father of Zenobia and once a wealthy man who fell from grace as a forger, remarried, and had another child, Priscilla.

Complications begin to unfold rapidly as the characters cannot help wanting to pair off. We learn that Zenobia loves Hollingsworth, but he favors Priscilla, who turns out to be Zenobia's poor half-sister. Between Coverdale and Hollingsworth there exists a tormented affection, begun when the blacksmith nurses the poet through a severe fever contracted early in his stay. When Coverdale recovers, he declines to be his "brother" in his "great scheme of good," even though Hollingsworth pleads, "[T]here is not a man in this wide world, whom I can love as I could you. Do not forsake me!" (*Works* III, 133)

Additional complications are introduced with the sinister figure of Westervelt, a mesmerist who has used Priscilla to entertain paying audiences as the Veiled Lady. He claims an intimate prior acquaintance with Zenobia, perhaps (though we are never certain) as her husband. In a twist that further enriches the story, Zenobia, rejected by Hollingsworth in favor of Priscilla, drowns herself in the

Charles River. Hollingsworth is overcome by guilt but eventually finds redemption through marriage to Priscilla. Coverdale, now an aimless man, returns to society after confessing that he also had been in love with Priscilla. All four characters at the center of the novel fail dramatically in their quest to recover human wholeness and communal harmony.

So many motives, so many unanswered questions: these deep waters can leave some of my students puzzled. To help them find clarity and closure, I begin with a discussion of Miles Coverdale, whose narrative point of view is replete with traps for the unsuspecting reader. On the one hand, there is much to admire about him; he is charming and funny, and his voice – easygoing, satirical, and unapologetic about his likes and dislikes – is quite irresistible. My students understandably develop an attachment to him. But on the other hand, as I pointed out early on in our discussions, he cannot be trusted at all times. Unless we remain alert, we can be lured into his distorted view of the situation, just as the utopian isolates members from their former lives and leads them astray.

The first clue is his name which, like the name of the community itself, is ironic. Miles Coverdale was the courageous sixteenth-century scholar who completed the translation begun by William Tyndale of the first complete Bible in English, and his first name is the Latin *miles*, meaning "soldier." Hawthorne's narrator intends to translate into a ballad the truth of what he sees and hears, but unlike his namesake, he never finishes the job. Hardly a soldier for Christ, the narrator is an Epicurean dilettante with a penchant for lassitude who lacks any real religious conviction, doesn't feel bound by the truth, and is guided by misplaced priorities. He distorts facts and misinterprets events. Wittily self-critical, he even admits that he exaggerates and adds details from his imagination. After a lengthy description of Hollingsworth in Chapter 9, for example, he asserts, "Of course, I am perfectly aware that the above statement is exaggerated, in the attempt to make it adequate . . . Let the reader abate whatever he deems fit" (*Works* III, 71). His pen, he confesses later, allows itself "a trifle of romantic and legendary license" (*Works* III, 181).

Both as a cold observer and a skeptic, Coverdale (whom we might take as Hawthorne's satirical self-portrait) is a caricature of the literary artist as a kind of intellectual predator who masks his intentions and identity (hence his name, *Cover*dale). Nonchalant and detached from others, he is eager to poach other people's ideas and then insert them into his own literary work while lamenting his ruthlessness. His favorite retreat is atop a white-pine tree where, hidden "owl-like" among the branches, he spies on the others (*Works* III, 99); or, while on holiday at an inn in a nearby town, where he spends time pulling aside his bedroom curtains to watch Zenobia, Priscilla, and Westervelt, who are also coincidentally staying in a house on the other side of the street.

We sympathize with him because he is socially isolated. Meaningful encounters take place between other people, far away, in the distance (he sees himself as the

"Chorus in a classic play" [*Works* III, 97]). Because he regards his friends as actors in a drama taking place on the private stage of his own imagination, he cannot become one of them or gain a direct gateway to their innermost feelings. As readers, we share Coverdale's voyeurism, and enjoy piecing together the clues in his observations.

Into this setting, Hawthorne inserts perplexing details. Chapter 13, "Zenobia's Legend," for example, relates (from a third-person point of view) her fable about a silvery veil and a young man named Theodore who bets his male friends that he would be able to reveal the true identity of the Veiled Lady. One evening, he sneaks into her dressing room where he hides until she arrives after her performance. Somehow, she senses his presence and calls him forward. The visibly surprised Theodore says that he is determined to discover her identity. She tells him to either kiss her through the veil before lifting it, in which case they will be bound together in a marriage-like relationship, or skip the kiss and straightaway lift the veil, but then he will never know happiness again. Because Theodore fears that her appearance would be less than pleasant, he decides he would rather see her face before kissing her. He lifts the veil to see her pale, lovely face only for an instant. Then she disappears, and he pines for another look for the rest of his life. The point becomes clear: Theodore's life is ruined because he has violated the Veiled Lady's privacy and succumbed to his carnal impulses, and yet has betrayed his romantic ideal with a cowardly act. Like Coverdale, lacking faith, he yearns to lift the veil hiding the truths of another character's life.

Thus, the fable resonates closely with the novel's general theme of veiling and masks. The residents dress up, play roles, act, and mask their true intentions and identities. Everyone seems to be guarding a secret. Priscilla, the Veiled Lady, is "insulated." Zenobia's name is a pseudonym, "a sort of mask in which she comes before the world." Old Moodie hides behind his alias and wears a patch to cover his past. Westervelt, with his gold teeth, has a face, says Coverdale, that "might be removable like a mask" (*Works* III, 95). Hollingsworth hides behind his grandiose philanthropic project, to rescue criminals by treating them with kindness. Meanwhile, Coverdale retreats behind his window as a voyeur; even his name connotes a disguise as he hides from others (Male 1955: 280).

When we first meet this "knot of dreamers," they are on the run from "the rusty iron frame-work" of urban and industrial life in quest of a better life, and they imagine that their "reformation of the world" is a Paradise, an Arcadia built upon "the blessed state of brotherhood and sisterhood, at which [they] aimed" (*Works* III, 12, 13, 19). But their dream of reforming the world quickly devolves into a devastating tragedy. Tensions, different ideas, passions, and ideologies start to bubble to the surface, exposing just what a fantasy this Utopia really is.

Zenobia is passionate, sensual, wealthy, artistic, glamorous – and hidden. Her public name, a sort of mask, comes from the Greek, meaning "life of Zeus" (ironic, given the Greek god's abuse of women). Like her namesake, she is a myth, mysterious and hard to pin down, as she espouses a feminist philosophy. Early on, she seems to pull the community together with her warmth and amiability. But in our minds, her connection with Margaret Fuller (1810–1850), briefly a resident at Brook farm, upends any comfortable assumptions about utopian life as we recall that Fuller, too, died by drowning (though not by suicide).

In 1848, Fuller gave birth to an illegitimate child. In May 1850, along with her child and her lover, Giovanni Angelo Ossoli, and carrying the draft of a book on the Italian revolution of 1848–1849, Fuller boarded the ship *Elizabeth* in Livorno bound for New York. On 19 July 1850, with land in sight, her ship was caught in a violent hurricane. It ran aground on a sandbar off Fire Island, only a few hundred yards from the beach, and split open. Neither her body nor Ossoli's were recovered, whereas their child, Nino, drowned in the arms of a steward. Hawthorne pours his heartbrokenness over this news into the discovery of Zenobia's horribly rigid and mutilated drowned corpse, leading one critic to refer to this scene as "the most dramatic and remarkable set piece in all of Hawthorne's work" (Hartley 1967: 106).

A key to understanding the group collected at Blithedale is Eliot's Pulpit, a place that she, Hollingsworth, Priscilla, and Coverdale frequent on Sunday afternoons. The actual site is a rock outcrop, shaded by the canopy of a tree, with a shallow cave below it. John Eliot (1604–1690) had once preached there to the Indians and translated the Bible into their own language; so in keeping with this tradition, Hollingsworth occasionally offers what Coverdale calls "a treasury of golden thoughts" (*Works* III, 119). Hawthorne uses this landmark in two episodes.

On the first occasion, in Chapter 14, Coverdale provides an elaborate description of a typical Sunday at Blithedale. Given the characters' aspirations, the reader expects to read about a blissful afternoon together at the foot of Eliot's Pulpit, where they are in the habit of going to sit and relax on Sundays. But the scene shows them not resting in harmony while Hollingsworth obliges with a sermon. They argue bitterly about women's capacities, and Coverdale sees both women are in love with Hollingsworth, to his chagrin. In the second scene, in Chapter 25, Coverdale paints a picture of spiritual and psychological discord. Verbal fights between Hollingsworth and Zenobia (over his rejection of her) as well as between Coverdale and Zenobia (over his view of women) finally destroy the Blithedale community once and for all. The community's ultimate disintegration occurs in a scene strongly suggestive of the Puritan witch trials.

Priscilla, on the other hand, who represents a very different type of womanhood from that of Zenobia, is from Coverdale's perspective, "shadowlike" (*Works* III, 77). She is a young, poor but spiritually empowered woman who is exploited by the demonic Westervelt to provide entertainment as the Veiled Lady, apparently while under hypnosis. Hawthorne took her name from the New Testament, a helper to Paul, the perfect model of an obedient woman. At the end, Coverdale confesses to the reader that he had been in love with her himself.

The ex-blacksmith and philanthropist Hollingsworth believes that kindness can indeed reform criminals. Given his dominance in the plot, we can understand why Hawthorne originally intended to name the novel after him. There is much to recommend him. He proves to be a compassionate, warmhearted nurse to the ill Coverdale, providing "more than brotherly attendance" (*Works* III, 41). He is deeply religious and aspires to reform mankind. Both Zenobia and Priscilla fall in love with him, but the latter ends up marrying and caring for him.

But Hollingsworth is willing to allow the innocent, spiritual Priscilla to become the subject of Westervelt's devilish and absurd experiments. He also ruthlessly uses Zenobia by encouraging her affections, believing that her supposed wealth might be used to support his reform ideas. Once he sees that this is no longer possible, he rejects her, and when she dies he has to bear the burden of guilt. Hollingsworth eventually escapes from committing the Unpardonable Sin because he repents, confesses, and does penance after taking Zenobia's warning seriously: "Are you a man? No; but a monster! A cold, heartless, self-beginning and self-ending piece of mechanism!" (*Works* III, 218) In his desolation, he spends the rest of his life with a contrite heart, believing it was he who killed Zenobia.

Her accusations and the guilt he feels over her suicide turn him away from evil. His heart is not hardened. The narrator tells us, "there was something of the woman moulded into the great, stalwart frame of Hollingsworth; nor was he ashamed of it, as men often are of what is best in them, nor seemed ever to know that there was such a soft place in his heart" (*Works* III, 42). Yet, within a page, Hollingsworth responds, "And you call me tender! . . . I should rather say, that the most marked trait in my character is an inflexible severity of purpose" (*Works* III, 43).

Every time we read Hawthorne's work, we walk away enlightened with a deeper insight into the mystery shrouding our hearts. As well-intentioned as the members of the group may be, human nature is flawed, and there is no technical fix (as we saw in "Earth's Holocaust"). Reform must be individual, not collective; from within, not without. Each person must experience a change of heart, a rebirth of the spirit. If we ignore this truth, as he shows us, we do so at our own peril.

Sir Thomas More (whose work Hawthorne had read) embraced this truth as far back as 1516 when he entitled his satiric masterwork *Utopia* – which in Greek quite literally means "nowhere." Utopia is also "eu-topia" – meaning, ironically, a "good place," a happy place. Like Brook Farm and all utopian experiments before and since, Blithedale is in fact a very unhappy place. Hawthorne understood that the utopian spirit is authoritarian and brutally selective. All such schemes ultimately leave the participants still yearning for reconciliation with the wholeness and harmony from which humanity feels estranged. In everyone is the memory of a lost Eden.

Thus Brook Farm did not turn out to be the place where Hawthorne would take his new bride. Instead, after their wedding and while *The Blithedale Romance* was going through the press, the newlyweds travelled by carriage from Boston, where the ceremony had occurred, to Concord where they moved into the Old Manse, a roomy house on the Concord River very near the Old North Bridge. Hawthorne had rented it from the Rev. Samuel Ripley, a Waltham minster who had inherited the property from his father, Ezra, in 1841. Unsurprisingly, this lovely house with its garden planted for the couple by Thoreau, and not the communal dormitories of Brook Farm, provided the idyllic setting which Hawthorne had sought to start a new life with the woman he adored.

12

The Marble Faun (1853–1860)

Hawthorne, London, 1860, photograph by J.J.E. Mayall, London.
Source: National Portrait Gallery, Smithsonian Institution; transfer from the National Gallery of Art; gift of the A.W. Mellon Educational and Charitable Trust, 1942; frame conserved with funds from the Smithsonian Women's Committee.

> *Nobody, I think, ought to read poetry, or look at pictures or statues,*
> *who cannot find a great deal more in them*
> *than the poet or artist has actually expressed.*
> —Nathaniel Hawthorne, *The Marble Fawn* (*Works* IV, 379)

Upon opening *The Marble Faun; Or, the Romance of Monte Beni* (1860), some of my students feel a slight sinking of the heart, and truth be told, so do I. By now, we have drawn close to Nathaniel and his family. We have discovered a lot about his life and the creative endeavors that went into its writing and personality in general. We have covered a substantial body of his work. But we know something that

The Life of the Author: Nathaniel Hawthorne, First Edition. Dale Salwak.
© 2023 John Wiley & Sons Ltd. Published 2023 by John Wiley & Sons Ltd.

he did not (but may have sensed). We are aware of the fact that this will be his last completed romance, that he will have passed on four years later, and that we wish that were not so. Like our preceding generations, we have surrendered to his hypnotic spell – and we want it to continue.

For many reasons, *The Marble Faun* has long been a favorite among readers and has elicited a wide range of interpretations and elaborations. It reverberates with poignant questions about Hawthorne's lifelong preoccupation with the loss of unfeigned innocence, the inconceivable power of the Past, the cauldron of sin, guilt and repentance, death, and the relationship between art and nature.

Played out against the backdrop of Italian history, past and present, it is also his longest and most elusive novel, with surprising time shifts, a misleading narrator, extensive literary references, ambiguities, and conflicting viewpoints, all intended to suggest the unfolding turmoil in the minds of the four central characters. Because the resolution is intentionally ambiguous, in a second edition Hawthorne reluctantly added a penitential postscript in answer to baffled readers' demands, as he wrote, for "further elucidations respecting the mysteries of the story" (*Works* IV, 463). Yes, he does provide answers, but many questions still remain unanswered, most notably whether or not one of the characters, Donatello, inspired by the fourth-century BC *Faun of Praxiteles*, has pointed ears hidden beneath his hair.

Set in the mid-nineteenth-century, the novel tells of two American artists – the New England sculptor Kenyon, who arrives in Rome to study the Ancients and develop his talent; and Hilda, a free-spirited Puritan with a "pretty and girlish face" and "a hopeful soul," who, since arriving in Rome, has "ceased to aim at original achievement" and instead creates brilliant copies of old Italian masters (*Works* IV, 57, 63, 462). They befriend a mysterious, dark-eyed New England painter, Miriam, daughter of the Puritans, who has rebelled against her father's expectation that she marry her cousin, who possesses, the narrator points out, traits that are evil, treacherous, and vile; and Count Donatello, a young Italian Catholic, who bears a striking resemblance to the fourth-century BC Greek sculptor Praxiteles's statue of a Faun in the Capitoline Museum. We spend a year with them and see Rome, the Tuscan countryside, and Monte Beni through their eyes.

The action is not far advanced before Miriam has a chance encounter in the catacombs of St. Calixtus with Antonio, a Capuchin monk (and artist's model), whom she regards mysteriously as "the evil spirit which blasted her sweet youth and compelled her . . . to stain her womanhood with crime" (*Works* IV, 190). Reminiscent of Chillingworth spying on Dimmesdale and Westervelt haunting Zenobia, the stranger (as the incubus, or succubus, the most interesting and puzzling of characters here) continues to stalk Miriam throughout the city.

Then, during one nighttime excursion to Capitoline Hill, he approaches her, imbuing her with "a cold, sick despair" (*Works* IV, 171). Donatello, now passionately attached to Miriam, engages in a physical scuffle with the tormentor and throws him off the Tarpeian Rock, the traditional punishment for traitors, later noting that he did what Miriam's eyes had commanded him to do. From the shadows, the innocent Hilda helplessly witnesses the murder.

For the rest of the novel, Hawthorne traces the movement of paranoia and guilt through the characters, all of whom feel responsible for the murder. We watch as they become lost, alienated, suffering from "an insatiable instinct that demands friendship, love, and intimate communion, but is forced to pine in empty forms; a hunger of the heart, which finds only shadows to feed upon" (*Works* IV, 114). The final paradox is that all the characters are united in their loneliness and their separateness. They do their best to look past their individual tragedies and to share whatever comfort they can (*Works* IV, 114). Donatello and Miriam accept responsibility for their sin. Kenyon and Hilda return, sadder but wiser, to America – thus bringing to a close what Charles Card Smith in the *North American Review* (April 1860) called "the greatest of his works" (Crowley 1970: 25). What immediately impresses us concerning *The Marble Faun* is how much Hawthorne cares about his characters, how fully he understands their isolation and estrangement. There is not a trace of disparagement in his treatment of any of them.

Donatello is forever transformed from a happy, carefree child of nature (like Adam before the Fall) into a man riddled with guilt and remorse (like Adam after the Fall). Living in Rome has destroyed his youthful happiness, but the experience has made him more perceptive about the human condition. In a sense, through him, the novel might be seen as a coming-of-age story, as he leaves behind the sensuality and selfishness of his youth, transitioning to the maturity and intelligence expected with adulthood. Eventually, he and Miriam reconcile, but he gives himself up to justice and is imprisoned.

Hilda, pure as the doves she watches from her tower, then crushed by the secret that she now carries, tends a shrine to the Virgin Mary in her tower and (though not a Catholic) confesses to a priest in St. Peter's. No longer able to derive pleasure in the pictures she used to copy, she considers herself overwhelmed with guilt. Never again will she wander about Rome "as securely as she has been accustomed to tread the familiar street of her New England village, where every face wore a look of recognition" (*Works* IV, 387). She bars her door to her friend Miriam and proclaims of Donatello that no fall could be happy and no evil a source of good. It is the only confession that restores her peace of mind.

Kenyon undergoes his own purgation as well. He meets the changed Donatello and Miriam in the Compagna, where he learns about her mysterious past. As the detached observer of life (there is usually at least one such character in Hawthorne's work), he has apparently suffered a tragic emotional experience in his youth which helps explain why Miriam calls him "as cold and pitiless" as the marble in which he works (*Works* IV, 129). His masterpiece, a statue of Cleopatra, depicts her "latent energy and fierceness" – thereby conveying his intuitive comprehension of human passion (*Works* IV, 126). He also sculpts Hilda's hand in marble as a symbol of purity (which he worships). He encourages the reunion between Donatello and Miriam in Perugia, near the statue of Pope Julius, and upon Miriam's advice, retreats to the Corso at the height of the Carnival to be reunited with Hilda, who agrees to marry him while still doubting her own innocence.

Deeply depressed, Miriam (a native of Rome) also never escapes her guilt and disappears. "Young as she is," says Kenyon, "the morning light seems already to have faded out of her life" (*Works* IV, 105). In her studio, Donatello finds paintings of murderous women: Jael (who drove a tent stake through the temple of the sleeping Sisera), Judith (who decapitated the Assyrian general, Holofernes), Salome (daughter of Herodias who asked for the head of John the Baptist), and Beatrice Cenci (a Roman noblewoman who murdered her abusive father) – suggesting her willingness to use violence against an oppressor. Like Hester Prynne's needlework on her scarlet letter, Miriam's art "can only dramatize or embellish her guilt, [for] all other themes are closed to her" (Onderdonk 2003: 85). However, the plot never reveals what purpose she serves in life. "[T]here was something in Miriam's blood, in her mixed race, in her recollections of her mother – some characteristic, finally in her own nature – which had given her freedom of thought, and force of will" (*Works* IV, 430).

To many readers of *The Marble Faun*, however, the greatest surprise comes from the scenes in which the characters debate the fall of Adam – a paradox that has found recurrent expression in Hawthorne's thought. Was it the *Felix Culpa* (Fortunate Fall) or *Infortunatus Culpa* (Unfortunate Fall)? Miriam wonders whether the murder had not been a blessing in disguise, a means of education, whereby the "simple and imperfect nature" of Donatello had been brought "to a point of feeling and intelligence, which it could have reached under no other discipline." She says, "Was that very sin – into which Adam precipitated himself and all his race – was it the destined means by which, over a long pathway of toil and sorrow, we are to attain a higher, brighter, and profounder happiness, than our lost birthright gave? Will not this idea account for the permitted existence of sin, as no other theory can?" (*Works* IV, 434–435).

Kenyon, on the other hand, warns her that she is trending towards "unfathomable abysses" and that "Mortal man has no right to tread on the ground where you now set your feet!" (*Works* IV, 434–435). Yet later, he raises similar questions with Hilda: "Is Sin, then – which we deem such a dreadful blackness in the Universe – is it, like Sorrow, merely an element of human education, through which we struggle to a higher and purer state than we could otherwise have attained? Did Adam fall, that we might ultimately rise to a far loftier Paradise than his?" (*Works* IV, 460). To this, the Puritanical Hilda responds, "This is terrible; and I could weep for you, if you indeed believe it. Do not you perceive what a mockery your creed makes, not only of all religious sentiment, but of moral law, and how it annuls and obliterates whatever precepts of Heaven are written deepest within us? You have shocked me beyond words!" (*Works* IV, 460).

Is Miriam speaking for Hawthorne? Or is Kenyon? Whose perspective does Hilda echo? The novel does not give a clear, unequivocal resolution to these sublime mysteries. At the very least, Hawthorne seems to concur, as the novel shows, that although God is not the author of evil, He is able to bring good from it. The Fall can never be sufficiently condemned and lamented; likewise, when all its consequences are considered, it can never be sufficiently celebrated (Kehl 2013: 28–30).

The Marble Faun is not only Hawthorne's most perplexing novel but also his boldest and most geographically expansive. Written with great love, he drew upon his time in Rome with sylvan interludes in Tuscany and the Campagna. More than two-thirds consists of wave after wave of vivid details about Italian landscapes, art and architecture adapted from his notebooks; in fact, it is illuminating to trace his creative process by comparing the final text with his sources – as Brenda Wineapple (*The New York Times*, 1 November 1998) and Alba Amoia (*The Nathaniel Hawthorne Review*, Spring 1998) have done. Views of papal and ancient Rome, of various Italian objects – antique, pictorial, and statuesque – "fill the mind, everywhere in Italy, and especially in Rome," Hawthorne wrote, "and cannot easily be kept from flowing out upon the page" (*Works* IV, 3).

Much of Hawthorne's Rome still remains unchanged. In the late-nineteenth-century, like all good pilgrims, American tourists to the Eternal City often took along handsomely illustrated editions of *The Marble Faun*, as I have done on three occasions, as a guidebook to the city, to retrace the steps of the main characters and therefore, of Hawthorne himself. One of my literature professors who taught this novel urged us to concentrate on mapping out the characters' movement, particularly where they intersect. My own students do the same; and I am now referring to that sketch as I recall some of the Roman landmarks that accompany the action in the novel.

The Italians have an expression for a quality in art that the English language has still not found an equivalent word: sprezzature or the ability of an artist to make his work seem effortless. Hawthorne displays this everywhere in *The Marble Faun*. Here, he follows the painter's technique, who puts on canvas those features essential to the setting. Each one as Hawthorne describes it is entirely real. Who can forget his accounts of St. Peter's, the Via dei Portoghesi, the Barberini Palace, the Church of the Cappuchini and the Cappuchini cemetery, the Pantheon, the Colosseum, the Catacombs of San Callisto, the Pincian Hill, the Campagna, the Trinita dei Monti church, the Capitoline Hill, the Carnival, the Fountain of Trevi, or the superbly dramatic chapter at the Tarpeian Rock (which he first saw by moonlight in the company of the Swedish novelist Frederica Bremer)?

As every visitor soon discovers, Rome's long indelible past is always a part of its present. Hawthorne excels in showing his characters in relation to the setting. Paragraph by paragraph, page by page, the scenes are sensorial delights.

His examination of the influence of European culture on American travelers laid the groundwork for later gems of American travel-writing, like Mark Twain's *The Innocents Abroad* (1869) and the novels of Henry James, such as *Roderick Hudson* (1875) and *The Portrait of a Lady* (1881).

But my students must be careful. So much has been written about what's exceptional within the novel's pages – the mystery, the questions, the characters, the settings – that it is easy to lose sight of the man behind the work. We can't separate the dancer from the dance. We must study the artist in order to know the work. What led to its writing? What did Hawthorne intend? What was he looking for?

To recapture the circumstances under which he wrote *The Marble Faun*, I once again invite my students to sit back and project themselves across a wide stretch of time. Hawthorne's Italian novel is a bridge between two languages as well as between two cultures. Reading it requires an informed understanding of the places and time in which the narrative was shaped. Otherwise, we risk judging the past by the standards of the present or basing our interpretation on a myopic worldview. The farther afield culturally or the further back in time we go, the greater the effort we must put in to see the narrative through the prism of the time in which it was created. "You must remove your 21st-century eyeglasses," I remind them, "and be transformed into readers of an earlier time and place."

Everything Hawthorne had experienced up to this moment laid the foundation for future events. He couldn't have developed the prescience at the time, of course, but what he did and saw and thought during the previous 53 years prepared him for the opportunities he would have and the people he would meet while abroad. Had he failed in his academic studies, re-directed his ambitions as a writer, never met and married Sophia, he wouldn't have enjoyed the positive transformations that the experience would bring to his life and work. "What we are doing now," I say to my students, "is preparing ourselves for people we will meet and opportunities we will have ten, twenty, thirty or more years later." That's a wonderful philosophy, and Hawthorne embraced it fervently.

We start in the year 1853 when Franklin Pierce had become the fourteenth president of the United States. Eleven days later, in return for Hawthorne's loyalty to the Democratic Party and, more particularly, for the campaign biography that he had written (along with the encouragement of Ticknor), President Pierce offered him the coveted (and hoped for) position as United States Consul at Liverpool. He would begin the assignment on 1 August, replacing Col. Thomas Crittenden of Kentucky. The area he covered would extend to include the town of Manchester and thereby increase his annual salary by another $3000.

Hawthorne knew his ancestral home of England well, but only through the works of Shakespeare and Wordsworth and Shelley. Here, at last, was an opportunity to travel overseas and escape the various nets of his Puritan past. He accepted the assignment to favor his friend Pierce, take advantage of the financial security it promised, and learn about the customs and social fabric of the Continent. He could also fulfill Sophia's long-cherished dream of visiting a part of the world (especially Italy) that she had appreciated since she was 15, when she had begun to study drawing and read *Corinne, or Italy* (1807), Madame de Staël's fictionalized Anglo-American guidebook to Rome. Given his weariness of literary effort, he thought the experience abroad might also inspire him with ideas and plots for future work. Perhaps he would recapture his muse.

The history of Liverpool goes back to 1190 when the site was called "Liuerpul," meaning a pool or creek with muddy water. The borough, founded by royal charter in 1207 by King John, comprised seven streets in the shape of the letter "H." It remained a small settlement until its trade with Ireland, and coastal parts of England and Wales was overtaken by trade with Africa and the West Indies, which included the slave trade (ironically, given Hawthorne's strong feelings against slavery). The world's first wet dock was opened in 1715 and Liverpool's expansion continued. By the start of the 1800s, a large volume of trade was passing through, and the Liverpool and Manchester Railway was opened in 1830. The population grew rapidly, from 77 000 in 1801 to nearly 400 000 in 1853, and the place had earned a reputation as "the second city of the Empire" and "the New York of Europe." The importance of commercial and political links between Liverpool and the United States (just in 1851, a thousand ships sailed from there to the New World), made this indeed a prestigious appointment – and both Hawthorne and his wife knew it (Seed 2020: xiii).

At 12 noon on 6 July, therefore, after two months of frenzied preparations, 49-year-old Nathaniel, along with Sophia, their three children, servants Mary and Ellen Hearne, and publisher William D. Ticknor set sail from Boston Harbor for England aboard the 150-passenger Cunard Line ship *Niagara*. Hawthorne was accorded the honor of a seat at the Captain's table. Captain Leitch, one of the most popular of the Cunard Commanders, was the same man to guide the Hawthornes home seven years later.

They arrived in Liverpool on Sunday morning, 17 July. He would hold the post for four years (1853–1857), remain in England two years longer, travel to France, live two winters in Rome, summer and autumn in Florence, before returning to England. He would then return to Concord on 28 June 1860, with $20,000 in savings and a newly published novel that soon became an international bestseller.

During those seven years, he also produced two voluminous books – *The English Note-books* (covering 1853–1860) and *The French and Italian Note-books* (1858–1859) – and collected material for what would become the charming and at times contentious *Our Old Home* (1863), a counterpart to Washington Irving's *Sketch-Book*. (These books rivaled those of Irving, the first American author to make a living from his work.)

Elegant, provocative, and entertaining, his nonfiction from this time gives an expatriate's point of view, with perceptive observations about writers of his time, portraits of family and acquaintances, as well as reminiscences of his frequent wanderings. Moreover, *The French and Italian Note-books* became a source for *The Marble Faun* and, as Henry James observed, for his sometimes ambivalent but ultimately celebratory response to European civilization's aesthetic and historical legacy. He could never have written this novel, James said, had he not spent "many hours of exquisite appreciation of the lovely land of Italy" (1984 [1879]: 126).

To a man with such powers of observation and such desire for using them, his time in Liverpool presented all sorts of challenges to which he rose with remarkable energy and conscientiousness. He wrote:

> The duties of the office carried me to prisons, police-courts, hospitals, lunatic asylums, coroner's inquests, death-beds, funerals, and brought me in contact with insane people, criminals, ruined speculators, wild adventurers, diplomatists, brother-consuls, and all manner of simpletons and unfortunates, in greater number and variety than I had ever dreamed of as pertaining to America; in addition to whom there was an equivalent multitude of English rogues, dexterously counterfeiting the genuine Yankee article. (*Works* V, 31)

His six-hour days at the Consulate office, on the other hand, were, for the most part routine, not unlike those he had performed at the Boston and Salem Custom Houses, though the work was far more important and demanded patience. From his fifteen-feet-square "dusky and stifled chamber" on the second floor of the Washington Buildings, Brunswick Street, near the old docks, he wrote close to a hundred official dispatches to the State Department (which have been collected and published) related to the consulate business (*Works* V, 9).

As Consul, too, he was obliged to meet every visiting American, some of whom sought just to satisfy their ego by having an audience with Hawthorne. At times, he solved the many problems they presented – deaths, crimes, breakdowns. On occasion, he had to pay out of his own pocket to support shipwrecked sailors and half-mad vagabonds. He paid for seamen's funerals and had to wait for reimbursement, which was often delayed. One recurring mercantile issue concerned conflicts between American seamen and their officers, and Hawthorne treated this matter with such seriousness that he wrote to the State Department about it. He concluded the "Consular Experiences" in *Our Old Home* with the words: "Liverpool, though not very delightful as a place of residence, is a most convenient and admirable point to get away from" (*Works* V, 39–40).

His reputation had preceded his arrival. *Tanglewood Tales* (1853) and the reissue of *Mosses from an Old Manse* (1854) kept increasing his fame, and rightly so.

The popularity of *The Scarlet Letter* and *The House of the Seven Gables*, both of which had been pirated and sold throughout the country, helped to open the door to the city's leading citizens. Moreover, his presence was expected at a succession of dinner parties, house tours, and civic banquets, considering that the American Consul at Liverpool was a public personage.

He was invited, for example, to a state dinner given by the Mayor to the judges and the grand jury. Called upon to speak, Hawthorne – who didn't like being lionized, ever reluctant to participate on such occasions – chronicled his experience from 15 August 1853:

> Afterwards the Bar, and various other dignitaries and institutions were toasted; and by-and-by came a toast to the United States and me as their representative. Hereupon, either "Hail Columbia" or "Yankee Doodle," or some other of our national tunes (but Heaven knows which) was played; and at the conclusion – being cornered, and with no alternative – I got upon my legs and made a response. They received me and listened to my nonsense with a good deal of rapping; and my speech seemed to give great satisfaction. My chief difficulty lay in not knowing how to pitch my voice to the size of the room; as for the matter, it is not of the slightest consequence. Any body may make an after-dinner speech, who will be content to talk onward without saying anything. My speech was not more than two or three inches long; – and considering that I did not know a soul there, except the Mayor himself, and that I am wholly unpractised in all sorts of oratory, and that I had nothing to say, it was quite successful. I hardly thought it was in me; but being once on my legs, I felt no embarrassment, and went through it as coolly as if I were going to be hanged. (*Works* XXI, 17–18)

It is noteworthy that he was also one of the finest novelists of his generation, and we have some measure of the true distinction of a remarkable man who, with grace, elegance, humor, and genuine modesty (as the above passage conveys), would never have admitted to having been in any way exceptional.

But a public man must also learn to find the luxury of contemplative time. When he could, his favorite leisure activity, like some of his characters (I think, for example, of the protagonist in "Sights from the Steeple" and "Wakefield"), was strolling through the city. He became the perennial observer seeking out "the darker and dingier streets," the most interesting sites in any place, "inhabited by the poorer classes" (*Works* XXII, 18). To his credit, he wrote of these walks with an uneasy mixture of fascination and fear: "The scenes there are very picturesque in their way; at every two or three steps, a ginshop; also filthy in clothes and person, ragged, pale, often afflicted with humors; women, nursing their babies at dirty bosoms; men haggard, drunken, care-worn, hopeless, but with a kind of patience, as if all this were the rule of their life" (*Works* XXII, 18–19).

A favorite haunt was Henry Young's bookshop on Castle Street, where he sometimes met with his friend, Henry Bright. Over time, the nook where the two met came to be known as "Hawthorne's corner." The proprietor, Henry Young, recalled:

> [This] dark-haired, remarkably quiet, gentlemanly looking man . . . walked into my shop and, without saying a word to any person or any person speaking to him, proceeded to investigate the books. In a little time he took from the shelf a [sic] uncut copy of *Don Quixote* in two volumes, illustrated by Tony Johannot, asked me the price, paid me the money and requested me to send the book to Mr. Hawthorne at the American Consulate. . . After a while he became more familiar and would ask about some of the rarer books, but more for information than purchase. (Griffiths 1918: 57–58)

Detailed vignettes of the Mersey ferries, the Necropolis, the West Derby Workhouse, Conway Castle, Furness Abbey, itinerant musicians, and numerous other city scenes also stirred his imagination, causing him to feel that his life had eventually been deepened and enhanced.

At such times, the inevitable prejudices of Salem and Concord seemed far, far away. In a journal entry from 28 December 1854, sitting at the fireside with his family close by, he expressed contentment as he reflected on Christmas day:

> For a long, long while, I have occasionally been visited with a singular dream; and I have an impression that I have dreamed it, ever since I have been in England. It is, that I am still in college – or, sometimes, even at school – and there is a sense that I have been there unconscionably long, and have quite failed to make such progress in life as my contemporaries have; and I seem to meet some of them with a feeling of shame and depression that broods over me, when I think of it, even at this moment. This dream, recurring all through these twenty or thirty years, must be one of the effects of that heavy seclusion in which I shut myself up for twelve years, after leaving college, when everybody moved onward and left me behind. How strange that it should come now, when I may call myself famous and prosperous! – when I am happy, too – still that same dream of life hopelessly a failure!" (*Works* XXI, 148–149)

Though it took some time to adjust, he eventually came to appreciate the appeal of English life. He was helped by his constant companion, Francis Bennoch, a merchant of Wood Street, Cheapside, London, whose house his family would occupy during the summer of 1856. Kind, hospitable and generous, he watched over Hawthorne "like a brother . . . constantly planning a day's happiness for his friend" after Ticknor had left for America (Fields 1872: 77, 89).

Bennoch also emerged as the inspiration behind one of the subordinate characters in the posthumously published *Dr. Grimshawe's Secret* (1882). After her husband's death, Sophia inscribed her edition of *Passages from the English Notes* (1871) to "Francis Bennoch, Esq., the dear and valued friend, who by his generous and genial hospitality and unfailing sympathy, contributed so largely (as is attested by the book itself) to render Mr. Hawthorne's residence in England agreeable and homelike" (Ticknor 1913: 65).

Two years into their stay, on 5 September 1855, Hawthorne and Sophia finally made the first of several visits to London – in his words, "the dream-city of my youth" (*Works* V, 215) and "a world in itself" (Ticknor 1913: 51). On 23 November 1855, he told Ticknor, "I think I never should be weary of London, and it will cost me many pangs to quit it finally, without a prospect of returning. It is singular, that I feel more at home and familiar there, than even in Boston, or in old Salem itself. Being the great metropolis of the world, it is every man's home" (*Works* XVII, 409).

I remember my own feelings when first visiting there in January 1973 to begin chronicling Hawthorne's international travels and the comfort it gave me to say, as he implied about his own initial visit, that I genuinely felt at home in this vibrant, intriguing, noisy, sprawling, compelling metropolis. Like Hawthorne, the moment my feet touched the ground, I sensed that I belonged there, glad to be walking the same streets that he walked, visiting many of the sites he came to know, staying where he stayed.

Europe and London certainly became a source of literary inspiration for Hawthorne. Now more than 45 years and many visits later, I can imagine a scene that represents what London specifically and the Continent generally mean to me. I could picture myself lost in a maze of winding streets on a dark, cold night, suddenly seeing a castle on a hill with warm light blazing from all its windows. From many centuries come the emblematic sounds of music and voices as I walk nearer. I somehow feel a comforting assurance that there is food and warmth inside the castle and that I will hear the music clearly and talk with its inhabitants plainly. This image might resonate within anyone who has been there. Certainly, it would have with Hawthorne.

One cannot experience life abroad without respecting the overarching influence of history. Hawthorne went on literary pilgrimages to the sites related to writers whose work he knew and admired, including the likes of Pope, Johnson, Goldsmith, Wordsworth, Coleridge, and De Quincey. He attempted to trace his own lineage and searched for his surname, albeit without success, on a tombstone in an ancient graveyard. He wrote in his notebook from the time: "My ancestor left

England in 1630. I return in 1853. I sometimes feel as if I myself had been absent those two hundred and eighteen years [*sic*] – leaving England just emerging from the feudal system, and finding it on the verge of Republicanism. It brings the two far separated points of time very closely together, to view the matter thus" (*Works* XXI, 138).

I can understand his intense longing to find his ancestors. Over the years, I have come upon the resting places of numerous literary luminaries. Standing on these hallowed grounds, I try to connect what I know of the writer with the mortal body that lies buried. Once, I chanced upon a slim volume in the British Library that led me to the burial site of one of my ancestors on the maternal side: Stephen Bachiler, born in 1561 in southern England. A man of character and unusual accomplishments, he entered St. John's College, Oxford when he was twenty. Following his graduation with a B.A. in 1586, he settled as Vicar of The Church of the Holy Cross and St. Peter in the little village of Wherwell, Hampshire, on the River Test, where he became sympathetic to the beliefs and problems of the Puritans.

While unsuccessful in finding the gravestones of the original William Hathorne, Hawthorne began considering the story of an American character named Middleton, who seeks out his ancestral home in the hope that he might now prove to be its heir. This became the theme underpinning two later abandoned works, *The Ancestral Footstep* and *Doctor Grimshaw's Secret*. On 12 April 1855, he even began to sketch the idea of a new romance. In a journal entry, he set down a brief outline for the plot:

> In my Romance, the original emigrant to America may have carried away with him a family-secret, whereby it was in his power (had he so chosen) to have brought about the ruin of the family. This secret he transmits to his American progeny, by whom it is inherited throughout all the intervening generations. At last, the hero of the Romance comes to England, and finds that, by means of this secret, he still has it in his power to procure the downfal [*sic*] of the family. It would be something similar to the [Greek] story of Meleager, whose fate depended on the firebrand that his mother had snatched out of the flames. (*Works* XXI, 162)

He would soon abandon this, however, because his creative instincts were drawing him toward a different theme. He later picked it up again, unsuccessfully, when back in Concord.

The same month (7 April) while dining at the home of Liverpool friends, Mr. and Mrs. J.P. Heywood, he met Mr. and Mrs. Peter Ainsworth of Smithills Hall, who told him about a legend that provided the central haunting image in his proposed new romance. When Catholic Queen Mary occupied the throne in 1553, many Protestants left the country to escape persecution, but the

Protestant curate George Marsh continued preaching. He was arrested, examined, condemned, and burned at stake for heresy in April 1555. As he left Smithills Hall, where he had been questioned, he stamped his foot on the flagstone outside of what is now the Withdrawing Room, as a declaration of his faith and refusal to convert to Catholicism. Blood issued from his foot, slid along the stone pavement, and left a "footprint of faith" printed in blood. "[T]here it has remained ever since," Hawthorne wrote in his journal, "in spite of the scrubbings of all after generations" (*Works* XXI, 160). Above the footprint hangs a plaque that reads: "FOOTPRINT of the Reverend George Marsh of Deane MARTYR Who was examined at Smithills and burnt at Chester in the Reign of Queen Mary."

Smithills Hall remains one of the oldest and best-preserved manor houses in the North West of England in Bolton, Lancashire, on the edge of the West Pennine Moors. In August, following that dinner, Hawthorne visited the Hall and saw the footprint. At one of the rear entrances, the impression (preserved in a glass and metal frame) still exists in a noticeable flagstone measuring two to three feet square. Clearly visible as a dark-brown stain in the smooth gray surface of the stone, it is said to bleed once a year.

In London, some of Hawthorne's most contented hours were passed alone in long rambles through innumerable narrow lanes and courtyards, where no one greeted him and where he could study faces and behavior, soaking up the scenes while "peeping into all the odd holes and corners" he could find (*Works* XVII, 387). On 6 December 1857, he wrote:

> I have walked the streets a great deal in the dull November days, and always take a certain pleasure in being in the midst of human life, – as closely encompassed by it as it is possible to be anywhere in this world; and in that way of viewing it there is a dull and sombre enjoyment always to be had in Holborn, Fleet Street, Cheapside, and the other busiest parts of London. It is human life; it is this material world; it is a grim and heavy reality. I have never had the same sense of being surrounded by materialisms and hemmed in with the grossness of this earthly existence anywhere else; these broad, crowded streets are so evidently the veins and arteries of an enormous city. London is evidenced in every one of them, just as a megatherium is in each of its separate bones, even if they be small ones. Thus I never fail of a sort of self-congratulation in finding myself, for instance, passing along Ludgate Hill. (*Works* XXII, 368)

In many ways, the scenes Hawthorne described resemble the urban life I came to know during my travels there 116 years later. London still teems with people from diverse backgrounds and classes. Little has changed.

Back in Liverpool, its gray skies, damp air, and frigid weather – as if right out of a Charles Dickens novel – proved to be detrimental to his wife's always fragile health. During their second winter, Sophia developed a serious bronchial infection. It was decided that she and the girls with their companion and tutor, the American governess Ada Shephard, should spend the next nine months in the southern climate of Portugal, at the home of Hawthorne's friend, former publisher, and United States minister to the Court of Lisbon, John O'Sullivan and wife, Susan, with a side trip to Madeira. Therefore, on 12 October 1855, they departed from Southampton aboard the steamer *Madrid*, leaving Nathaniel and son behind in Liverpool, at Blodgett's boarding-house, 133–135 Duke Street. Given that it was the first time in 13 years that husband and wife had suffered such a separation, they were both crestfallen.

On 7 April 1856, he wrote to her: "Oh, my wife, I do want thee so intolerably. Nothing else is real, except the bond between thee and me. The people around me are but shadows. I am myself but a shadow, till thou takest me in thy arms, and convertest me into substance. Till thou comest back, I do but walk in a dream" (*Works* XVII, 465). In another entry (dated 16 January), he wrote: "Nothing gives me any joy . . . I am like an uprooted plant, wilted and drooping. Life seems so purposeless as not to be worth the trouble of carrying it any further" (*Works* XXI, 407).

Their letters also retail day-to-day activities, share news about the children, and send endearments. In others, Hawthorne constantly refers to her illness, offering advice. Though written more than 160 years ago, these letters have timeless appeal: they seem to speak to us as directly and urgently as if we were overhearing present-day confidences. Their language is imaginative, passionate, full of wit and, sometimes, highly erotic. Such vividly individual letters focus our attention and bring to life the circumstances that shaped them.

On 12 June 1856, Sophia returned to her husband, restored to health and full of restless energy and longing to visit the Continent. That opportunity soon presented itself. Pierce had lost the Democratic nomination for President. On 13 February 1857, Hawthorne submitted his letter of resignation, and on 12 October 1857 gave the office up to his replacement, Nathaniel Beverley Tucker from Virginia, who remained consul until 1861.

Hawthorne left England with his family on a bone-piercing, chilly 5 January 1858, in the coldest winter for 20 years in Paris and Rome. After a brief stay in Paris and Marseilles, they moved on to Rome, arriving on 20 January at midnight, half-frozen in the wintry rain. Except for a summertime stay in Florence, they lived there for a year and four months, settling into a ten-room suite at 37, Via Porta Pinciana.

Finally, after years of hoping, Sophia's dream was coming to fruition. She wrote to her sister Elizabeth of her deep and tender acquaintance with the eternal city:

"I am in Rome – Rome, <u>Roma</u> – I have stood in the Forum, & beneath the Arch of Titus at the end of the Sacra Via. I have wondered about the Coliseum [*sic*], the stupendous grandeur of which equals my dream & hope & I have seen the sun kindling the open courts of the Temple of Peace, where Sarah [Clarke] said years ago – that my children ought to play" (*Works* XIV, 906).

Unlike his wife, Nathaniel did not fall speedily in love with the Eternal City, but quite the reverse. Europe had not figured previously in his thoughts or in his fiction, other than in Dimmesdale's invitation to find life in pleasant Italy and in Clifford Pyncheon, who proposes leaving the dismal House of the Seven Gables to live in Paris, Naples, Venice, and Rome. Nathaniel reacted adversely to the weather (he developed a cold on arrival) and disliked what he saw (dated 3 February 1858): "Cold, nastiness, evil smells, narrow lanes between tall, ugly, mean-looking, white-washed houses, sour bread, pavement, most uncomfortable to the feet, enormous prices for poor living, beggars, pickpockets, ancient temples and broken monuments with filth at the base, and clothes hanging to dry about them, French soldiers, monks, and priests of every degree, a shabby population smoking bad cigars" (*Works* XIV, 54). He deplored the nude statues (of Venus, for example) and paintings as well as the city's overall noise and filth: "old Rome does seem to lie here like a dead and mostly decayed corpse," he continued 3 February 1858, "retaining here and there a trace of the noble shape it was, but with a sort of fungous [*sic*] growth upon it, and no life but of the worms that creep in and out" (*Works* XIV, 54). His health continued to suffer: "I never knew that I had either bowels or lungs, till I came to Rome," he wrote to Ticknor on 4 March 1859, "but I have found it out now, to my cost" (*Works* XVIII, 163).

In the meantime, Hawthorne's presence in Rome did not go unnoticed. Writing under the pseudonym "Pericles," *The New York Times* correspondent for 4 April 1859 stated: "Hawthorne I frequently see in the street, swinging along in a sort of land-measuring pace, smoking, and occasionally looking out from under his shaggy brow and otherwise tenacious face." He also reported that Hawthorne seems "to be engaged on some new work, the subject of which is not even known to his wife" (Mays 1983: 187).

Yet Nathaniel's spirits were restored with the onset of spring. Although he had little feeling for art, to please his wife he visited museums, galleries, ancient sites, gardens, cathedrals, and catacombs – sometimes with the children, sometimes with Sophia alone – unconsciously collecting majestic images that would soon be coalesced into his new novel. He was impressed by the value of the Catholic Church (which figures prominently in *The Marble Faun*), concluding that its form of worship, available anytime day or night, meant that "a great deal of devout and reverential feeling is kept alive in people's hearts" (*Works* XIV, 98). He called the confessional the "most precious privilege of all," and used it in the novel to allow one of his characters, Hilda, to find peace for her troubled conscience (*Works* IV,

355). Toward the Church Hawthorne's attitude, like Hilda's, was a grateful appreciation for the solace that it offered to its participants.

At nighttime, they strolled all the way to the Fountain of Trevi and saw the statue of Neptune, God of the sea, and the Grand Arch of Constantine. As in England, he kept recording his observations of scenes and persons in a notebook.

His company was largely confined to other Americans living abroad (there were 1500 in Rome at the time). He met only a few Italians. Although he paid attention to political developments, including the founding of a revolutionary Roman republic in 1848, its suppression by the French invasion of 1849, and the process of national unification in 1859–1860, his interest was aesthetic, not political. He befriended sculptor William Wetmore Story and his wife Emelyn, as well as poets William Cullen Bryant and Robert and Elizabeth Browning. He also met with a small cadre of American artists including Cephas Thompson, Benjamin Akers, Emma Stebbins, Louise Lander, and Harriet Hosmer. Then, one day he saw something that transformed his outlook.

On 18 April 1858, Hawthorne awoke to Rome as a possible setting for the romance growing in his mind. As the family visited the Villa Borghese, he made a great discovery: two statues of Fauns, one copied from Praxiteles. What he saw became an obsessive image, his *donnée*, for the novel to come: "I like these strange, sweet, playful, rustic creatures, almost entirely human as they are, yet linked so prettily, without monstrosity, to the lower tribes by the long, furry ears, or by a modest tail; indicating a strain of honest wildness in them. Their character has never, that I know of, been wrought out in literature; and something very good, funny, and philosophical, as well as poetic, might very likely be educed from them" (*Works* XIV, 173).

On 22 April, he looked at the Praxiteles original in the sculpture gallery of the Capitol. The charming likeness of a Faun, or Resting Satyr, dating back to the fourth-century BC, looked human until one saw the pointed ears and tail. Hawthorne, however, was not shocked. The figure conveyed an ease like that of Eden, he said, reinforcing the lighter side of the animalistic instinct of humanity, "with something of a divine character intermingled." He saw the Faun as "neither man nor animal, and yet no monster, but a being in whom both races meet on friendly ground." "I can do something with this," he thought, and he would. In the novel, the faun-like Donatello seems to have "nothing to do with time" and to have a "look of eternal youth in his face." He appears almost part animal rather than altogether human, albeit "in a high and beautiful sense," immature and simple, a child of nature. Hawthorne revisited the Capitol on 30 April and took notes because, he wrote, "the idea keeps recurring to me of writing a little Romance about it" (*Works* XIV, 178–179, 191–192).

In May, the family moved to Florence for the summer, where he worked haltingly at the new romance. On 1 August, they moved again to the north, where they stayed for the next two months at the Villa Montano while he continued to sketch out the new book. On Friday, 1 October 1858, they left, with their sights set again on the Eternal City, settling with the family in a seven-room apartment at 68 Piazza Poli. By February, he had completed a rough draft.

Of his new book, Hawthorne told Ticknor on 6 April 1860 that he had never "thought or felt more deeply, or taken more pains" (*Works* XVIII, 262). He carried some apprehension about it, considering the fact that his last work of fiction, *The Blithedale Romance*, had appeared seven years earlier. On 4 March 1859, he had confessed to Ticknor: "I shall do my best upon it, you may be sure; for I feel that I shall come before the public, after so long an interval, with all the uncertainties of a new author. If I were only rich enough, I do not believe I should ever publish another book" (*Works* XVIII, 164).

All during this time, much weighed upon him. He had recently lost people he cared about, including his sister Louisa and friend Margaret Fuller by drowning, his mother, as well as Sophia's mother on 11 January 1853 and father on 1 January 1855. He was also profoundly worried about the United States as it moved toward Civil War, writing to Ticknor on 7 July 1854: "[Y]ou seem to be in such a confounded muss there, that it quite sickens me to think of coming back. I find it impossible to read American newspapers (of whatever political party) without being ashamed of my country. No wonder, then, if Englishmen hate and despise us, taking their ideas of us and our institutions from such sources" (*Works* XVII, 237).

Then on 24 October 1858, his eldest daughter, Una, while on a sketching expedition at the Colosseum, contracted malaria (the Roman Fever) and almost died. She took until 27 February 1859 to recover, though not fully. "Carriages were constantly driving to the door with enquiries," Sophia recalled. "People were always coming . . . Magnificent flowers were always coming, baskets and bouquets, which were presented with tearful eyes . . . Everyone who had seen Una in society or anywhere came to ask" (Lathrop 1923 [1897]: 370).

At the peak of the family's anxiety, Franklin Pierce arrived with his wife, Jane. The presence of his old friend was a great morale booster for Hawthorne and the entire family, although Pierce was now showing signs of advancing age. The man had become a mere shadow of himself. Tragically, just before taking office Pierce had lost a son in a railway accident, and two more sons had died afterwards. These losses weighed heavily on the Pierces.

On 19 April 1859, the day of Pierce's departure, Hawthorne recorded in his journal what the visit had meant to him. "Never having had any trouble, before, that pierce into my very vitals," he said, "I did not know what comfort there might be in the manly sympathy of a friend; but Pierce has undergone so great a sorrow of his own, and has so large and kindly a heart, and is so tender and so strong, that he really did us good, and I shall always love him the better for the recollection of these dark days. Thank God, the thing we dreaded did not come to pass" (*Works*

XIV, 518). There's reason to believe that Pierce's arrival was a necessary catalyst for completing the new novel.

The family returned to England on 23 June 1858, where they finally settled upon the tiny seaside town of Redcar in Yorkshire on 6 October 1859 – "the most secluded spot [he] ever met with" (*Works* XVIII, 192). The Hawthornes welcomed the privacy as Nathaniel prepared the manuscript of his Italian romance for the publishers. Sophia read and re-read it while encouraging her husband to reassert himself as the writer he'd not been for seven years. Though he had hoped to return home in July, work on his book stretched into weeks. He wrote to Ticknor on 6 October: "I have been constantly occupied with my book, which required more work to be done upon it than I supposed. I am now, I think, within a fortnight of finishing it" (*Works* XVIII, 191). On 8 November 1859, in her journal Sophia recorded that her husband had completed the book. He stayed to oversee its publication in England (with the title *The Transformation*).

Retrospectively, he says in his much-studied preface that Italy was "chiefly valuable" to him as the setting since it afforded him "a sort of poetic or fairy precinct, where actualities would not be so terribly insisted upon, as they are, and must needs be, in America" (*Works* IV, 3). He hoped to inspire in the reader, he says in the opening chapter, "a vague sense of ponderous remembrances; a perception of such weight and density in a by-gone life . . . that the present moment is pressed down or crowded out, and our individual affairs and interests" would therefore become less real (*Works* IV, 6). He laments that in his native land, "No author without a trial, can conceive of the difficulty of writing a Romance about a country where there is no shadow, no antiquity, no mystery, no picturesque and gloomy wrong, nor anything but a common-place prosperity, in broad and simple daylight, as is happily the case with my dear native land" (*Works* IV, 3). No place ever took so strong a hold on his being. Hawthorne considered it his best work.

The book was published first in England (by Smith, Elder & Co., which paid £600 for the English copyright) on 28 February 1860, as *The Transformation*. In early March, it was published in America by Ticknor and Fields as *The Marble Faun: Or, The Romance of Monte Beni*, to overwhelming praise. In the *Atlantic Monthly* for April 1860, James Russell Lowell called Hawthorne the nineteenth-century's "purely original writer" and Donatello the most imaginative character in the book. The novel embodied, he wrote, "the most august truths of psychology, with the most pregnant facts of modern history" (Crowley 1970: 321, 322). Henry James (1984 [1879]), who considered Hawthorne America's first outstanding contribution to national literature of its own, later commended *The Marble Faun* for its "light threads of symbolism" and said that "some of the finest pages in all Hawthorne are to be found in it" (132, 133).

As it turned out, the American edition sold 14 500 copies before the end of the year. The size of the English print run is unknown. "I have been much gratified by the kind feeling and generous praise contained in the notices you send me," he wrote to Ticknor on 6 April. "After so long absence and silence, I like to be praised too much. It sounds like a welcome back among my friends" (*Works* XVIII, 262).

The overall consensus was that Hawthorne was again at the top of his form. He had recovered his muse. Life in England had helped him throw off the shackles of New England experience and of his shameful Puritan past to embrace a deeper, broader past and present, that of Rome itself. What could he possibly teach the Europeans? He came from an exceptionally young and, as some would suggest, naïve country. He came to learn and then take what he learned, filter it through the magic of his fertile imagination, and produce the novel.

Hawthorne leaves many questions unanswered. What was Miriam's past history? What was the model's claim upon her? What passed between them when she knelt before him after her Sylvan dance? How did the model's corpse get into the Church of the Capuchins? What role did she play in Donotello's eventual incarceration? By now, these mysteries and more should no longer take us by surprise. They are the author's way of reminding us, as he has done throughout his career, that life is ambiguous and that there aren't always easy answers to the questions thrown at us. "The actual experience of even the most ordinary life," he writes, "is full of events that never explain themselves, either as regards their origin or their tendency" (*Works* IV, 455).

Although the novel leaves us in the company of many long-standing mysteries, with patience they can also provide intense pleasure. From such explorations of what a work of art really offers – where it comes from, how it succeeds or fails – students develop a respect for the gamut of meanings behind words and a genuine appreciation for the richness of languages and cultures other than their own. And, perhaps most importantly, they learn to examine the evidence in any text before rushing to form their opinions about its accuracy, its truth, and its implications.

On 16 June 1860, as the Hawthornes prepared to leave the Continent along with the Fieldses aboard the *Europa*, the sister ship of the *Niagara*, no doubt he sensed that he would not be returning. It must have engulfed him with melancholy, a foreboding of transience, as it now does for us as we continue to follow his journey and look to his final years. All good things, after all, have to come to an end.

13

The Final Years (1860–1864)

The Wayside, complete with author's tower, 1861. Source: Nathaniel Hawthorne's house - The Wayside/Lebrecht Authors/Bridgeman Images.

> *Some strange, vast, sombre, mysterious truth, which he seemed to have searched for long, appeared to be on the point of being revealed to him; a sense of something to come; something to happen that had been waiting long, long to happen; an opening of doors, a drawing away of veils, a lifting of heavy, magnificent curtains, whose dark folds hung before a spectacle of awe; – it was like the verge of the grave.*
>
> —Nathaniel Hawthorne (1883), *Doctor Grimshawe's Secret* (270)

"Nothing gold can stay" (1923), said Robert Frost in a poem by the same title, a reality Hawthorne confronted with growing concern in his own work, as indeed we must face in ours. Like him, who knew so well the absorbing satisfaction of the creative instinct, we discover how quickly time passes if we are immersed in what

The Life of the Author: Nathaniel Hawthorne, First Edition. Dale Salwak.
© 2023 John Wiley & Sons Ltd. Published 2023 by John Wiley & Sons Ltd.

we love to do. If we find our true calling, and recognize that we have a purpose that guides our very existence, then we don't want its challenges and pleasures to end.

Throughout his adult life, Hawthorne had aspired to and worked toward literary success as a way to support himself and his family while enriching the lives of his readers. After his profound dissatisfaction with *Fanshawe* and the subsequent false starts and blockages that all writers encounter, the publication of *The Scarlet Letter* and many wondrous tales brought him fame and relative security, albeit accompanied by the censure of some fellow New England readers. While fascinated with his ambiguities, they resented his depiction of their Puritan past and their portrayal in the preface.

Still unsure of himself and his future, Hawthorne began a search for a better understanding of his artistic identity. This prompted him to delve deep into New England's past with *The House of the Seven Gables*; then to Brook Farm and the resulting *The Blithedale Romance*; then, he sought artistic nourishment in England, France, and Italy among a group of American expatriates, leading to *The Marble Faun*; and finally, he returned to Concord on 28 June 1860 – feeling apathetic, unstrung, and creatively spent, no longer a man of radiant spirits. Although he would start four fresh novels, he finished none of them. Much to his distress, he was facing what most creative geniuses dread: the decline of his powers. Intimations of mortality, which had haunted him his entire life, now seemed ever closer.

While resuming life at The Wayside, the first and only piece of real estate he ever owned (and the eighth home he lived in), 56-year-old Nathaniel felt that the end of his time was near. In *The Marble Faun*, the narrator (speaking for Hawthorne) reflects tellingly on the personal impact of the expatriate's life:

> [T]he years, after all, have a kind of emptiness, when we spend too many of them on a foreign shore. We defer the reality of life, in such cases, until a future moment, when we shall again breathe our native air; but by-and-by, there are no future moments; or, if we do return, we find that the native air has lost its invigorating quality, and that life has shifted its reality to the spot where we have deemed ourselves only temporary residents. Thus, between two countries, we have none at all, or only that little space of either, in which we lay down our discontented bones. (*Works* IV, 461)

Anyone who has stayed abroad for too long and then returned home will connect with this letdown. As Thomas Wolfe would write eloquently in *You Can't Go Home Again* (1934), we can never fully go back to our friends, back to our early years, "away from all the strife and conflict of the world, back home to the father

you have lost, and have been looking for, . . . back home to the old forms and systems of things which once seemed everlasting but which are changing all the
time – back home to the escapes of Time and Memory" (95). A lot had changed for
Hawthorne and his country, and not all of it had been pleasant. "I lose England
without gaining America," he wrote to Bennoch on 17 December 1860; "for I have
not really begun to feel at home here" (*Works* XVIII, 352). Like George Webber in
Wolfe's novel, Hawthorne realized that no one can return to his hometown and
expect everything to remain the same. The forces of time and change are too
strong, and change is the only constant.

During the first month after his return, friends called on him and were received
cordially. But other than attending monthly meetings of the all-male Brahmin
Saturday Club (to which Emerson had introduced him) for dinner and talk, he seldom engaged with others outside his family and a few close friends. Higginson
(1879) recalled "the imperturbable dignity and patience with which he sat through
a vexatious discussion, whose details seemed as much dwarfed by his presence as if
he had been a status of Olympian Zeus" (4). When he decided to talk, Fields (1872)
remembered, "it was observed that the best things said that day came from him" (55).

At times, he was seen on the way to Walden Pond, either alone or in company
with his son. Bronson Alcott often noticed him gliding along, ghost-like, by the
rustic fence separating their two estates, or on the way to Sleepy Hollow Cemetery.
"He seems not at home here in his temperament and tendencies," Alcott wrote in
his journal on 17 February. "See how he behaves, as if he were the foreigner still,
though installed in his stolen castle and its keeper, his moats wide and deep, his
drawbridges up on all sides, and he secure within from invasion" (1938: 335–336).
Struck by the unmistakable change in his physical appearance, William Dean
Howells (1968 [1900]) reflected: "Hawthorne's *look* was different from that of any
picture of him that I have seen. It was sombre and brooding, as the look of such a
poet should have been" (49). Within a year of their return, Sophia confided to his
publisher, Ticknor, that her husband was "low in tone and spirits . . . he has lost
the zest for life" (Meltzer 2007: 135).

When the weather cooled, he cultivated a habit of walking back and forth on
the hillside above his house, where the bank descended sharply, with dwarf pines
and shrub oaks on the far side of it. He wore a path on the hilltop there, as would
Septimius Felton in the aborted romance published posthumously in 1872.
Perhaps ideas for that story germinated in his mind while looking down upon
Lexington Road beneath him, imagining how it appeared while awash with
marching British soldiers: "'I really believe they are,' [says] Septimius, his cheek
flushing and growing pale, not with fear, but the inevitable tremor, half painful,
half pleasurable, of the moment. 'Hark; there was the shrill note of a fife! Yes, they
are coming!'" (*Works* XIII, 20)

Ceaseless financial worries added to his stress. In early August, he and his wife had ordered renovations for The Wayside to accommodate the size of their family. Just the cost of enlarging and improving their home, the main part extended upward by three stories and the west wing by two, rose to $2000 – exceeding his initial calculations by a distressing four times. The work dragged on through the middle of May 1861 as Ticknor continued to advance him the required funds (including $484 for timber and building materials, $32.23 for a new carpet, another $500 for house repairs), often making him feel the anguish of a mendicant. "If I escape absolute beggary, I shall thank Heaven and you," he wrote to Ticknor on 30 January 1861. "What will be the use of having a house, if it costs me all my means of living in it?" (*Works* XVIII, 361)

A new third-floor tower room, 20 feet square and pine-built, served as a study and retreat from the carpenters' noise. To reach it, he climbed a narrow wooden staircase and entered through a trapdoor. Once inside, he drew the curtains and slid a chair over the entrance to keep out interruptions. He had modeled the tower on the haunted castle Villa Montauto in Florence (the prototype of Donatello's Monte Beni), where they had happily spent the summer of 1858 while he worked on *The Marble Faun*. Every morning, Hawthorne closeted himself in his new retreat, an echo of the upstairs chamber of his Herbert Street childhood home. On the wall, Sophia had hung a motto attributed to his son Julian: "There is no joy but calm" (Higginson 1879: 5). As his family below re-adjusted to Concord life, he tried in vain to finish the new romance, *The Ancestral Footprint*, begun and abandoned while in England, but he lacked the enthusiasm and drive to complete it.

"[T]here seem to be things that I can almost get hold of, and think about," he wrote in his journal; "but when I am just on the point of seizing them, they start away, like slippery things" (Schmidt 2014: 333). He made little progress despite changing the title to "Etherege" and then to "Grimshawe." "I spend two or three hours a day in my sky-parlor, and duly spread a quire of paper on my desk," he wrote to Ticknor on 16 February 1861; "but no very important result has followed, thus far" (*Works* XVIII, 363).

I can feel his frustration, his isolation in that low-ceilinged upper room where I now sit as I make notes for this chapter. There's a slightly dusty smell, reminiscent of a secondhand bookshop. From the thinly frosted gabled windows, I feel privileged to see what Hawthorne saw. Through spindly trees, the snow extends across the meadows to Walden Woods, sparkling like diamonds; then the Alcott house and the road to Concord village; a dark and deep patch of woodland here and there; and beyond, the Fitchburg railroad tracks. The sound of a train whistle at night still conjures up my visits. How many mornings, I wonder, had he spent there, intent on his dream game and absorbing the entire landscape? Thoreau claimed that this house (like the Manse) was haunted, in this instance, by a man who believed a generation or two ago that he was immortal. Was that a rustle? A footstep? A whisper?

Along with these concerns, he was profoundly anxious about his eldest daughter, Una, who suffered a recurrence of malaria in mid-September that lasted until November. "We are in great trouble on account of our poor Una, in whom the bitter dregs of that Roman fever are still rankling, and have now developed themselves in a way which the physicians foreboded, and forewarned us of," he wrote to Fields on 21 September 1860. "I do not like to write about it, but will tell you when we meet. Say nothing" (*Works* XVIII, 319).

Because of her father's nerves, Una had to be shifted to the house of her aunt, Mary Mann, and cousin Horace, Jr., who lived in the center of town, so that the Concord doctor could attend her at night when necessary. Treatments included dunking her in a tub of frigid water (against which she rebelled frantically), phrenology, magnetism and, as a desperate measure, electric shock treatment using a galvanic battery. This last attempt did seem to improve her condition, but she was never able to regain her vibrancy and robustness. The mental strain upon her father was exhausting, to say the least.

Most disconcertingly, he had returned to discover an angry country. War clouds were on the brink of bursting. A Southern Confederate government was formed on 8 February 1861. Abraham Lincoln was inaugurated on 4 March. On 12 April, in the Confederates' drive to preserve slavery, they captured Fort Sumter in South Carolina, and thus the Civil War began. Federal troops were rushed from the North to protect Washington and were billeted in the Capital. Volunteers were rushed to enlist on either side. Where was his great republic headed?

Although a pacifist, Hawthorne, like most Northern Democrats, was vocal in his support for the cause of the Union. As battles raged and the death toll mounted, as the nation turned into purgatory, and southern slave states were increasingly seceding, he wrote to Fields on 12 October: "For my part, I don't hope (nor, indeed, wish) to see the Union restored as it was; amputation seems to me much the better plan . . . I would fight to the death for the Northern slave-states, and let the rest go" (*Works* XVIII, 412). Who could write with the country so shaken? Throughout his life, he believed that writers created their boldest imaginative success when they kept a stable routine at home. "The war continues to interrupt my literary industry," he wrote to Ticknor on 16 May 1861; "and I am afraid it will be long before Romances are in request again, even if I could write one" (*Works* XVIII, 379).

Every day brought fresh news of disaster as he continued to pray for peace. On 26 May 1861, he wrote to Bridge: "One thing, as regards this matter, I regret, and one thing I am glad of; – the regrettable thing is, that I am too old to shoulder a musket myself; and the joyful thing is, that Julian is too young." In this letter, he also confessed that he did not quite understand what they were fighting for, or the certitude of the anticipated result. "If we pummel the South ever so hard," he wrote, "they will love us none the better for it; and even if we subjugate them, our next step should be to cut them adrift" (*Works* XVII, 380, 381). On 8 March 1863, he wrote to Bright that he soon felt "a sense of infinite weariness. I want the end to come, and the curtain to drop, and then to go to sleep" (*Works* XVIII, 543).

Then, in a remarkable letter sent sometime in July 1861 to his friend Bennoch, he connected the turmoil of his own day with the revolutionary past that brought America forth as a nation. He was of the view that young men under the age of 50 should be excluded from fighting conflicts because their elders had allowed the wars to develop. "[W]e seem to have little, or, at least, a very misty idea of what we are fighting for. It depends upon the speaker, and that, again, depends upon the section of the country in which his sympathies are enlisted . . . All are thoroughly in earnest, and all pray for the blessing of Heaven to rest upon the enterprise" (*Works* XVIII, 387).

Understandably, at such a time, Hawthorne became preoccupied with the subject of death and life thereafter. Ever since he had read William Godwin's *St. Leon: A Tale of the Sixteenth Century* (1799) as a young man, he had been deeply interested in immortality. Set in Europe during the Protestant Reformation, it tells the story of an impoverished aristocrat who obtains the philosopher's stone and the elixir of immortality. But much to his distress, endless riches and immortal life prove to be curses rather than gifts, transforming him into an outcast.

As early as 25 October 1836, Hawthorne's American notebook entries point to his interest in the subject: "Curious to imagine what murmurings and discontent would be excited, if any of the great so-called calamities of human beings were to be abolished, – as, for instance, death." In an entry from 1840, he wrote, "The love of posterity is a consequence of the necessity of death. If a man were sure of living forever here, he would not care about his offspring." On 1 June 1842, he added, "The advantages of a longer life than is allotted to mortals – the many things that might then be accomplished" (*Works* VIII, 23, 186, 241).

After he had abandoned the idea of an English romance, Hawthorne took up the theme of the Elixir of Life with a focus on two men – a young student named Septimius (in "Septimius Felton" and "Septimius Norton," which he soon gave up after changing their names, adding new details, and refining the dialogues) and an old apothecary named Dolliver, for which we have three chapter-length segments along with a handful of notes (published posthumously as *The Dolliver Romance* in 1876). *Septimius Felton, Or the Elixir of Life* (found after his death), would be published in 1872, along with another fragment, *The Ancestral Footstep*, in 1883. In these unfinished novels, we witness a contest between their author and his work, beneath which flows a current of psychological anguish.

He had sketched the story for Fields by mid-September 1861, projecting fifteen scenes. The complete story, found only in the "Septimius Felton" draft, is set against the battle of Concord at the start of the American Revolution. As a young ministerial student and poet, Septimius has brooded about the limitations of life. After killing a young British soldier, he finds on his body a manuscript containing an immortality-conferring formula. Septimius becomes obsessed with the manuscript as he tries to decipher it, and ends up alienating himself from family, friends, and country: "he knew nothing, thought nothing, cared nothing about his country, or his country's battles" (*Works* XIII, 165).

He then meets Sybil Darcy, whom we later learn had been the British soldier's lover. Eventually, he creates the elixir and persuades Sybil (who had set out to avenge her lover's death but falls in love with Septimius) to drink it. She does so, but falls dying, poisoned, because the elixir has contained one incorrect ingredient. Septimius disappears from Concord. There are rumors that he has laid claim to an English estate through his distant relationship to the slain British officer.

During the latter half of 1863, Hawthorne began a new approach to the theme, *The Dolliver Romance*, in which he continued to consider the concept of the man who does not die (based on the idea Thoreau had shared with him). But he could not complete this either. He reported to Fields that it was now taking a very different shape when compared with the original version, which is why he abandoned the idea in 1864, even though Fields had proposed running it as a serial story in the *Atlantic* starting that January.

"I don't see much probability of my having the first chapter of the Romance ready so soon as you want it," he wrote to Fields on 24 October 1863. "There are two or three chapters ready to be written, but I am not yet robust enough to begin, & I feel as if I should never carry it through" (*Works* XVIII, 605). In another letter (dated 17 January 1864), he wrote, "Seriously, my mind has, for the present, lost its temper and its fine edge, and I have an instinct that I had better keep quiet. Perhaps I shall have a new spirit of vigor, if I wait quietly for it – perhaps not" (*Works* XVIII, 634). On 25 February 1864, unable to get the new romance off his mind, he wrote to Fields: "I cannot finish it, unless a great change comes over me; and if I make too great an effort to do so, it will be my death" (*Works* XVIII, 641). At home, on the desk in his study, half the novel was waiting; the other half was still buried inside him somewhere. Words did not seem to come.

"The best we have or can produce is only the tip of the iceberg," wrote George Steiner for the flyleaf of his *My Unwritten Books* (2008). "Behind every good book, as in a lit shadow, lies the book which remained unwritten." Had Hawthorne lived to carry it out, the work would have doubtlessly been the vehicle for a profound and pathetic drama based on the instinctive yearning of a man for immortality. Perhaps someone will come along and complete the work, just as David Madden (2011) did with Dickens's incomplete *The Mystery of Edwin Drood* (1870). In the meantime, we are left with a mystery.

That Hawthorne never finished this novel does not diminish his achievement, however, but it does alter our view of it. "Unfinished novels prod us to relinquish conventional approaches to reading and to seek literary pleasure elsewhere than narrative unity," wrote Grant Shreve (2018). "They demand that we attend to dead ends as well as to false starts, to charged silences as well as to verbal excesses. They ask us to see what meanings can be gleaned from a process that has not yet hardened into the product. Though their plots may be arrested, this fact does not make them any less arresting" (11).

In hopes of improving his spirits and his health, on the clear and frosty morning of 6 March 1862, with Ticknor, he set out for Washington via New York, New Jersey, and Philadelphia. Their month-long stay in the Capital (his first since April 1853, also with Ticknor) to see firsthand the nation at war engaged Hawthorne's interest. Their stopping-places were "thronged with soldiers," he wrote, and upon the train station in Washington, they were met by "lines of soldiers, with shouldered muskets" (Ticknor 1913, 264). However, they were disappointed upon learning that they had just missed seeing 60 000 troops cross the Potomac on their march toward Manassas.

During his stay, he visited with Horatio Bridge, now chief of a bureau in the Navy Department, as well as members of Congress. In addition to touring Union military installations along the Virginia border, he met Vice President Hannibal Hamilton at Fortress Monroe and Major General George B. McClellan at Fairfax Seminary. He sat with the Secretary of War Edward M. Stanton (who appointed him to a civil commission to report about the condition of the Army of the Potomac) and the Secretary of the Treasury Salmon B. Chase. Along with a delegation from Massachusetts, he called on the new president.

With finances ever on his mind, Hawthorne wrote to Una on 16 March, "By a message from the State Department, I have reason to think that there is money enough due me from the government to pay the expenses of my journey. I think the public buildings are as fine, if not finer, than any we saw in Europe" (*Works* XVIII, 438).

Back home in Concord on 10 April, he returned to work on an essay with "renewed vigor of body and cheerfulness of spirit" (Ticknor 1913: 282). In all of his writings, Hawthorne tried to observe closely and set down the truth as he saw it. He never spared any topic from questions or scrutiny and treated many with mild irony or plain wit. A case in point was his dryly satirical article, submitted anonymously to the *Atlantic* for the July 1862 issue, entitled, "Chiefly About War-Matters, by a Peaceable Man," in which he sought to articulate his observations from his visit to the Capital.

"No nation ever came safe and sound through such a confounded difficulty as this of ours," he notes. "There is no remoteness of life and thought, no hermetically sealed seclusion, except, possibly, that of the grave, into which the disturbing influences of this war do not penetrate" (Woodberry 1902: 283). The outbreak of war gave death a newfound prominence in both private and public life. Hawthorne understood loss, but not to this extent. The sheer savagery of the war compelled him to ask with intensified urgency, "What is Death?" Ironically, its threat distracted him from his work:

> the general heart-quake of the country long ago knocked at my cottage door, and compelled me reluctantly to suspend the contemplation of certain fantasies, to which, according to my harmless custom, I was endeavoring to give a sufficiently life-like aspect, to admit of their figuring in a Romance. . . [I]t seemed at first a pity that I should be deprived from such unsubstantial business as I had contrived for myself, since nothing more genuine was to be substituted for it. But I magnanimously considered that there is a kind of treason in insulating one's self from the universal fear and sorrow and thinking one's idle thoughts in the dread time of civil war; and could a man be so cold and hard-hearted, he would better deserve to be sent to Fort Warren than many who have found their way thither on the score of violent, but misdirected sympathies. (*Works* XXIII, 213)

Fields, the magazine's editor, liked the essay but proposed trimming down certain satirical passages about Washington officials and southerners because he believed they would outrage the feelings of many readers. Hawthorne acquiesced, but replaced the deleted passages with footnotes written in the voice of an agitated, dogmatic editor. Read as a satire; we cannot help but see the Peaceable Man and the footnotes added by his fictitious editor courageously lampooning the state of the country, not only the hubris of the slave-holding South but also the censorious North.

Fields was also concerned about the piece's irreverent tone toward Lincoln, worrying that English readers would gloat over the descriptions. In the original draft, Hawthorne had written that the president appeared to be "about the homeliest man I ever saw, yet by no means repulsive or disagreeable." In fact, he wrote, "I liked this sallow, queer, sagacious visage with the homely human sympathies that warmed it and, for my small share in the matter, would as lief have Uncle Abe for a ruler as any man whom it would have been practicable to put in his place."

Left with no other choice, Hawthorne cut the entire interview, albeit grudgingly. In a letter to Fields dated 23 May 1862, he said that it was "the only part of the article really worth publishing. Upon my honor, it seems to me to have a historical value – but let it go" (*Works* XVIII, 461; Fields subsequently did publish it in its entirety in April 1871). "What a terrible thing it is," he griped in the same letter, "to try to let off a little bit of truth into this miserable humbug of a world!" (*Works* XVIII, 461) Despite its rather unsympathetic views on the president, it remains the only authentic pen-portrait that we have of him.

Given his manifold worries and increasingly fragile health, it is remarkable that Hawthorne even tried to produce as much as he did in his final four years, raising important questions that inspire us to re-visit his heart as a man and as a writer. How could he be expected to devote his attention to what seemed utter trivialities in comparison to the war? Why would he want to begin a new novel when he had very little chance of completing it?

The answer to these questions was what he had always before learned and applied from experience: that he must continue to work even under unfavorable conditions, as he had done his entire life. No one has "enough" time to finish what needs completion. No man escapes death; therefore, he must, in faith, accept the human condition soberly and humbly entrust the creative life and future to God.

To help my students understand and apply Hawthorne's philosophy to their own lives, I like to direct them to C.S. Lewis's sermon, "Learning in War-Time," delivered at St. Mary the Virgin Church, Oxford, on 22 October 1939, almost two months after the war had broken out with Germany's invasion of Poland. The title sums up his thesis. Lewis argues that there never has been an era without crises, alarms, difficulties, and emergencies. If mankind had deferred the quest for knowledge and beauty until life and everything in it was secure, then the search for progress and betterment would never have begun.

We must, therefore, learn to resist the distraction of excitement that jeopardizes our focus on the tasks we have been given. We must not succumb to frustration as we recognize that we cannot always bring our planned projects to conclusion with ease. We must face fear head-on and avoid imagining that our suffering is greater than it is. This is exactly what Hawthorne did. Unlike his father, who was struck down before he barely realized himself, Hawthorne brought to fruition a lifetime of cherished dreams.

If only he could return to England, he thought. Perhaps the sea-voyage and the "old home" would restore his spirits. Alas, it was too late in life for him to even consider such a trip; and so he wrote about it by drawing upon his notebooks to produce a series of sketches, covering his enriching consular experiences and life in England, for the *Atlantic* (October 1860 and August 1863).

When Fields suggested making a book of them, Hawthorne agreed. He polished, tightened, and rearranged the material but had difficulty deciding whether to dedicate the book to Bennoch or the controversial Pierce. He finally insisted on the latter – "As a slight memorial of a college friendship, prolonged through manhood, and retaining all its vitality in our autumnal years" – despite his publishers' vehement objections.

He did so, he explained, as an expression of loyalty, but others saw it as a slavish and foolish political act (*Works* V, xxvii). Northern readers were outraged. They accused the former president of treason because of his opposition to the Civil War and his subsequent attacks on the Lincoln administration. Emerson even tore the dedication page out of his complimentary copy. Nevertheless, Hawthorne reconciled himself to the consequences, and the volume appeared 19 September 1863 in both England and America under the title *Our Old Home: A Series of English Sketches*.

This wonderfully quotable book is an engaging and human part-memoir and part-travelogue intended, as he says in the preface, "for the side-scenes, and backgrounds, and exterior adornment, of a work of fiction . . . [I]t has been utterly thrown aside, and will never now be accomplished. The Present, the Immediate, the Actual, has proved too potent for me. It takes away not only my scanty faculty, but even my desire for imaginative composition, and leaves me sadly content to scatter a thousand peaceful fantasies upon the hurricane that is sweeping us all along with it" (*Works* V, 3–4). We join him on his leisurely rambles as he shares his many observations, insights, and reflections while mingling critical comments with sensitive appreciation. Philip McFarland (2004) pointed out that Hawthorne's humor, patriotism, and compassion are the book's greatest strengths (280–281).

He is at his humorous best, for example, when he describes his office and focuses on "a fierce and terrible bust of General Jackson, pilloried in a military collar which rose above his ears" along with a copy of the New Testament for administering oaths, "greasy, I fear, with a daily succession of perjured kisses" (*Works* V, 8, 9). Or when he writes of his appearance at a London civic banquet, never having stood in a posture "of greater dignity and peril" and deciding it "sage policy here to close these Sketches, leaving myself still erect in so heroic an attitude" (*Works* V, 345).

His patriotism emerges bold and clear when he expresses his annoyance at English condescension to his native land. British sympathy for the Confederate side irritates him. As much as he loved England, he found it to be stultified by class, by tradition, by the stale burden of history. By contrast, America was a land of opportunity, change, and a better future.

And there is compassion, as when he writes movingly of the social inequalities (worker and aristocrat, slum-dweller and businessman, pauper and Lord). Haunting images of extreme poverty on the streets of Liverpool depressed him. "How superficial are the niceties of such as pretend to keep aloof! Let the whole world be cleansed, or not a man or woman of us all can be clean" (*Works* V, 299). He writes of the pitiful children. "Unless these slime-clogged nostrils can be made capable of inhaling celestial air, I know not how the purest and most intellectual of us can reasonably expect ever to taste a breath of it. The whole question of eternity staked there. If a single one of those helpless little ones be lost, the world is lost!" (*Works* V, 282) My students find this chapter riveting as it confronts them with how we ignore the homeless while living comfortably ourselves. Equally, it elicits a desire to struggle against bland acceptance of it all.

One of the most poignant and meaningful of sections is titled "Recollections of a Gifted Woman." Here, he recalls his one (hourlong) London visit he made on 29 July 1856 with Delia Bacon, upon the encouragement of her friend and his sister-in-law, Elizabeth Peabody. Acting on a kind impulse, he helped to place and anonymously finance the publication of her book, *The Philosophy of the Plays of Shakspere* [*sic*] *Unfolded* (1857), which she had been researching and writing while in London over the past three years.

Published on 20 March by Ticknor and Fields in a volume of almost 700 pages, her book attributes the plays to Francis Bacon, Sir Walter Raleigh, and Edmund Spenser – all members of an alleged secret society of play-writing Elizabethan courtiers. She argues (without any extrinsic evidence) that *Julius Caesar* (1599), *Coriolanus* (1605/1608), and *King Lear* (1606) were actually Republican polemics produced within Elizabeth's and James's court (and therefore coded attacks on the Tudor and Stuart monarchies). Sophia opined that the argument was brilliant. While Hawthorne found the book "d–d hard reading" and didn't believe her theory, he told Ticknor that it "contains wonderfully good matter, nevertheless" and wrote an introduction to the book (Ticknor 1913: 185). "It was a very singular phenomenon," he writes; "a system of philosophy growing up in this woman's mind without her volition – contrary, in fact, to the determined resistance of her volition – and substituting itself in the place of everything that originally grew there" (*Works* V, 106).

From that visit, he came away liking her and feeling compassion for an impoverished lady who was in a state of near-despair because she had no idea how to get her book into print. Soon after the book's appearance and poor reviews (one calling the theory "a nullity [that] will not bear the least serious handling" [Peel 1857: 493]), she suffered a severe psychotic breakdown and was taken by a nephew back to the United States. She died on 2 September 1859 in the Hartford Retreat, an asylum in Hartford, Connecticut. He concludes his essay in *Our Old Home*:

> [W]hen, not many months after the outward failure of her life-long object she passed into the better world, I know not why we should hesitate to believe that the immortal poet may have met her on the threshold and led her in, re-assuring her with friendly and comfortable words, and thanking her (yet with a smile of gentle humor in his eyes at the thought of certain mistaken speculations) for having interpreted him to mankind so well.

Eventually, Hawthorne came to regard her as "unquestionably . . . a monoma-niac" whose ideas were "erroneous." And yet, in *Our Old Home* he says that Bacon was "in a certain sense" right. "Shakespere [*sic*] has surface beneath surface," he writes, and Bacon was able to recognize a depth in the plays that "scholars, critics, and learned societies, devoted to the elucidation of his unrivalled scenes, had never imagined to exist there" (*Works* V, 106, 116).

Finally, although he praises England's antiquity and literary giants as a whole, readers reacted most adversely to his few, minor uncomplimentary references to English women, as seen, for example, in the following offending passage: "I have heard a good deal of the tenacity with which English ladies retain their personal beauty to a late period of life; but . . . it strikes me that an English lady of fifty is apt to become a creature less refined and delicate, so far as her physique goes, than anything that we Western people class under the name of woman" (*Works* V, 48).

The North American Review (October 1863) commented: "Things present them-selves grotesquely to Mr. Hawthorne. He takes hold of them by some other than the usual handle, and offers to our view just the parts and aspects of them which it is conventionally fit to keep out of sight." *Blackwood's Magazine* (November) commented that his description of womanhood is not exactly good-natured. "We wish we could quote some pleasanter passages respecting our people, but there are really none." Henry Bright for the *Examiner* (dated 17 October) wrote: "Whatever Mr. Hawthorne may like in England, he certainly does not like us Englishmen. With us he is neither struck nor pleased. Englishmen, and English women more especially, seem to be his positive aversion." *Punch* for 17 October declared: "We have often credited you with literary merit, and your style, dear boy, puts to shame a good many of our own writers who ought to write better than they do . . . You have written a book about England, and into this book you have put all the caricatures and libels upon English folk, which you collected while enjoying our hospitality. Your book is thoroughly saturated with what seems ill-nature and spite" (Crowley 1970: 391, 392, 396, 402).

None of this surprised him. On 18 October 1863, he wrote to Fields, "The English critics seem to think me very bitter against their countrymen, and it is perhaps natural that they should, because their self-conceit can accept nothing short of indiscriminate adulation; but I really think that Americans have more cause than they to complain of me. Looking over the volume, I am rather sur-prised to find that, whenever I draw a comparison between the two peoples, I almost invariably cast the balance against ourselves" (*Works* XVIII, 603).

The English critics' first responses seemed little more than howls of indigna-tion, ignoring the possibility that Hawthorne's comments on their country might have some validity. Hawthorne asserted his right to say what he thought was true:

"it is very possible that I may have said things which a profound observer of national character would hesitate to sanction, though never any, I verily believe, that had not more or less of truth. If they be true, there is no reason in the world why they should not be said" (*Works* V, 5). Ironically, the controversy helped to generate large sales on both sides of the Atlantic. With the first printing of 3500, then another 2000, and many re-prints thereafter, 15 000 copies were in print by 1880. Hawthorne and his publishers always had a shrewd eye for publicity.

By November 1863, however, once the rage had died down, others corrected the misreadings. The (London) *Times*, for example, came forward with a more nuanced approach: "As we glide over these easy pages, we feel ourselves in the company of a gentle, kindly, pure-minded character who, however hard he may try to smite us, cannot hurt us much and might as well be pelting us with sugar plums and smothering us in roses . . . Mr. Hawthorne's book is quite different from what – judging by the preface and some of the opinions that have been passed upon it, we were led to expect . . . Mr. Hawthorne scarcely ever takes off his gloves; they are excellently well-padded and his blows fall on us like eiderdown . . . We can no more be offended with him because he says we are fat and rotund than we expect him to be offended with us because we think his countrymen lank and lean" (Crowley 1970: 10).

Around this time, Hawthorne suffered several sad losses. On 2 December 1863, Mrs. Franklin Pierce (Jane) died, leaving her husband alone (none of their three children had lived past the age of 11). Hawthorne could not turn away from his friend even though his own health was failing. On a bone-chilling day, he traveled to the funeral at the Old North Cemetery in Concord, New Hampshire, where he stayed from 4 to 6 December. There beside the open grave, the bereaved Pierce was seen pulling up the collar of Hawthorne's coat to protect his friend against the freezing wind.

On the following 29 March, the still unwell and fatigued Hawthorne set off with Ticknor to Philadelphia. They got as far as New York but were forced to stay over-night in the Astor House until the bad weather let up. Eventually, they were able to leave and arrived safely at the Continental Hotel in Philadelphia on 7 April. Hawthorne's spirits and energy did improve somewhat, but ironically Ticknor, who had always been the embodiment of health and vitality, was afflicted with a particularly severe cold. Hawthorne did his best to look after him, even summoning doctors and a nurse, but to no avail. His condition worsened and at the Continental Hotel early Sunday morning, 10 April, he died of pneumonia at the age of 53. Hawthorne was crestfallen, reiterating "over and over again that he should have died and not Ticknor" (Ticknor 1913: 322).

Shortly after Ticknor's eldest sons had retrieved the body, George William Childs arrived to accompany the distraught and grieving Hawthorne back to Boston. From there, he made his way alone to Concord, arriving on 14 April.

Years later, the family came to know that Ticknor had risked his own health for his friend when, during a drive to Fairmount Park in Philadelphia, he removed his coat and wrapped it about Hawthorne. As Pierce had done for Hawthorne at the funeral of his own wife, so Ticknor had given all that he had to protect his friend.

This small gesture typified the man. Ticknor, founder of one of the leading publishing houses in the nineteenth century, Ticknor and Fields, had been as we have seen a man of great personal charm and unselfish devotion to his friends, none more than Hawthorne, who had depended upon him for guidance and counsel ever since he contracted for *The Scarlet Letter*. We need only to glance through the collection of Hawthorne's letters to him to realize Ticknor's "constant thoughtfulness," for he was "untiring in his rendering of small as well as large services" – financial as well as personal (Ticknor 1913: 36).

Of her husband's arrival home, Sophia wrote to Fields a few days later, "[A]s soon as I saw him, I was frightened out of all knowledge of myself, – so haggard, so white, so deeply scored with pain and fatigue was the face, so much more ill he looked than I ever saw him before. He had walked from the station because he saw no carriage there, and his brow was streaming with a perfect rain, so great had been the effort to walk so far . . . He needed much to get home to me, where he could fling off all care of himself and give way to his feelings, pent up and kept back for so long" (Ticknor 1913: 324–325).

Sophia sat with him, and listened empathetically, as he spoke of his remorse over the death of his valued friend. "The wheels of my small *ménage* are all stopped," she continued. "He is my world and all the business of it" (Ticknor 1913: 325). He was buried at Mount Auburn cemetery. A message from a Washington official expressed the sentiments of the distinguished company gathered for the event: "I find, everywhere, they who best knew him, loved him best. And I know of no higher or worthier testimony" (Ticknor 1913: 326).

Since the autumn of 1863 Hawthorne had been a very sick man – yet he did not know why, nor was it ever explained satisfactorily. Everything continued to weigh heavily on him. On 5 April 1864, Sophia wrote in alarm to Horatio Bridge: "I have felt the wildest anxiety about him, because he is a person who has been immaculately well all his life, and this illness has seemed to me an awful dream which could not be true. But he has wasted away very much, and the suns in his eyes are collapsed, and he has no spirits, no appetite, and very little sleep" (Bridge 1893: 16). Sophia pleaded with him to see a doctor, but Hawthorne, who had an aversion to being touched and handled and mistrusted the medical profession, refused.

After Ticknor's funeral, arrangements were made for a change of scene for Hawthorne, who sat brooding for his friend, and he went to Boston to meet Franklin Pierce, who had agreed to take him to northern New England.

Sophia hatched a scheme for Dr. Oliver Wendell Holmes to see Hawthorne as if by chance at the Boston hotel where he was staying.

Holmes caught up with him on 10 May, noting (in a report that was published in the *Atlantic* for July 1864) that "he seemed to have shrunken in all his dimensions, and faltered along with an uncertain, feeble step, as if every movement were an effort." He concluded that his condition was "very unfavourable. There were persistent local symptoms, referred especially to the stomach, – 'boring pain,' distension, difficult digestion, with great wasting of flesh and strength. He was very gentle, very willing to answer questions, very docile to such counsel as I offered him, but evidently had no hope of recovering his health. He spoke as if his work were done, and he should work no more" (Fields 1872: 121–122).

On 18 May, Hawthorne and Pierce drove by carriage from Centre Harbor to Plymouth, New Hampshire, gateway to the White Mountains and at the very southern end of the region along the Pemigewasset River. They stopped at the Pemigewasset House for rest and sleep, a massive wood-framed hotel that no longer exists, having burned down in early 1909. In a letter to Horatio Bridge, Pierce described what happened next:

> After taking a little tea and toast in his room, and sleeping for nearly an hour upon the sofa, [Hawthorne] retired. A door opened from my room to his, and our beds were not more than five or six feet apart. I remained up an hour or two after he fell asleep. He was apparently less restless than the night before. The light was left burning in my room – the door open – and I could see him without moving from my bed. I went, however, between one and two o'clock to his bedside, and supposed him to be in a profound slumber. His eyes were closed, his position and face perfectly natural. His face was turned towards my bed. (Woodberry 1902: 292)

A few hours later, on 19 May (Hawthorne's father's birthday), Pierce returned to his friend's room:

> I awoke again between three and four o'clock and was surprised – as he had generally been restless – to notice that his position was unchanged – exactly the same that it was two hours before. I went to his bedside, placed my hand upon his forehead and temple, and found that he was dead. He evidently had passed from natural slumber to that from which there is no waking, without the slightest movement. (Bridge 1893: 15; Fields 1872: 123)

While packing up his friend's belongings, Pierce came upon an old pocket-book. Inside he found his own picture, which his friend had obviously taken with him wherever he had traveled.

Like the traveler in "The Ambitious Guest," Hawthorne died at a hotel in the White Mountains. Like his father, he died away from home and family. Like his friend Ticknor, he died with a loving companion at his bedside. In *The Blithedale Romance*, the narrator Coverdale, speaking of Hollingsworth, seems prophetic when he says, "Happy the man that has such a friend beside him, when he comes to die! . . . How many men, I wonder, does one meet with, in a lifetime, whom he would choose for his death-bed companions!" (*Works* III, 42)

From what did he die? We shall never be certain. Some theories have been posited. Pierce believed he died of paralysis. The consensus is gastrointestinal cancer. But there is mystery here as there was mystery in his passing. What does seem clear is that upon sensing his imminent death, Hawthorne left home to die in the dignity of solitude and to spare his wife the grief and shock associated with the loss of her husband. Now she would forever remember him as he was when he was alive. He saved his family the image of his death so that he could remain alive in their memories. That is the extent to which he loved his family (Robuck 2015: 389–390).

Upon hearing the news, Rose said that when her father left for the New Hampshire trip, both parents sensed the parting was to be forever. "I could hardly bear to let my eyes rest upon [my mother's] shrunken, suffering form on this day of farewell," she wrote. "My father certainly knew, what she vaguely felt, that he would never return." She continued: "The last time I saw him, he was leaving the house to take the journey. . . Like a snow image of an unbending but an old, old man, he stood for a moment gazing at me. My mother sobbed as she walked beside him to the carriage. We have missed him in the sunshine, in the storm, in the twilight, ever since" (Lathrop 1923 [1897]: 114).

At his funeral on 23 May at The Church of the First Parish in Concord, most of the friends who had gathered at Ticknor's graveside a few weeks before assembled once again. Pallbearers included Longfellow, Emerson, Alcott, the attorney George Wallace Hillard, Holmes, and Elizabeth Norton. Franklin Pierce sat with the family. The incomplete manuscript for *The Dolliver Romance* lay on his coffin. The Unitarian minister James Freeman Clarke, who had joined them 22 years earlier in marriage, delivered the eulogy: "God placed him here to glorify New England life and pour over it the poetical beauty which was in his heart . . . I know no other thinker or writer who had so much sympathy with the dark shadow, that shadow which the theologian calls sin, as our friend. He seemed to be the friend of all sinners, in his writings" (McFarland 2004: 296).

To Oliver Wendell Holmes, the day was so bright that he thought it "looked like a happy meeting"; and to Emerson, "there was a tragic element in the event . . . and in the painful solitude of the man, which, I suppose, could not longer be endured, and he died of it" (Richardson 1995: 552). Henry James said that he wept on the day Hawthorne passed away. Longfellow, in his memorial poem "Hawthorne," which appeared in the August 1864 issue of *the Atlantic* (under the title "Concord") wrote of his friend:

> There in seclusion and remote from men
>> The wizard hand lies cold,
> Which at its topmost speed let fall the pen,
>> And left the tale half told.
>
> Ah, who shall lift that wand of magic power,
>> And the lost clue regain?
> The unfinished window in Aladdin's tower
>> Unfinished must remain! (29–36)

He was buried at Author's Ridge in the appropriately named Sleepy Hollow Cemetery, Concord, in a spot on a gentle hill under a canopy of leaves and beneath tall white pines, where Thoreau, the Alcotts, Ellery Channing, Emersons, and Sophia's sister, Elizabeth, are also buried.

After Nathaniel's death, the family moved to Germany and then to England, settling in Liverpool. Sophia continued to live for her children while working on behalf of her husband. Between 1864 and 1868, she re-read, copied, and edited for publication (with the help of her cousin, George Palmer Putnam) the intimate journal they had kept together, as well as his massive American, English, French, and Italian notebooks.

As Randall Stewart has traced, she made hundreds of changes that would make the text more acceptable to her children and a larger Victorian audience, to ensure that he "should appear before the world only with elegance" (Matthiessen 1941: 212). She deleted or revised, for example, every passage in which Nathaniel had expressed skepticism about marriage, womanhood, America, or Christianity, and suppressed references to smoking, drinking, or sexual desire. For Hawthorne's "whores," she substituted "women"; for "swilling," "drinking"; for "smell," "odor"; for "swap," "exchange"; for "not witty to kill," "not very witty" (Crews 1966: 14). "It is a vast pleasure to pore over his books in this way," she wrote on 11 November 1865. "I seem to be with him in all his walks and observations" (Bridge 1893: 193–194).

Julian wrote that she copied to reanimate her relationship with her husband: "from a short time after his departure until the hour came for her to join him, she always had a feeling that he was near her, – that their separation was of the senses only, not spiritual" (Lawrence and Werner 2005: 9). In addition to excerpts from their private journal in the *Atlantic* and passages from the American and English notebooks, Sophia published *Notes in England and Italy* in 1869. She died in London of typhoid pneumonia on 26 February 1871, aged 61, with Una and Rose at her side.

"Her face looked more and more like an angel's," Una wrote (who held her hand as she died and assisted in preparing the body for burial); "a delicate color stayed upon the cheeks, a lovely smile upon the slightly parted lips; her beautiful white hair was brushed a little back from her face, under a pretty cap, and her waxen hands lay softly folded against each other upon her breast" (Hawthorne, 1884: II, 370–371). On the last day of her vigil, Una removed the wedding ring from her mother's finger and placed it on her own.

She was buried in Kensal Green Cemetery, London (the same site for Una, who died on 10 September 1877, aged 33), under a white marble headstone with words she would have been proud of: "Sophia, wife of Nathaniel Hawthorne" and on the foot-stone: "I am the Resurrection and the Life" (Hawthorne 1884: 351). There they remained far away from Hawthorne.

But the story does not end here.

One day in 2006, I said to my summer class, "Well, I'm here, but my heart is elsewhere." I then explained that in 2004, some devotees had approached his descendants and officials to inquire about the possibility of reburying Sophia and Una in Concord. On 1 June 2006, their remains were exhumed and sent to the United States. Joan Deming Ensor, one of the four surviving great-grandchildren, said on this occasion, "It was a wonderfully happy marriage and they never wanted to be separated – his letters were full of longing when they were – and this is very fitting after the two have been apart for so long" (Zezima 2006).

On the afternoon of 26 June at 2:30 pm, when I was meeting with my class, the reburial (paid for by The Servants of Relief for Incurable Cancer, a Roman Catholic order of nuns founded by Nathaniel and Sophia's youngest daughter, Rose, along with private donations) was accomplished.

Their remains were taken from the New Church of the First Parish (rebuilt after a fire in 1899 had burned the original to the ground) to the cemetery in the horse-drawn carriage that was believed to have carried Hawthorne's body to his grave. There were around 35 people walking behind the coffin in silent procession as it was carried by pallbearers. At the private ceremony, mourners read correspondence among the family members and biblical verses. They placed flowers and significant objects in the coffin, which was slightly open and held both the mother and her daughter. It was resealed and reinterred appropriately beside Nathaniel Hawthorne. The family and religious order then gathered at the Old Manse, the Hawthornes' former home, both for a public service and afternoon refreshments (Zezima 2006).

Standing at their gravesite, as I am now, beneath a delicately hued sky, there is a soft caressing breeze. The sunbeams down "like a benediction," as Mark Twain wrote, a line that seems particularly befitting as I reflect on Sophia's words, sent to her daughter, Rose, after Nathaniel's demise: "Our own closed eyelids are too often the only clouds between us and the ever-shining sun. I hold all as if it were not mine, but God's, and ready to resign it" (Twain 1903: 21; Lathrop 1923 [1897]: 114).

Sophia Hawthorne, 1861. Source: Silsbee and Case/Peabody Essex Museum.

Julian, Una, and Rose. Source: Silsbee and Case/Peabody Essex Museum.

Conclusion

When Mozart was three years old, he first sat at his sister's clavier in the family house in Salzburg "to find notes that like one another" (De Ayala and Guéno 2000: 34). That became his life's work. At the end of the semester, I enjoy sharing this bit of history with my students because in it, I hear a metaphor for Hawthorne as writer, who strove to find *words* that like one another. Few pursuits are more satisfying than to fall in love with language, as a musician falls in love with the melody, to discover our thoughts and communicate them convincingly and eloquently.

Like music, writing is about rhythm and timing, sensing our audience, and seeing and hearing ourselves *through their eyes and ears.* It's about anticipating. It's about becoming so locked into our subject that we can tell when a point needs to be re-emphasized or when a question is shaping itself. It's about knowing, immediately, if the reader will follow the narrative, and if not, why not.

My students and I find this and more in Hawthorne's best work. Alert to every scene and detail, he truly possessed each word he used, not just in meaning but also in sound and rhythm. He understood the etiquette of good writing. With his incomparable eloquence and irony, said L.P. Hartley (1967), "hardly a paragraph he wrote could have been written by anyone else" (141). Henry James (1984 [1879]) captured his appeal and importance as one of the most individual and recognizable of authors when he wrote:

> His work will remain; it is too original and exquisite to pass away; among the men of imagination he will always have his niche. No one has had just that vision of life, and no one has had a literary form that more successfully expressed his vision . . . He combined in a singular degree the spontaneity of the imagination with a haunting care for moral problems. Man's conscience was his theme, but he saw it in the light of a creative fancy which added, out of its own substance, an interest, and, I may almost say, an importance. (145)

The Life of the Author: Nathaniel Hawthorne, First Edition. Dale Salwak.
© 2023 John Wiley & Sons Ltd. Published 2023 by John Wiley & Sons Ltd.

What a noble way to spend one's years! What a powerful, potentially life-altering example with which to leave our students.

And yet, in spite of such positive assessments and the ever-growing body of writings about the man and his writings, in spite of the numerous imitations and reinventions, movies, dramatic presentations, and readings resulting from his work (most of which remain in print), there is a prevailing attitude among some teachers (to whom I referred at the start of this book) that Hawthorne is mostly irrelevant to our times. Why should we be bothered, so the condescension runs, with unlocking the "impenetrable" mysteries of a nineteenth-century writer, a dead white Western male at that, who promotes sexism, misogyny, racism, and elitism? Even if these charges are accurate or useful – and I don't believe they are – now is the time to re-visit them. Underlying motives are important. So, what's really going on here?

For at least 15 years, there has been a debate on campuses worldwide about whether or not teachers of literature should issue disclaimers – or "trigger warnings" – because certain texts could traumatize students. Some have even gone so far as to offer "no fear literature" – meaning stories from which controversial passages have been toned down, outright removed, or translated into modern English after removing allegedly offending passages.

Proponents point to Joseph Conrad's *Heart of Darkness* (1899), for example, as possibly upsetting to readers who have been victims of racism. Or to F. Scott Fitzgerald's *The Great Gatsby* (1925), in which allusions to suicide and domestic abuse could cause some readers to relive similar personal experiences. Or to *The Scarlet Letter*, which ostensibly excuses adultery and misogyny.

This approach is condescending and infantilizing. It presumes that students are so fragile, or so frightened by the printed word, that they need to be insulated from the corrosive aspects of life as communicated through literature. The problem with this mindset is that almost anything could trigger an unpleasant memory. I can't imagine the long list of warnings that I would need to add, if required, to my courses in the Bible as literature or the works of Shakespeare! Once begun, this flawed game will never end.

As an undergraduate, I discovered that whenever I felt uneasy with someone's writing – William Golding's, for example – it was probably a sign for me to reread and rethink. No one likes to be reminded, as I was when reading *Lord of the Flies* (1954), of the potential for unabashed barbarism within the human heart. Yet ignoring such qualities does not expunge them from the world.

During my five decades of teaching in the college classroom, any objections raised by students to an assignment could usually be attributed to a misreading of the text because they overlook the irony or are looking at it through the lens of modern times. I have responded by trying to turn their disgust or disagreement into teachable moments, to reveal to them the real meaning and implications of the text.

I have had to explain, for example, that in dealing with his family's shame from involvement in the Salem witch trials in *The Scarlet Letter*, Hawthorne was trying to expose, not promulgate, fanatical Puritanism. Or that his purpose in *The House of the Seven Gables* is not, as some students have asserted, to promote occultism and witchcraft, but to leave behind his apparently cursed past and examine it through the distance and prism of art.

I do not include alerts when I'm teaching Hawthorne, but that does not preclude the possibility of sensitive topics forming part of my course. I can understand when topics being discussed might set off memories of sexual assault, child abuse, domestic violence, or homophobia. Further, I can appreciate the importance of being sensitive to veterans in our classes who may be suffering from post-traumatic stress disorder (PTSD).

But should trigger warnings be mandated for all literature? For someone as compassionate, empathetic, and humane as Hawthorne? Isn't the purpose of our kind of education to challenge students to think in new and diverse ways? I believe that what is important is not the warning itself but my own awareness that subjects could affect students in deeply personal ways; therefore, I choose to address them head-on with a certain courtesy, just as I have tried to do in this book, just as I believe Hawthorne would want us to do.

Classic writers like Hawthorne tell us something about the way we live, from the vilest faults in our souls to the most glorious triumphs of the human spirit. Through his work, he allows us to experience situations that we would likely shrink from in life. He speaks powerfully to the central concerns of his time or any time, ours included. He pulls us quite uncynically across deep waters.

The psychological themes of Hawthorne's that come alive in my classroom are among the ones that I have discussed in the preceding chapters. They include his urgent interest in the effects of sin (both secret and disclosed), guilt and penitence, religious hypocrisy, sexuality, history and national identity, the inconceivable power of the past, death, art, and the imagination – themes that, if they are honest with themselves, most students have encountered and explored (or will) at some time in their lives.

Something visceral to the students' experience has also shown them the truth of such timeless, universal themes as jealousy and reconciliation, humility and hubris, great love and great hatred. Animated, often passionate class discussions may revolve around crises or conflicts between parents and children, between siblings, or between husbands and wives. Hawthorne's themes touch on many recognizable aspects of ordinary human life – the earthier the better.

Students are also eager to determine how those whom we consider towering figures managed to become what they are. These young readers are instinctively interested in the opponents and situations the protagonists had to struggle against and, above all, the conflicts the characters had to surmount and resolve within themselves. These events are hugely important to students and become so to their teachers.

In other words, a complete moral universe, from nobility to perfidy, comes alive when class members focus on Hawthorne's portrayal of the human condition – the situations characters face, the choices they make, and the ways those choices play out. The narratives illustrate a variety of aspects of our common humanity, about which the author has no illusions, and students quickly recognize reflections of their own world in a milieu that had (perhaps) previously seemed so opaque and unrealistic.

Over and over in the pages of Hawthorne, they discover that, like themselves, even the most confident and gifted individuals have known bitter and lonely hours. Even the strongest endured pain, both physical and emotional. Even the most loyal suffered betrayal. With such a crowd of witnesses to the confusion, complexity, and challenges inherent in living a moral life on Earth, students come to understand that only through great struggle does any human being grow in body and mind and spirit.

For those who are open to the experience, however, the class is not just a matter of learning about the texts, the characters, and the traditions; it is also an invitation – sometimes, a challenge – to examine their own and others' belief systems. This is Hawthorne's real greatness. I have come to the realization that, like the author himself, most of my students long to tackle serious questions and that they will work hard to understand anything if they determine it is important and relates to their circumstances. Some of the more mature individuals may be clear-eyed (like Hawthorne) about the paradoxes in life and in their own nature; they may know what they want and need from their studies, and they find it.

But for the majority – who are young, uncertain, searching, perhaps lost – somewhere deep within their innermost being, they want to know how best to live, what to care about and why, and what life means; moreover, they seem to want answers to these mysteries from a perspective that science cannot always offer. As we have discovered, this yearning – wanting to know what matters – is a deep and recurrent theme throughout Hawthorne's life and as a consequence, his writings. Many of my students begin to understand over the course of a semester or longer that his fiction and nonfiction can help guide them in addressing their own concerns.

We conclude our studies, as I conclude this book, by admitting that there is no obvious reason as to why the son of a seafaring captain should go on to become in little more than 30 years the immortal writer that we have discussed. How could one man have seen, felt, and known so much? How could he write with such insight? In his essay "The Salem of Hawthorne" (1884), his son, Julian, said that he found himself "being constantly unable to comprehend how such a man as I knew my father to be could have written such books. He did not talk in that way;

his moods had not seemed to be of that color" (6). Some say that the man was obsessed, that he burned with overwhelming energy, that he had an intuitive grasp over the vagaries and potentialities of human nature, or that he was divinely inspired. Others suggest that he read voluminously and observed incessantly, or (obviously) had an extraordinarily fertile imagination, a restless mind, and a sure sense of self-worth.

As we have discovered, the truth lies somewhere within all these possibilities. When artists perform with peers of the highest caliber, they are inspired to greater heights in their own work. Hawthorne was certainly aware of his competition. He learned that, while delving deep, in order to survive as a writer he had to attract his audience with pleasing tales and novels. Just as his work continues to mean different things to individual readers, so too Hawthorne himself has been a different person to individual biographers, always subject to interpretation. Getting to know him as a person, as I have tried to do in this study, opens up new ways of reading his work in our post-romantic world.

We do know, however, that Hawthorne lived in an environment where his innate talents could be fulfilled, that he remained fully responsive to all experiences, occupations, interests and powers of the body, soul and mind, and that he worked very hard to give expression to all this in some of the most eloquent prose ever written in the English language.

We also know that, like all of us, although he (understandably) had spells of unhappiness and melancholia, his correspondence and journals, his children's books and sentimental tales reveal a man capable of great warmth and enthusiasm with his friends and family, far more engaging and approachable than presumed by some of his critics. He was not a misanthrope. He was not always the recluse, the eccentric, the alienated or underground man that he was made out to be. His darkness has been overstated.

He was, rather, an enchanting, often intentionally amusing storyteller who cared about his readers and stayed true to his talent. At the same time, he protected his privacy so that he could get on with his work. He wrote in a determined voice that we can trust and rely on, remarkable for its sympathetic insights into human frailty. He left us with an array of images and characters and events that surprise us and stay with us for the rest of our lives, inspiring us to overcome our preconceived limits, impelling us to shed our hypocrisy, and challenging us to listen to the quiet, divine voice of conscience. In the midst of fulfilling his sacred devotion to literature, he was, as we have seen, a loyal friend, a devoted husband, and an appreciative family man. Fields (1872) likened him to Milton's Raphael, "an 'affable' angel, and inclined to converse on whatever was human and good in life" (87).

And yet, there remain dark, hidden mysteries that have clung to him for a century and a half. This should not surprise or dismay us. "Never say you know the last words about any human heart!" wrote Henry James for the opening sentence of *Louisa Pallant* (2020 [1879]: 3). Indeed: Biographers never have the last word. All this and more is what it means to fall under his spell. This is why many of us continue to read him and shall continue to do that. This is why we attend conferences and produce books or essays on him and talk about him with our students and other readers.

And this is why, 159 years after his death on 19 May 1864, despite his critics and his own personal and professional disasters, he deserves a special place in the pantheon of American letters – still baffling, never completely or finally understood, always "the Sphinx that he wished, or was condemned, to be" (Hartley 1967: 141). "The long shadow cast from that creative act haunts us still and will continue to do as long as American fiction lasts" (Coale 1985: 217).

The gravesites of Nathaniel and Sophia with Una, Sleepy Hollow Cemetery, Concord, Massachusetts. Source: Dale F. Salwak (Author).

References

Abel, D. (1963). *American Literature Volume Two: Literature of the Atlantic Culture.* Woodbury, NY: Barron's Educational Series.

Alcott, B. (1938). 1861. In: *Journals* (ed. O. Shepard). Boston: Little, Brown.

Allen, B. (2003). The Surveyor of Customs. *New York Times.* October 5. https://www.nytimes.com/2003/10/05/books/the-surveyor-of-customs.html (accessed 20 July 2021).

Amis, M. (2014). *The Zone of Interest.* New York: Knopf.

Amis, M. (2020). *Inside Story.* New York: Knopf.

Argersinger, J.L. and Person, L.S. (ed.) (2008). *Hawthorne and Melville: Writing a Relationship.* Athens: University of Georgia Press.

Auerbach, N. (1982). *Woman and the Demon.* Cambridge: Harvard University Press.

Auster, P. (2003). Introduction. In: *Twenty Days with Julian and Little Bunny By Papa* (ed. N. Hawthorne). New York: New York Review of Books.

Bachelard, G. (1964). *The Poetics of Space.* Boston: Beacon Press.

Baker, C. (1996). *Emerson Among the Eccentrics: A Group Portrait.* New York: Viking.

Balthus [Balthasar Klossowski] (2001). *Vanished Splendors: A Memoir.* Transl. Benjamin Ivry. New York: HarperCollins.

Bannatyne, L.P. (2011). *Halloween Nation: Behind the Scenes of America's Fright Night.* Gretna, LA: Pelican Publishing.

Baym, N. (1976). *The Shape of Hawthorne's Career.* Ithaca: Cornell University Press.

Beauregard, M. (2016). *The Whale: A Love Story.* New York: Viking.

Bellow, S. (1994). *It All Adds Up: From the Dim Past to the Uncertain Future.* New York: Viking.

Bertrand, R. (1946). *Ideas That Have Harmed Mankind: Man's Unfortunate Experiences with His Self-made Enemies, Including Sadistic Impulses, Religion, Superstition, Envy, Economic Superiority, Creeds, and Other Evil Things.* Girard, KS: E. Haldeman-Julius.

Bloom, A. (1987). *The Closing of the American Mind.* New York: Simon and Schuster.

The Life of the Author: Nathaniel Hawthorne, First Edition. Dale Salwak.
© 2023 John Wiley & Sons Ltd. Published 2023 by John Wiley & Sons Ltd.

Borges, J.L. (1968). *Other Inquisitions: 1936–1952*. Transl. L. C. Simms. New York: Simon and Schuster.

Brady, K. (1985). Hawthorne's editor/narrator: the voice of indeterminacy. *CEA Critic* 47.4 (Summer): 27–38.

Bridge, H. (1893). *Personal Recollections of Nathaniel Hawthorne*. New York: Harper and Brothers.

Brontë, C. (2000). January to December 1848. In: *The Letters of Charlotte Bronte: Volume Two 1848–1851* (ed. M. Smith). Oxford: Oxford University Press.

Bryant, W.C. (2009 [1824]). *Poems*. Charleston, NC: BiblioLife.

Burns, J.M.G. (1982). *The American Experiment: The Vineyard of Liberty*. New York: Knopf.

Bustillos, M. (2013). By Anonymous: Can a Writer Escape Vulnerability? *The New Yorker*, 18 November 2013. https://www.newyorker.com/books/page-turner/ by-anonymous-can-a-writer-escape-vulnerability (accessed 10 March 2021).

Campbell, J. (1949). *The Hero with a Thousand Faces*. New York: Pantheon Books.

Cantwell, R. (1948). *Nathaniel Hawthorne: The American Years*. New York: Rinehart.

Caro, R.A. (2019). *Working: Researching, Interviewing, Writing*. New York: Knopf.

Chandler, E.L. and Hawthorne, N. (1931). Hawthorne's *Spectator*. *The New England Quarterly* 4.2 (April): 288–330.

Chaucer, Geoffrey. 1961. General prologue. *The Works of Geoffrey Chaucer*. 2nd edition. Ed. F.N. Robinson. Boston: Houghton Mifflin, 1961.

Chukovsky, K. (1971). *From Two to Five*. Rev. ed. Transl. Miriam Morton. Los Angeles: University of California Press.

Clarke, H.A. (1913 [1910]). *Hawthorne's Country*. Garden City, NY: Doubleday, Page & Company.

Cleaveland, N. and Packard, A.S. (1882). *History of Bowdoin College: with Biographical Sketches of Its Graduates*. Boston: James R. Osgood.

Coale, S.C. (1985). *American Romance from Melville to Mailer*. Lexington, KY: The University Press of Kentucky.

Coale, S.C. (2001). Mysteries of mesmerism: Hawthorne's haunted house. In: *A Historical Guide to Nathaniel Hawthorne* (ed. L.J. Reynolds). Oxford: Oxford University Press.

Connolly, Cyril. 2008 [1938]. *Enemies of Promise*. Rev. ed. Chicago: University of Chicago Press.

Crews, F.C. (1966). *The Sins of the Fathers: Hawthorne's Psychological Themes*. Oxford: Oxford University Press.

Crowley, J.D. (1970). *Hawthorne: The Critical Heritage*. New York: Barnes and Noble.

Cryer, D. (2004). An Engrossing Look at the Life of Nathaniel Hawthorne. *Chicago Tribune*, 24 January. https://www.chicagotribune.com/news/ct-xpm-2004-01-04-0401020017-story.html (accessed 21 February 2021).

Davies, R. (1997). *The Merry Heart: Reflections on Reading, Writing, and the World of Books*. New York: Viking Penguin.

De Ayala, R. and Guéno, J.-P. (ed.) (2000). *Brilliant Beginnings: The Youthful Works of Great Artists, Writers and Composers*. Transl. John Goodman. New York: Henry N. Abrams.

De La Mare, W. (1969). *The Complete Poems of Walter De La Mare*. London: Faber.

Delano, S.F. (2004). *Brook Farm: The Dark Side of Utopia*. Cambridge, MA: Harvard University Press.

Dickinson, Emily (1873). Of our deepest delights. Amherst College Archives and Special Collections. https://www.themorgan.org/exhibitions/online/emily-dickinson/13 (accessed 11 October 2021).

Elie, P. (2003). *The Life You Save May Be Your Own: An American Pilgrimage*. New York: Farrar, Straus and Giroux.

Eliot, T.S. (1918). The Hawthorne aspect. *Little Review* 5.4 (August): 47–53.

Eliot, G. (2008 [1859]). Chapter LIV: The Meeting on the Hill. In: *Adam Bede* (ed. C.A. Martin). Oxford: Oxford University Press.

Emerson, Ralph Waldo (1903–1904). The American Scholar. *The Complete Works of Ralph Waldo Emerson*. Centenary Edition, ed. Edward Waldo Emerson. 12 vols. Boston: Houghton Mifflin.

Emerson, R.W. (1969). *The Journals and Miscellaneous Notebooks of Ralph Waldo Emerson*, vol. VII, 1838–1842. Cambridge: Harvard.

Fields, J.T. (1872). *Yesterdays with Authors*. Boston: James R. Osgood.

Gaeddert, L.A. (1980). *A New England Love Story: Nathaniel Hawthorne and Sophia Peabody*. New York: Dial Press.

Goldstein, J.S. (1945). The literary source of Hawthorne's Fanshawe. *Modern Language Notes* 60.1 (January): 1–8.

Goldstein, Laurence (1988). A Scarlet 'A' for Accountability: Prudence, Not Prurience, Inclines Us to Judgment. *Los Angeles Times*, 10 September. www.latimes.com/archives/la-xpm-1988-09-10-me-1389-story.html (accessed 11 November 2020).

Greene, G. (1954). *The Power and the Glory*. New York: Bantam.

Griffiths, J.L. (1918). *The Greater Patriotism: Public Addresses*. Los Angeles: University of California Libraries.

Hansen, K.P. (1991). *Sin and Sympathy: Nathaniel Hawthorne's Sentimental Religion*. Frankfurt am Main: Peter Lang.

Hartley, L.P. (1953). *The Go-Between*. New York: Stein and Day.

Hartley, L.P. (1967). *The Novelist's Responsibility*. London: Hamish Hamilton.

Hawthorne, N. (1838). Political portraits with Pen and Pencil, No. 8, Jonathan Cilley. *Democratic Review* 3 (September): 67–76.

Hawthorne, N. (1883). *Doctor Grimshaw's Secret* (ed. J. Hawthorne). London: Longman, Green.

Hawthorne, J. (1884). The Salem of Hawthorne. *Century Magazine* 28.1 (May): 3–17.

Hawthorne, M. (1940). Nathaniel Hawthorne at Bowdoin. *The New England Quarterly* 13.2 (June): 249–279.

Hawthorne, J. (1984 [1878]). *Nathaniel Hawthorne and His Wife*. Boston: James R. Osgood.

Hendrix, H. (2009). From early modern to romantic literary tourism: a diachronical perspective. In: *Literary Tourism and Nineteenth-Century Literature* (ed. N.J. Watson). Houndmills, Basingstoke: Palgrave Macmillan.

Herbert, T.W. (1993). *Dearest Beloved: The Hawthornes and the Making of the Middle-Class Family*. Berkeley: University of California Press.

Higginson, T.W. (1879). *Short Studies of American Authors*. Boston: Lee and Shepard.

Holmes, R. (2000). *Sidetracks: Explorations of a Romantic Biographer*. New York: Pantheon Books.

Howells, W.D. (1968 [1900]). *Literary Friends and Acquaintances: A Personal Retrospect of American Authorship* (ed. D.F. Hiatt and E.H. Cady). Bloomington: Indiana University Press.

Idol, J.L. Jr. and Jones, B. (ed.) (1994). *Nathaniel Hawthorne: The Contemporary Reviews*. Cambridge, UK: The Cambridge University Press.

Jacob, F. (1993). *The Logic of Life: A History of Heredity*. Princeton, NJ: Princeton University Press.

James, H. (1907). *The Novels and Tales of Henry James*. New York: Charles Scribner's Sons.

James, H. (1934). *The Art of the Novel: Critical Prefaces*. Chicago: University of Chicago Press.

James, H. (1984 [1879]). *Hawthorne*. Ithaca, NY: Cornell University Press.

James, Henry. Louisa Pallant; The Bostonians. 2020 [1879]. In: *The Collected Works of Henry James*. Vol. 10 (of 36). London: Throne Classics.

Keats, J. (1991). *Complete Poems* (ed. J. Stillinger). Cambridge: Harvard University Press.

Keats, J. (2002). 1816-1817. In: *The Selected Letters of John Keats*. Rev ed. (ed. G.F. Scott). Cambridge: Harvard University Press.

Kehl, D.G. (2013). *Jack Lewis and His American Cousin, Nat Hawthorne: A Study of Instructive Affinities*. Eugene, OR: Wipf and Stock.

Laffrado, L. (2010). Hawthorne's Literature for Children. *Nathaniel Hawthorne Review* 36.1 (Spring): 28–46.

Lahiri, Jhumpa. 2015. Teach Yourself Italian. *The New Yorker*, 7 December. www.newyorker.com/magazine/2015/12/07/teach-yourself-italian (accessed 2 January 2021).

Lathrop, R.H. (1923 [1897]). *Memories of Hawthorne*. New York: Houghton Mifflin.

Lawrence, D.H. (1977 [1923]). *Studies in Classic American Literature*. New York: Penguin.

Lawrence, N.R. and Werner, M.L. (ed.) (2005). *Ordinary Mysteries: The Common Journal of Nathaniel and Sophia Hawthorne 1842–1843*. Philadelphia: American Philosophical Society.

Le Carré, J. (2005). Introduction. In: *The New Annotated Sherlock Holmes, Vol. I: Sir Arthur Conan Doyle* (ed. L.S. Klinger). New York: W.W. Norton.

Lewis, C.S. (1958). *The Allegory of Love: A Study in Medieval Tradition*. Oxford: Oxford University Press.

Lewis, C.S. (1961 [1942]). *A Preface to Paradise Lost*. Oxford: Oxford University Press.

Lewis, C. S. 1965 [1949]a. The inner ring. In *The Weight of Glory and Other Addresses*. Grand Rapids, MI: William B. Eerdmans.

Lewis, C.S. 1965 [1949]b. Learning in war-time. In *The Weight of Glory and Other Addresses*. Grand Rapids, MI: William B. Eerdmans.

Lingeman, R. (2006). *Double Lives: American Writers' Friendships*. New York: Random House.

Loggins, V. (1951). *The Hawthornes*. New York: Columbia University Press.

Longfellow, H.W. (1864). Concord. *The Atlantic* 14.82 (August): 169–170.

Longfellow, H.W. (1876). *The Masque of Pandora and Other Poems*. Boston: James R. Osgood.

Lovecraft, H.P. (1994 [1927]). *Supernatural Horror in Literature*. Hopewell, NJ: Ecco Press.

Madden, D. (ed.) (2011). *The Mystery of Edwin Drood (1870)*. Uthank Books.com.

Male, R.R. Jr. (1955). Toward *The Waste Land*: the theme of *The Blithedale Romance*. *College English* 16.5 (February): 277–283, 295.

Marshall, M. (2005). *The Peabody Sisters: Three Women Who Ignited American Romanticism*. New York: Houghton Mifflin.

Martin, Terence. 1983. *Nathaniel Hawthorne*. Rev. ed. Boston: Twayne.

Matthiessen, F.O. (1941). *American Renaissance: Art and Expression in the Age of Emerson and Whitman*. Oxford: Oxford University Press.

Mays, J.O.'.D. (1983). *Mr. Hawthorne Goes to England: The Adventures of a Reluctant Consul*. Burley, Ringwood, Hampshire: New Forest Leaves.

McFarland, P. (2004). *Hawthorne in Concord*. New York: Atlantic Monthly Press.

Meltzer, M. (2007). *Nathaniel Hawthorne: A Biography*. Minneapolis, MN: Lerner Publishing.

Meyers, J. (1985). *Hemingway: A Biography*. New York: Harper & Row.

Miller, E.H. (1991). *Salem Is My Dwelling Place: A Life of Nathaniel Hawthorne*. Iowa City: University of Iowa Press.

Millington, R.H. (ed.) (2011). *Nathaniel Hawthorne, The Blithedale Romance*. New York: W.W. Norton.

Milton, J. (1909). *The Complete Poems of John Milton*. The Harvard Classics, vol. 4. New York: P.F. Collier & Son.

Nabokov, V. (1980). Good readers and good writers. In: *Lectures on Literature: Austen, Dickens, Flaubert, Joyce, Kafka, Proust, Stevenson* (ed. F. Bowers). New York: Harcourt, Brace, Jovanovich.

Naipaul, V.S. (1995). *A Way in the World: A Novel*. New York: Knopf.

Newman, L.B.V. (1979). *A Reader's Guide to the Short Stories of Nathaniel Hawthorne*. Boston: G.K. Hall.

Niemeyer, M. (ed.) (2016). *The Divine Magnet: Herman Melville's Letters to Nathaniel Hawthorne*. Asheville, NC: Orison Books.

Nietzsche, F. (2019 [1873]). *The Use and Abuse of History*. Transl. Adrian Collins. Mineola, NY: Dover.

Oates, J.C. (2003). *The Faith of a Writer: Life, Craft, Art*. New York: HarperCollins.

Oates, J.C. (2005). *Uncensored: Views and (Re)views*. New York: HarperCollins.

Onderdonk, T. (2003). The marble mother: Hawthorne's iconographies of the feminine. *Studies in American Fiction* 31.1 (Spring): 73–100.

Parker, H. (1996). *Herman Melville: A Biography. Vol. I, 1819–1851*. Baltimore: The Johns Hopkins University Press.

Parker, H. (2002). *Herman Melville: A Biography. Vol. II, 1851–1891*. Baltimore: The Johns Hopkins University Press.

Peel, S.R. (1857). Shakespeare in modern thought. *North American Review* 85 (July): 491–513.

Petridou, G. (2016). *Divine Epiphany in Greek Literature and Culture*. Oxford: Oxford University Press.

Plato (2013 [375 BC]). *Republic. Books 1–5*. Eds. and transl. Chris Emlyn-Jones and William Preddy. Cambridge: Harvard College.

Poe, E.A. (1950 [1846]). The philosophy of composition. In: *Selected Prose and Poetry* (ed. W.H. Auden). New York: Holt, Rinehart and Winston.

Proust, M. (1982 [1923]). *Remembrance of Things Past, Vol. 3: The Captive, The Fugitive and Time Regained*. Transl. C. K. Scott Moncried. New York: Vintage.

Quindlen, A. (2004). *Imagined London: A Tour of the World's Greatest Fictional City*. Washington DC: National Geographic.

Reynolds, David S. 1993. Naughty Sophie Hawthorne. *The New York Times*. 7 February. www.nytimes.com/1993/02/07/books/naughty-sophie-hawthorne.html (accessed 1 March 2021).

Rezneck, S. (1935). The social history of an American depression, 1837–1843. *The American Historical Review* 40.4 (July): 662–687.

Richardson, R.D. Jr. (1995). *Emerson: The Mind on Fire*. Berkeley: University of California Press.

Ripley, S. (1840). Brook farm letters. *The Bulletin of the Boston Public Library* 12 (March): 93–114.

Risjord, N.K. (2001). *Representative Americans: The Romantics*. London: Rowman & Littlefield.

Riviere, F. (1998). Martin Amis, the art of fiction no. 151. *The Paris Review* 146 (Spring): 5–17.

Robuck, E. (2015). *The House of Hawthorne*. New York: New American Library.

Rossetti, D.G. (1887). II Literary Papers: Hake's Madelone. and Other Poems. In: *The Collected Works of Dante Gabriel Rossetti* (ed. W.M. Rossetti). London: Ellis and Elvey.

Sanchez-Eppler, K. (2004). 7: Hawthorne and the writing of childhood. In: *The Cambridge Companion to Nathaniel Hawthorne* (ed. R.H. Millington), 143–161. Cambridge, UK: Cambridge University Press.

Schmidt, M. (2014). *The Novel: A Biography*. Cambridge: Harvard University Press.

Seed, D. (ed.) (2020). *American Travelers in Liverpool*. Liverpool: Liverpool University Press.

Shakespeare, William. (2015). Coriolanus, Hamlet, Julius Caesar, King John, King Lear, Macbeth, The Merchant of Venice, Othello, The Tempest, Timon. In: *The Norton Shakespeare*. 3rd ed. Ed. Stephen Greenblatt, Walter Cohen, Suzanna Gossett, Jean E. Howard, Katharine Eisaman Maus, Gordon McMullan, New York: W.W. Norton.

Shelden, M. (2016). *Melville in Love: The Secret Life of Herman Melville and the Muse of Moby-Dick*. New York: HarperCollins.

Shreve, G. (2018). In Praise of Unfinished Novels. *The Millions*. 21 February. https://themillions.com/author/grant-shreve (accessed 1 June 2021).

Smith, Rev. Sydney (1820). Who reads an American book? *Edinburgh Review* 33 (January): 69–80.

Sophocles (2021 [429 BC]). *Oedipus Tyrannos*. Transl. and ed. Emily Wilson. New York: W.W. Norton.

Spenser, E. (1909 [1590]). Cant. X. In: *Spenser's Faerie Queene. Volume I, Books I-III* (ed. J.C. Smith). Oxford: Oxford University Press.

Spiller, R.E. (1929). The verdict of Sydney Smith. *American Literature* 1.1 (March): 3–11.

Steiner, G. (2008). *My Unwritten Books*. New York: New Directions.

Stern, I. written with Chaim Potok (1999). *My First 79 Years*. New York: Knopf.

Stoddard, R.H. (1853). Nathaniel Hawthorne. *National Magazine* 2 (January): 17–24.

Tapley, H.S. (1931). Hawthorne's 'Pot-8-O' club at Bowdoin College. *The Essex Institute Histories Collection* 18 (July): 225–233.

Theroux, P. (2011). *The Tao of Travel: Enlightenments from Lives on the Road*. New York: Houghton Mifflin Harcourt.

Thwaite, A. (1996). *Emily Tennyson: The Poet's Wife*. London: Faber and Faber.

Ticknor, C. (1913). *Hawthorne and His Publisher*. Boston: Houghton Mifflin.

Turner, Arlin. 1958. Introduction. In *The Blithedale Romance* by Nathaniel Hawthorne. New York: W.W. Norton.

Twain, M. (1903). *The Adventures of Tom Sawyer*. New York: Harper and Brothers.

Updike, J. (2007). *Due Considerations: Essays and Criticism*. New York: Knopf.

Valenti, P.D. (1987). Sophia Peabody Hawthorne's continuation on Christabel. *Nathaniel Hawthorne Review* 13.1 (Spring): 14–16.

Valenti, Patricia Dunlavy (1990). Sophia Peabody Hawthorne: A Study of Artistic Influence. *Studies in the American Renaissance* (January): 1–21.

Valenti, P.D. (2004). *Sophia Peabody Hawthorne: A Life, Volume 1, 1809–1847*. Columbia: University of Missouri Press.

Valenti, P.D. (2011). Sophia Peabody Hawthorne and 'The-What?': creative copies in art and literature. *The Nathaniel Hawthorne Review* 37.2 (Fall): 48–72.

Valenti, P.D. (2015). *Sophia Peabody Hawthorne: A Life, Volume 2, 1848–1871*. Columbia: University of Missouri Press.

Van Doren, M. (1949). *Nathaniel Hawthorne: A Critical Biography*. New York: Viking Press.

Warren, A. (1935). Hawthorne's reading. *The New England Quarterly* 8.4 (December): 480–497.

Wilson, E. (1977). 1946–1949. In: *Letters on Literature and Politics 1917–1972* (ed. E. Wilson). New York: Farrar, Straus, Giroux.

Wilson, A.N. (1999). *God's Funeral: The Decline of Faith in Western Civilization*. New York: W.W. Norton.

Wineapple, B. (2003). *Hawthorne: A Life*. New York: Knopf.

Winters, L. (1993). *Willa Cather: Landscape and Exile*. Cranbury, NJ: Associated University Presses.

Wise, T.J. and Alexander Symington, J. (ed.) (1932). *The Brontes: Their Lives, Friendship and Correspondence in Four Volumes*. Oxford: Shakespeare Head.

Wolfe, T. (1934). *You Can't Go Home Again*. New York: Charles Scribner's Sons.

Wolff, T. (2003). *Old School: A Novel*. New York: Random House.

Woodberry, G.E. (1902). *Nathaniel Hawthorne*. New York: Houghton Mifflin.

Woodson, T. (1986). A new installment of Hawthorne's *Spectator*. *Nathaniel Hawthorne Review* 12.2 (Fall): 1–2.

Woolf, V. (1976 [1972]). A sketch of the past. In: *Moments of Being: Unpublished Autobiographical Writings* (ed. J. Schulkind). New York: Harcourt Brace Jovanovich.

Wordsworth, W. (2012 [1850]). Lines written a few miles above Tintern Abbey and *The Prelude*. In: *The Norton Anthology of English Literature*, 9e (ed. S. Greenblatt). New York: W.W. Norton.

Zezima, Katie (2006). Historic Literary Coupe Are Reunited After 142-Year Separation. *The New York Times*. 27 June. www.nytimes.com/2006/06/27/us/27hawthorne.html (accessed 2 September 2020).

Index

The Life of the Author: Nathaniel Hawthorne, First Edition. Dale Salwak.
© 2023 John Wiley & Sons Ltd. Published 2023 by John Wiley & Sons Ltd.